LOVE, HATE AND

Psychosocial approaches to policy and practice

Lynn Froggett

17.99

CW00572487

First published in Great Britain in October 2002 by

The Policy Press
34 Tyndall's Park Road
Bristol BS8 1PY
UK

Tel +44 (0)117 954 6800
Fax +44 (0)117 973 7308
e-mail tpp@bristol.ac.uk
www.policypress.org.uk

© The Policy Press 2002

British Library Cataloguing in Publication Data
A catalogue record for this book is available from the British Library

ISBN 1 86134 343 4 paperback
A hardcover version of this book is also available

Lynn Froggett is based at the University of Central Lancashire.

The right of Lynn Froggett to be identified as author of this work has been asserted by them in accordance with the 1988 Copyright, Designs and Patents Act.

All rights reserved: no part of this publication may be reproduced, stored in a retrieval system, or transmitted in any form or by any means, electronic, mechanical, photocopying, recording, or otherwise without the prior permission of The Policy Press.

The statements and opinions contained within this publication are solely those of the editor and contributors and not of The University of Bristol or The Policy Press. The University of Bristol and The Policy Press disclaim responsibility for any injury to persons or property resulting from any material published in this publication.

The Policy Press works to counter discrimination on grounds of gender, race, disability, age and sexuality.

Cover design by Qube Design Associates, Bristol.
Printed and bound in Great Britain by Hobbs the Printers Ltd, Southampton.

Contents

Acknowledgments

There are a number of people who deserve special thanks for helping me see this project through. Chief among them are those who put up with long tracts of emotional unavailability. They are, first and foremost, my immediate family, Mark, Jonah and Leah, as well as friends who I neglected and who have forgiven me. Wendy Hollway bears most responsibility for the fact that it ever saw the light of day. Her initial judicious enthusiasm gave me the courage to show it to others. Tom Wengraf had the stamina to read two successive drafts and his eye for detail was invaluable. Sue Lees and Prue Chamberlayne both encouraged me with particular sections – especially the beginning and the end. Brid Featherstone read an early version and kept my spirits afloat in a very dejected moment. Nigel Parton's comments forced me to impose greater discipline on the first chapter; I am sure there should have been more of it throughout. John Lea also intervened on the side of rigour, but helped me to let go of it when I started to obsess. I owe especial gratitude to Bob Sapey who shared an office with me, chewed over ideas, and gave of his editorial eye and friendship with endless generosity. He also worked on the diagram in Chapter One, which was beyond my technical skill. I also want to thank the University of Central Lancashire for the short but precious sabbatical that allowed me to finish the typescript. Finally, I must acknowledge the patience of at least four cohorts of post-graduate students in health, social work and social policy whose questions and criticisms helped me to anchor the ideas in current practice. Despite all this invaluable commentary I cringe over the flaws of my own making which – in the nature of things – become clearer to me as time passes.

Note

The text contains case examples taken from practice. Any personal details which might identify individuals have been changed.

Part 1:
Introduction

Saleem was old and tired and poor. He had always known denigration and condescension. But now there was something more profoundly exhausting – the brittle competence and the endless efficiency. In this office his life had become opaque to him – inscribed in files which he couldn't read, in a language he barely spoke, and in something they called 'care plans' which mystified him. He had been a practical man, clever with his hands and he liked to think that if he had stayed in the old country he would have been a carpenter. Instead, there had been a life of sorts in the mill – now half-forgotten. He, a warrior and poet at heart, had let down his guard and the eternal grey cold had seeped into his soul. A terrible weakness had followed and he had been possessed by the jinn who taunted him endlessly. Now he had to carry this malice inside himself. The burden was too much for an old man – his body ached with its weight.

His had been a life of separations: from his village, his kin, his children. He dimly remembered a wife who had departed along with his hopes. He had long since lost a sense that there might be any help in this world – his paltry pension, the occasional hot meal from the luncheon club, handouts from local charities, tablets from the doctor. Now he had two choices: the solace of the local healers who he could barely afford, but who understood about the jinn, and the cold, and the lost dreams; or health and social services with their infernal care plans.

In this book I examine the changing relationships between users of services, professionals and managers in the post-war welfare state. I argue that while the 'old-welfarist' model was tainted by paternalism, the loss of relationship-based practice implicit in the new consumerism undermines the welfare project at its core. I pursue a case for its revitalisation based on a politics of recognition, and suggest that the recovery of narrative and biographical methods can provide a basis for this.

I was born in the aftermath of the Second World War and raised under the protection of the welfare state. Like most of my generation I was a direct beneficiary of free public services and expanding social provision. Later, as an employee I was guided by what I took to be an ethic of public service. Located as I was within the helping professions, I linked this with a sense of responsibility – understood as an ability to respond, not only to intimates but to the 'needs of strangers' (Ignatieff, 1994). I have spent most of my working life in large public sector institutions, in social services, health and education. Yet as far back as I can remember I have marvelled at the disparity between the public face and expressed aims of these organisations and the realities of their internal relationships and their interface with the wider community.

Having subsequently lived through the welfare 'dark age' of the Thatcher–Major years I cannot lightly consign these institutions (for all their imperfections) to history. I am aware that a loss of legitimacy for public welfare has been associated with costs far heavier than those that preoccupy the Treasury. By the time of Tony Blair's second term of office, public opinion had clearly shifted in favour of renewed investment in health and education (despite dire warnings of crisis, social services received hardly a mention). However, the balance of public versus private funding had become a hotly contested issue. The question turned on the extent and scope of responsibility among individuals and within institutions, and of institutions for individuals and families. Within the Blairite project, responsibility is largely seen in terms of contractual obligations, or reciprocity (I do to others as I would be done by, or as they merit, or as seems fair). Recognition of the 'other', the distinctive, needing, desiring person, is still absent from these calculations. And yet it is precisely for its inability to accommodate difference and contain need that 'old' welfarism has been so roundly condemned.

In this book I will draw on a tradition which links social responsibility to its psychosocial roots. It is first and foremost an achievement of the human infant, who in striving to become an individual realises that personhood has drawbacks, as well as pleasures, and that both come in the shape of other people. Recognition of others, starting with the first carer, is bound up with responsiveness to their needs which may well be in tension with one's own. In a good-enough environment small children develop an ability to respond to an ever-widening world and their 'response ability' is animistic. As adults we delight in this and nurture it: 'take care of teddy'; 'mind the poor little flower'. While rummaging in memorabilia I found an old Christmas card that my daughter had solemnly deposited in the garden when she had barely learnt to write: 'To the plants and animals – from your friend, Leah'. As children grow, however, this responsiveness is moulded by the social world in which they live. It acquires contours and limits prescribed by their culture, but these are personalised with capacities for loving and hating that are rooted in early intimacies. They learn who and what they are *not* responsible for and must exclude from recognition: rival gangs at school, the homeless beggar on the street, war victims in faraway countries seen on TV – perhaps people of other races, or abilities, or anyone very different.

Welfare institutions are an important part of the cultural shaping of responsibility. This much was recognised and given a morally conservative inflection within the New Labour project. I shall suggest that whether they do so for better or worse depends on how far they can sustain relationships based on recognition. This is the lens through which I intend to view three ideal type models of welfare and an emergent fourth alternative, all of which have been reflected with varying degrees of prominence in the changing welfare settlements of post-war Britain. It is an approach that could fruitfully be extended to comparative work – but that would be another book entirely.

Debates about the future direction of welfare policy and practice are notoriously vulnerable to polarisation. Increasingly they are infected with a certain fatalism born of the fear that globalisation leaves little room for manoeuvre within nation states. They take place among members of the public and among a number of academic, political and practitioner groups with quite different interests and disciplinary backgrounds. A conversation embracing all of these perspectives and agendas becomes very difficult and is easily submerged in the authoritative discourses of public policy analysis. Other voices could join in: those of users and advocates. The difficulty is that they often operate within different frames of reference and use different languages. Those who try to transgress boundaries often find it hard to make themselves understood on either side. The four welfare configurations identified in this book are an attempt to map the conceptual terrain on which such a conversation could take place. Each of them involves a distinctive set of relationships between people who give and receive help. These relationships are reflected in institutions and states of mind, and express themselves in different cultural representations of dependency, autonomy, rights, responsibilities, and mutuality.

There are a number of routes to understanding the kinds of welfare provision that have emerged in the second half of the 20th century, and I do not wish to claim priority for one over another. In directing my attention to the relational aspects of welfare work, I am remaining faithful to a particular understanding of its nature and purpose. I refer most often to social work, in part because it is what I know best, and in part because it represents the paradigmatic form in which publicly sponsored help responds to private need at any given time. Nevertheless, teachers, nurses, doctors, social administrators, social care workers and a number of other occupational groups all express different variants of this form. In any case, the boundaries between public sector professions are shifting and in some cases dissolving, as are those between the public and voluntary sector. The grid that I introduce in Chapter One and that has structured the rest of the book developed out of dialogue between practitioners from different backgrounds and was conceived as a means of mapping the complex changes in the post-war welfare state in such a way as to allow them to reflect on the commonalties and divergences of their professional perspectives. The market-oriented restructuring of public services during the course of the eighties and nineties has ensured that similar themes have emerged everywhere: the commodification of services, the tension between professional and managerial power, the instrumentalism of organisational cultures.

In proposing that a welfare politics based on recognition could move us beyond the limits of consumerism, I am, of course, drawing on the work of others. Fraser (1995) has explored the tensions between recognition and redistribution and more recently (2000) the role of recognition in identity politics. The most systematic theoretical approach to the subject has come from Honneth (1995) who identifies three moments in the struggle for recognition: the pursuit of love, rights and solidarity. Williams (1999) has extended many of the insights of this major work in attempting to identify the principles of 'good-enough' welfare. I have taken a look at four typologies of social relations of welfare in Britain and asked what kind of welfare environment can best allow principles such as these to operate. I understand the most important aspect of this environment to be the human relationships through which needs are understood and sometimes met, or denied. I am concerned with their oppressive potential but also with their rich possibilities and I do not consider that these will be realised within a predominantly individualist discourse of rights, choice, empowerment and accountability.

The point of view that I shall develop, informed by psychosocial theory, is that welfare depends on our becoming responsible self-actualising subjects in the context of irrevocable attachments to others. This requires that others recognise us as subjects, and for that they must be recognised in turn. Sustained recognition demands a continual open-ended dialogue that can only be fully realised if its participants perceive each other as of equal moral worth and reciprocal significance

The themes of recognition and dialogue appear explicitly in feminism and psychoanalysis, critical and political theory and social policy, and implicitly in the work of a number of writers from different backgrounds. I shall draw on these as I go along. They also appear in discussions of community regeneration and social action, of user participation, of anti-oppressive practice and partnership, and of 'thick' models of social justice, and the ethics of care. The parties to these debates come from user groups, advocates, community organisations and social movements including those of women, lesbians and gays, environmentalists, ethnic minorities and disabled people. They cross academic and professional boundaries and it seems to me that they are very much at issue in ecological models of welfare which stress agency and interdependence (Barnes and Prior, 2000).

I have always tried to understand relationships in terms of the connections between states of mind, interpersonal relations and the cultural and political world. This has made it difficult to find an intellectual home in any one discipline. I therefore draw on several (and worry terribly as a result) while warnings about facile transitions between levels and domains of analysis ring in my head. At a recent multi-disciplinary seminar on the very possibility of psychosocial analysis I heard someone asking 'why bother doing it at all?'. I mentally played back a reel of practice scenarios from my days as a social worker that had caused me much anxiety at the time. The realities of practice can sometimes overwhelm the capacity to hold on to complexity. As a practitioner, however, it would have made no sense to ask why I should 'bother' with the relationship between the psyche, culture and politics. There seemed to be no other choice. I shall refer to some of these experiences in illustrative vignettes throughout the book. However, for the moment I would like to present two examples from other authors.

It is commonplace to talk about collective states of mind: 'New York in shock', 'America thirsting for vengeance', 'Britain in mourning' – whole economies in 'depression'. These metaphorical over-simplifications have a ring of truth that captures important dimensions of public experience. At the same time it is obvious that within groups and organisations, individuals may be ambivalent or at odds with the prevailing mood. What, then, is the nature of the interaction between the individual and the group? What makes it possible to consider the congruence between the state of mind of a particular person, and the sense of shared feeling that sometimes pervades collectivities? Where is the boundary between them?

It is recognised that in the aftermath of disasters a disturbance of grief, shock, rage or confusion is felt throughout the affected community, and also in very personal and sometimes contradictory ways among individuals. In events like the attacks on the World Trade Center, or the collapse of the Hillsborough stadium, individual responses cannot be simply read off from the collective response, but neither can they be disconnected. The questions 'Why is this happening to us?' and 'Why is it happening to me?' are distinct but related. How each individual reacts depends on how the shared meanings of external events become bound to inner psychic material. Thus in traumatic situations all may register the source of the trauma but only some will be clinically traumatised.

Garland (1998) illustrates this by reference to a boy who was institutionalised and subjected to a desensitisation regime after the Hillsborough disaster. He was surrounded by continual planned reminders of the events he had witnessed in an effort to move him out of severe depression. Yet analytically informed analysis of his predicament highlighted the extent to which the photographs and tape recordings of the stadium mirrored and reinforced the boy's sense of deathliness and catastrophic personal guilt. This guilt had been released, but only partially produced, by the way in which he had projected[1] feelings of competitive aggression, rooted in family rivalries, onto the game. The match therefore enacted a personal psychic drama in which the opponents of his team were aligned with those who he unconsciously wished to annihilate. He then witnessed their violent deaths 'as if' by his own agency. This example shows how intra-psychic, interpersonal and socio-political levels of experience can intersect with each other. For that boy the match became a psychic event in which his personal rivalry could be enacted for him in a culturally sanctioned ritual of aggression whose wider social meanings were supplied by the 'political' alignments of league competition. To that *particular* boy at that moment in his life its dreadful ending in the collapse of the stadium signified the collapse of a rule-bound moral order in which his own destructiveness could be contained, and mirrored his inner catastrophe induced by a 'crushing' sense of guilt.

However, it is not only in individuals that this dynamic relation between particular histories and wider collective experience is played out. Larger groups and communities can react to events in unpredictable and seemingly irrational ways in which unconscious projections become intertwined with wider cultural and political anxieties. Shapiro and Carr (1991) describe the surprise of a vicar at the anger and resistance of his congregation when a new statue of the Virgin Mary was introduced. In general this was neither an excitable nor especially active group. The contemplation of the Virgin had been quite normal in this particular Anglican community, yet all of a sudden it had acquired overtones of distinctly 'un-English' forms of Christianity. It was not until the wider anxieties of the wider community were interpreted that the behaviour became intelligible. The Church attracted general goodwill even though it represented a religious minority within an urban population into which there had been influxes, first of Jews, and later of Asian Muslims. Despite the provocations of extreme Right-wing racist groups, it operated within a relatively harmonious social environment. Moreover, its role extended well beyond the boundaries of its own congregation in that it had come to symbolise stability and a form of 'English tolerance'. It thus provided an effective container[2] for unarticulated fears of division and fragmentation which were vulnerable to political exploitation. In this context, interference with the continuity of its adornment and the 'Englishness' of its practices threatened to undermine its role as a force for integration. The relation between an episode of seemingly irrational protest and wider political currents could only be explained by identifying the unconscious psychic 'bridges' between the inner worlds of a particular subsection of the community and the historical and actual experience of the parish as a whole. This episode reveals something of the way in which an institution exists in the mind as well as in social relations and bricks and mortar.

Once again we can understand the significance of this experience at different levels. Intra-psychic anxieties of division and fragmentation which the Church had hitherto successfully contained were enacted in an interpersonal quarrel about a change that might normally have been accommodated. This was reflected in worries about the erosion of a distinctive and valued dimension of the institutional culture – and expressed in a vehement determination to safeguard it from invasion by a cultural symbol (the Virgin Mary) which was *now* construed as alien. The wider socio-political context for this was the activity of Right-wing racists, which played ceaselessly on anxieties of 'intolerable' cultural and racial corruption. Note that no linear causal chain of reaction is suggested here. The political activities of these groups did not straightforwardly determine the dissent and division; they did not directly challenge the culture of the Church; nor did they, in and of themselves, provoke the anxiety of the members. Neither is it suggested that the unconscious concerns of the members somehow engineered the debate over the statue. Rather, we have a conjunction of unconscious dynamics which are rooted both in the predispositions of the members and their historical experience of the area, with political activity which shaped *the content* of their anxiety. In its expression, however, it was displaced onto a cultural artefact which was available to receive the projections of the congregation at *that point in time* because of the way in which its wider cultural meanings acquired a resonance with attributes (of 'un-Englishness') which the members were unconsciously trying to disown.

Outside-in and inside-out perspectives

I shall attempt to trace some of the links between intimate experiences of care, the institutions that provide formal and organised care, and the development of public policy. The argument takes in face-to-face encounters of individuals and interactions between large groups of people. In most of the welfare literature, the private lives of citizens have been of interest to the extent that they have been resistant to, or regulated by, public policy. This is a classically outside-in perspective. Inside-out approaches, which attempt to understand social relationships within groups in terms of how we *also* construct our world by projecting onto it our longings and loathings, have remained the province of psychoanalytic social theory. As a minority pursuit, this has often been identified with a form of reductionist drive theory in which instinctual life is seen as crudely determinant of social experience. Like all the straw men of social science it has encountered the ridicule of the methodologically correct. Since the 'sociological deluge' and the denouncing of psychoanalytically influenced models of casework by radical social scientists in the seventies, developments in psychoanalytic theory have been neglected, and even the basics are ignored on many training programmes. In the social policy arena they are seen as irrelevant, if not risible. Among professional publications, *The Journal of Social Work Practice*, which continues to encourage and develop psychodynamic thinking, remains an exception. Outside of psychoanalytic strongholds, such as the Tavistock Clinic, much therapeutic work has been influenced by humanistic psychology with little critical appraisal. Humanistic psychology has limited applicability with people who are subject to the more coercive functions of public services and is not easily linked with social analysis. The result has been a separation of the therapeutic and socio-political dimensions of welfare. Unfortunately, Jacoby's (1975) critique of conformist psychology went largely unheeded in the welfare field – leaving the way clear for the mystifications of a positive, rather than dialectical, humanism. His attack on Rogers' (1951, 1970) separation of psychic and material needs is ever more pertinent:

> it capitulates to the ideology of the affluent society which affirms the material structure is sound, conceding only that some psychic and material values might be lacking. Exactly this distinction sets up 'authenticity' and 'fulfilment' as so many more commodities for the shopper. (pp 48-9)

Jacoby's target at the time was what we might call the 'romantic' movement in alternative psychology. Personal growth and encounter groups took off as a middle-class leisure pursuit in the seventies, joined in the eighties with emerging forms of new-age spirituality. 'Enlightenment' became a cottage industry as niche markets developed in 'holistic' healing. Resistance to the 'loadsamoney' monotheism of Essex Man took the form of a proliferation of paths to religiosity stimulated by the growth of consumerist restlessness. The reverse side of romanticism was the appeal to 'hard-headed' pragmatism represented by the penetration of a managerialist ethos into everyday life. The Filofax, and later the electronic notebook, came to symbolise this as we were exhorted to 'manage' not only our diaries, but our life-plans, finances, children, sexuality, consumption, pets, health, and personal effectiveness. A route was thereby opened for the extension of technical–rational principles into the intuitive, the affective and communicative. Personal growth gave way to performativity, fulfilment to behavioural adaptation, enlightenment to material reward. The harmonious coexistence of these two options, the romantic and the pragmatic, involved a view of personal development as something that could be either massaged or managed, by-passing the discomforts and conflicts of the psyche. It is precisely this split that Rogers' version of humanistic psychology so effectively underwrites. The inner world is either idealised or denied depending on which school of thought we opt for as a means of curbing disquiet.

Despite an increasing mistrust of depth psychology from the sixties onwards, it was possible to maintain that, in a naturalised form, psychoanalysis remained a major paradigm - at least in social work (Payne, 1991). Care management did much to dislodge it during the nineties by shifting the emphasis towards rational, economic models of human behaviour. This technical–rational challenge has been all the more effective in that it has been articulated in the systematic institutional reforms demanded by the purchaser/provider environment. There are, however, a few signs that psychodynamic thinking in coming back into focus – for example, through the conjunction of psychosocial studies and applied social science in some university departments. What it continues to offer is a theoretical tradition that gives reflective definition to relational aspects of welfare work and potentially to welfare policy. It may be that the constraints of a managerialised environment actively prompt attention to relationships and emotions which then acquire a critical edge and suggest unexplored lines of political and social analysis. At any rate these issues refuse to go away - Howe's (1993) wide-ranging review of studies seeking the views of people on the receiving end of social work services shows that the quality of the experience is a recurrent theme. As Parton and O'Byrne (2000) point out, this refers not only to 'relationship', essential though it is, but also to the conversational experience and narratives through which people make sense of their dreams and desires as well as their distress.

The extrusion of depth psychology from welfare work in the seventies and eighties left us with social psychology as a means of linking the personal and the social. Social psychology illuminates intersubjective relations but leaves out too much. Honneth (1995) provides a detailed discussion of the work of G.H. Mead (1934), pointing out that while he thought little could be known of the inner world it should be accorded its place in moral development. The reason was that human beings are not entirely determined by their social circumstances, however crushing they appear to be. They maintain a capacity for resistance and the search for new ways of living. This applies to people who are oppressed and who need practical or emotional help, education or control as well as the increasingly beleaguered professionals who work with them.

The inner capacity for resistance comes from awareness of being an 'I', a desiring subject who is necessarily in tension with the 'me' – myself as the object of others' definitions. "The existence of the 'me' forces one to fight, in the interests of one's 'I', for new forms of social recognition" (Honneth, 1995, p 82). When social or health workers or teachers try to help people find a way out of a predicament by discovering their own resources, including the very capacity to use help, they search for ways to nourish the active subject who resists oppressive or demeaning ascriptions. Philp (1979), in an influential attempt to define the nature of social work, pointed out that what people who become clients all have in common is the fact that they are encumbered with an objective status that threatens to overwhelm their ability to appear to society and to themselves as subjects. He described the position of social work as representing the "final paradox of social science ... for while it attempts to remain in the form of objective knowledge, this objectivity is uncertain in the extreme because what it presents is a picture of the subject" (p 91).

The visual metaphor is apt here in that the observational standpoint of the social scientist, like that of the painter, is predominantly one of distance and separation from its object. This approach to knowledge of other people is reasonably well suited to the advocacy function that Philp had in mind. Even here, however, it has limitations which become obvious when advocacy extends beyond representation of interests, to giving voice – especially on behalf of those least able to be heard: people who do not use speech in conventionally intelligible ways, whether through impairment, trauma, disturbance, immaturity or oppression. It is here that meanings slide and evade interpretation and are too easily subject to professional definition. It may then be, as Booth and Booth (1996) say, that we have to 'lend them the words' – not *our* words, but the words that come closest to voicing the quality of their 'silence'. These can only be discovered through patient processes of negotiation in which we explore alternative languages until we are not so much speaking 'for' as speaking 'with'. Of course, advocacy in both senses is a crucial part of social work – but in some ways it is the easier part that allows the mobilisation of cleansing moral indignation, born of the fight against injustice. Real social work is dirtier than this. Listening is often a struggle against our fear, frustration and disgust. The people for whom we would fight turn into our internal persecutors, and the battle lines scatter into a melee of competing assailants. Objectivity does indeed become uncertain, and subjectivity too, both 'ours' and 'theirs'.

The tension between the 'I' and the 'me' affects both parties to the helping relationship and is a necessary and potentially productive aspect of the process, providing that it is recognised and worked with. The ascendancy of care management, however, has ensured the return of behaviourist methodologies in which the objective status of the 'me' is increasingly the only one admitted to discourse. Philp's paradox is unhappily resolved, because the social work goal, understood in terms of the restoration of subjectivity, disappears, and the virtues of practical material assistance are elevated over every other aspect of helping. A colleague once recalled his satisfaction when, after weeks of painstaking advocacy for a recently bereaved woman, he had helped her to resolve her housing problems. Then, on the eve of gaining her new tenancy, she killed herself. He reflected that we could be providing every state-of-the-art aid and adaptation, an adequate income for anyone reliant on state benefits, quality housing, first rate rehabilitation schemes and flying pigs as pets, but we would still be leaving a great deal of suffering untouched.

It is uncontentious to assert that political, social and cultural analyses are essential in the understanding of public welfare and it is a truism that the work itself involves emotional labour. We become deeply invested in, and unsettled by, what we do and, in the absence of other means of support, we are often impelled to develop defences which serve nobody very well. The wholesale retreat into rigidly applied instrumental procedure is just one of the more obvious strategies. One of the consequences of the loss of the psychodynamic tradition is an impoverishment of the language of feelings and relationships. Rather, they are acknowledged as an ever-present undertow – a residual substratum of experience which leads to emoting and intuiting but not thinking and communicating.

There are signs, however, that the tide is beginning to turn. The introduction to a recent text-book (Hughes, 1998) discusses the importance of addressing the multiple ways in which social welfare has been represented and contested among different sections of the British population. It also affirms the importance of exploring the ways in which dominant symbolic meanings emerge at any given time. In part these are the outcome of struggles over interests and identities, the question of precisely who is to be included in 'the people', and what are the attributes of the welfare subject. Hughes points out that the process of representation is not simply a question of the social construction of meaning at a cognitive level. Since meanings are always multiple and contested, the question remains as to why we invest in some rather than others at any given time:

> These processes are not just about ideas: 'articulation' is not simply moving words around so that they can mean something different. They are also processes through which identifications and attachments can be created – the symbolic means through which we can recognise ourselves and see where 'we belong'. By implication, they are simultaneously processes of rejection, detachment and non-recognition. They position 'others' who do not and cannot belong and who are not spoken for in the construction of this particular 'we'. This aspect of articulation (or social construction) means giving attention to affective or non-rational dimensions of meaning as well as the more instrumental or rational views about social interests and ideology. (Clarke et al, in Hughes, 1998, p 7)

This book explores the ways in which the non-rational can be thought about and articulated in the analysis of welfare relationships and institutions. It does this by attempting to understand the states of mind which impede or help us in recognising one another and links this to the problem of becoming active welfare subjects. In acknowledging the importance of a sense of belonging, it attempts to move beyond the rhetoric of social inclusion and the blind alley of identity politics to ask how a genuinely individuated response to human need can be grounded in new forms of social solidarity.

Scheme of the book

In Chapter One I develop a grid out of the intersecting principles of equality and attachment which I take to be central concerns of public welfare. I attempt to show diagrammatically how the significance of these principles has changed as the social relations of welfare have changed. I suggest that we need to analyse these relationships at different levels: politics, institutional cultures and interpersonal dynamics, and that in order to do this we need to understand something of how these relationships are implicated in states of mind. This gives me a way of depicting four different welfare configurations which have been prominent in post-war Britain. It also informs the structure of the rest of the book.

Chapter Two lays the theoretical groundwork for the subsequent analysis. I have tried to represent the key ideas as straightforwardly as possible. Inevitably this delays the development of my main argument but it avoids burdening the rest of the text with detailed theoretical exposition. Some readers will not be familiar with the Object Relations tradition - specifically with the work of Melanie Klein, Donald Winnicott, Wilfred Bion and, more recently, Jessica Benjamin. They will need it most. Others may choose a bypass strategy, returning for clarification as necessary.

The core themes are developed through Chapters Three to Five. They deal with successive configurations of post-war welfare which are conventionally analysed in terms of social policy: social democratic welfarism, the neo-liberal reaction, and the current 'third way' version of the mixed economy of care. In order to avoid repetition of this congested terminology and for want of any better terms, I have dubbed them 'old welfare', 'no welfare' and 'mixed welfare'. My concern is neither to supplant nor to correct the usual categories but to enquire into their psychosocial conditions and effects. I have departed from the assumption that institutions exist in the mind as well as in the external world (Armstrong, 1991) and I have tried to fill in a dimension that has been ignored in much of the writing currently available to welfare professionals – the states of mind implicated in successive welfare settlements. In any historical phase there are particular features of institutions which both reflect and shape these states of mind out of which our responses to the needs of others are formed. In Part 2 of the book I use a similar method of analysis to move onto more speculative territory – the possible outlines of a new welfare paradigm, elements of which are most clearly detectable in oppositional and grass-roots movements outside of the statutory sector.

It is perhaps worth stressing here what I am *not* doing. Clearly, a book which tries to deal with four dimensions of welfare in three different welfare settlements over more than half a century, and then identify new directions, would risk being over-ambitious and far too long. It would also mean re-treading a vast amount of well-worn ground, such as the immanent contradictions of Keynesianism, where I do not feel that I have anything very new to contribute. I do not intend, therefore, to produce yet another history of the welfare state, and I am not primarily concerned with the development of each welfare settlement in relation to whatever preceded it. My aim is to depict three ideal types of welfare configuration in which it becomes possible to discern heuristically the profile of the ideal welfare subject. This subject is variously the focus of competing welfare discourses, object of social engineering, hailed by emancipatory movements, and subsumed under economic categories. At the same time he or she is anchored in a body with its perpetual vulnerabilities, and surrounded by others with whom to share the dream of the good life. These are the themes that interest me and in order to concentrate on them, I begin each of the Chapters Three to Five with a pen picture of the welfare subject under consideration, before moving on to consider the psychosocial possibilities and limitations of his or her position. This substitutes for a conventional synthesis of historical material and provides a starting point which is more suitable for my purposes. I do not attempt this in the second part of the book, for the simple reason that such a subject has not yet emerged, and although I have some views as to the mental and emotional capacities that might be desirable, I am not in the business of producing a utopia. I prefer to concentrate on contributions to theory, practice and politics from a number of sources which seem to point to a new direction with partial, but increasing, coherence.

Chapter Three is centrally concerned with the collectivist impulses to reparation and generosity – and their limits – which underpinned consensual support for public welfare in the post-war period. Much has been written about the hostility of the New Right to the 'old welfarist' project. The restructuring of institutions which was initiated in the 1980s required as its condition a redirection of altruism towards the private sphere which was achieved through a sharpening of the boundaries of responsibility and the shaping of an actuarial consciousness. The competitive and individualist environment emerged out of active processes of splitting and is the subject of Chapter Four. Chapter Five asks how far the mixed economy of welfare under New Labour perpetuates or contains this splitting, and identifies in the Blairite vision of modernisation, patterns of idealisation and denigration which set severe limits to its capacity for responsiveness.

In the second part of the book, which deals with emergent themes, there is a change in the organisation of the argument. Essentially I am concerned with the question of how claims for recognition from 'below' – from user and advocacy groups and from social movements – can make themselves heard above an often empty consumerist rhetoric of choice and participation. Chapter Six addresses the theoretical and ethical concepts required to envisage a new welfare configuration based on attachment (or solidarity) and equality. It considers the issues of rights and redistribution and their relation to compassion and recognition, and an ethic of care. Chapter Seven picks up an issue which has episodically preoccupied writers on the nature of practice in the helping professions: its art-like qualities. It sees in the re-emergence of this theme a more adequate response to the uncertain environment of late modernity than the current empiricist evaluation agenda and the government's obsession with regulation. It also identifies the beginnings of a reorientation towards a psychosocial approach. It then goes on to develop a detailed example of a voluntary organisation which has made extensive use of the arts and attended to the aesthetic dimensions of its own practice. Chapter Eight turns from practice to politics and explores the affinity of deliberative and associational democracy with the kind of organisation depicted in Chapter Seven. A recurring theme in the second part of the book is the significance of storytelling. The final chapter pursues the importance of the aesthetic by identifying in a partly eroded narrative tradition a medium through which different voices can emerge and links this to recognition and an ethic of care.

Notes

[1] In this context, projection refers to the unconscious expulsion of unwanted or threatening psychic material onto the game in question, where it could be disowned. See Chapter Two for further explanation.

[2] In the Kleinian and object relations tradition of analytic psychotherapy, containment refers to the capacity of an individual, or in this case an institution, to mentally receive and hold the disorganised or troubling psychic material of another, rendering it more bearable. The prototype of all containment is that offered by the nursing mother to her baby. This concept will be further elaborated in Chapter Two.

ONE

Between fracture and solidarity

It can be a form of madness to live in a group.

Christopher Bollas, *Being a character* (1992, p 243)

The turn from 'factual truth' to 'meaning', which continues to engage much of social science, has stimulated interest in the production of meaning in institutional life. It arises in an interplay between rationality and desire, as an activity which is at once cognitive and emotional, dependent on both conscious and unconscious processes. The systems of interpersonal care that comprise the welfare state have a fundamental bearing on human vulnerability and well-being and bridge the divide between public and private lives. They are implicated in the construction of political and social identities while reaching at times into the most intimate areas of human experience. It follows that any adequate account of relationships in this arena should at least pose the problem of the connections and disjunctions between inner and outer worlds. After all, politics is formed in their interplay, as is ever more vividly illustrated in the rise and demise of its protagonists. Attempts at tracing the links are more likely to be found in the press than in academic discourse. We are fascinated by the private vulnerability of the powerful, the way it affects their public conduct and its wider ramifications. We are mesmerised by Thatcher's tears, the sexual adventurism of American presidents, the childhoods of terrorists. However, there has been very little exploration of the kind proposed in this book: the mindset generated by the institutions that are charged with managing vulnerability and dependency on behalf of society.

The social relations reflected and reproduced within welfare arrangements will be considered in four dimensions: states of mind, interpersonal relations, institutions and the socio-economic environment. T.H. Marshall (1963, 1971) conceptualised the post-war settlement in terms of three: the reciprocal relationships between individuals and the wider community, welfare institutions and structural inequalities of wealth or opportunity. In order to aid the task of organisation and simplification, I have developed a grid out of two intersecting axes (see Figure 1): one represents relations of attachment and separation between self and other (and therefore bears on the possibility of social solidarity); the other depicts relations of equality and inequality. The choice of these axes is consistent with my intention to consider the intra-psychic, interpersonal, institutional and political relationships implicated in welfare provision.

My two axes: attachment/separation and equality/inequality represent the intersection of the two dimensions of human welfare that have informed the construction of the welfare state. They are not eternal normative principles,

Figure 1: Successive paradigms in post-war British welfare

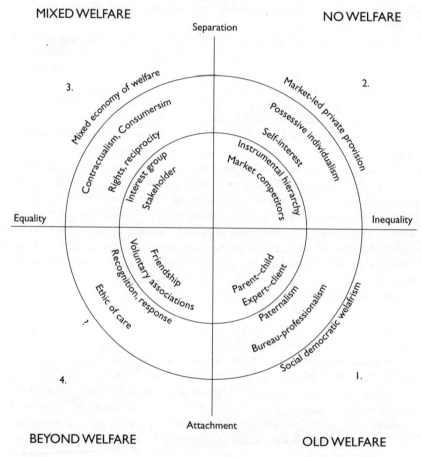

Linking:
Interpersonal relationships
Organisational and cultural principles
Political economy

MIXED WELFARE

Separation

NO WELFARE

3.

Mixed economy of welfare
Contractualism, Consumersim
Rights, reciprocity
Interest group
Stakeholder

Market-led private provision
Possessive individualism
Self-interest
Instrumental hierarchy
Market competitors

2.

Equality

Inequality

Friendship
Voluntary associations
Recognition, response
Ethic of care

Parent–child
Expert–client
Paternalism
Bureau-professionalism
Social democratic welafrism

4.

1.

Attachment

BEYOND WELFARE

OLD WELFARE

but neither are they randomly chosen. They juxtapose the relational concerns of practitioners with the social and economic preoccupations of policy makers. They have a very direct empirical bearing on the ways in which we experience our earliest relationships of dependency and care and the process of individuation that stems from them. They continue to influence the ways in which those relationships are constructed throughout our lives.

First, at the macro level, most public debate about the welfare state is in terms of *social and economic relations*, and the political intentions and conflicts behind policy and opinion formation.

Second, social relations of welfare are reproduced in the *institutional cultures* directly implicated in welfare provision, the values that inform them, and in formal and informal representations of help and helping.

Third, they are reflected in *interpersonal relationships* between people. A growing body of service evaluation attests to the fact that the quality of the helping relationship is at least as important as practical and financial assistance.

Fourth, they become bound to *intra-psychic* material. Helping relationships imply particular states of mind which mobilise a range of socially structured defences. The relative neglect of this dimension has entailed a silence about the ways in which welfare arrangements affect how, or whether, we become responsible caring subjects. It also means we are deprived of a language in which to speak of the irrational, chaotic, fearful experiences that accompany the sociologically defined categories of exclusion, poverty or disadvantage. This dimension is not represented on the grid, partly in the interests of graphic simplicity, and partly because it will require considerable further explanation. It could, however, be thought of as an innermost circle in which each quadrant represents a different state of mind and feeling (see Figure 2, page 47).

It is worth underlining at the outset that I am not claiming causal priority for any one of these dimensions. The fact that they evoke the metaphor of interlinked 'levels of experience' is unavoidable but potentially misleading. (It might be better to conceive of them as 'networked sites of experience' but there would be a loss of clarity in other respects.) There would be considerable difficulties in demonstrating that the content of personal anxieties derive in any linear way from the nature of the socio-political order or vice versa and I would be rightly open to the charge of methodological reductionism if I were to try. If I dwell more on the intra-psychic and interpersonal experiences of welfare subjects it is not because I claim that these in some aggregate sense determine the cultures or structures of welfare societies. Nor do I believe that the felt needs and anxieties of individuals and their capacity to care for one another are simply constructed by welfare discourses or determined by the nature of material provision. The deployment of welfare policy as an instrument of social engineering has been at best a provisional success.

The processes that interest me in this book do not have a clear point of origin and may operate in a circular fashion. For example, immigration does not in any simple sense cause the insecurity associated with the rise of the far Right. This only takes hold, and only among some people, when socially-structured defences, which assure a degree of predictability and a feeling of personal safety, are breached through unemployment, rising crime or whatever. We all share a propensity for the kind of anxiety that leads to scapegoating when under threat. The fact that it finds expression as virulent racist intolerance in certain populations under certain conditions reflects the undermining of social containers which allow the irrational components of this anxiety to be interpreted and held in check. This is precisely the aim of racist demagogic populism and certain types of crude media reportage.

I am not, therefore, suggesting that the various 'levels' of experience can be seamlessly translated into one another, or that it would be productive to try. There is a sense in which dynamics of the inner world are irreconcilable with the structured rationality of social institutions. For Freud (1930), who saw civilisation as being necessarily bought at the price of repression, this was just as well. Our symbolic world is too fluid, too diverse and too much of an imaginative construct to be straightforwardly anchored in the economy. Nevertheless it is difficult to see why one or other level of social analysis should be underprivileged in the consideration of systems which penetrate areas of life as intimate as birth, death, suffering and care.

Mr and Mrs B were a youngish couple who had recently moved into the area, registered for welfare benefits, acquired accommodation and presented themselves to social services with minor difficulties (form-filling) that they could probably have dealt with themselves. Mrs B was in an advanced stage of an uncomplicated first pregnancy. Their bringing themselves to social services' attention was puzzling in that it was done with vehement denunciations of helping professionals in general, and the social workers who took the referral in particular. Mr B, who had limited education, presented himself as one who, but for the misfortunes of life, would have been a brain surgeon, rocket scientist or world statesman. Mrs B assailed just about anybody who happened to cross her path with unprovoked and slanderous verbal attacks. There was seldom any direct exchange between the couple and they appeared to be relying on their shared hostility to social services (together with housing, social security and the health system) as the cement that held them together.

Formally, no action was required in that there was no hard information one way or the other to suggest that their child might not be appropriately cared for – just the sense that behind their respectively grandiose and aggressive presentations they were very lonely and frightened. It was clear that neither felt they could rely on the other and it was almost inconceivable that in this state they could consistently meet the emotional needs of a baby. Every visit to the office was an opportunity to co-opt receptionists, cleaners, social workers, managers and whoever happened to be in the waiting area into the staging of another episode in their family drama. It was so difficult to communicate directly with either of them that two social workers were allocated on the understanding that their roles would inevitably get split and they would have to work hard to integrate them. Sure enough, Mr B homed in on the younger one who had good academic qualifications, attempting to co-opt her into endless discussions on the meaning of life and the future of everything. Mrs B attached herself to the other who she saw as down-to-earth and gutsy, like herself. Both social workers were perfectly clear that they should resist these unrealistic projections and present themselves as both helpful and constraining, and united in the difficult work. Their task was to help the couple to build trust in each other by owning and communicating their personal vulnerabilities and frustrations.

In a very short space of time, however, friction arose between the two workers as each began to identify with 'her' client. The younger graduate entertained notions of encouraging Mr B to take up various courses at the local further education college (where he would almost certainly have been a disruptive presence and would have been further able to escape from the reality of his relationship and responsibilities). The worker positioned as ' down-to-earth' began to behave as if she was personally embattled when her line manager refused to approve all her requests. Between the two workers there was mute hostility, and an inability to focus on the impending arrival of the baby.

At the time the department had been subject to criticism in the local and national press because of its mishandling of certain well-publicised cases. It was also struggling with shortfalls in funding and the need to cut non-essential services. The atmosphere had become increasingly beleaguered with divisions developing between the self-styled 'hard-nosed realists', who wanted to axe all preventive work, and the so-called 'woolly-minded' who merely by holding to established definitions of their role were accused of having their heads in the clouds. It seemed that acrimony was only avoided by vigorous blaming of the government, the press, other agencies and the public. Meanwhile, staff were uncertain about where to look for support and worried about their futures. The supervision system, where the task of holding together contradictory pressures was mainly located, had all but collapsed.

The baby was born amid mounting concern at Mr and Mrs B's apparent loss of contact with reality. A week later they disappeared 'into thin air', leaving no forwarding address.

This example once again illustrates the intersection of different levels of experience. The social workers lost a sense of their task and the ability to cooperate. This might normally have been picked up in supervision. Supervision is an interpersonal encounter which, when it is working as it should, brings the reparative dimensions of a professional and organisational culture to bear on the work process. It thus aims to contain both the divisions and difficulties that arise between workers and the organisation, and those that develop between workers and clients. Containment is both an intra-psychic and interpersonal function. In psychodynamic supervision (Mattinson, 1975; Hughes and Pengelly,

1997) the supervisor reflects on their own emotional responses to the behaviour and affect of the workers since these may unconsciously reflect the dynamics of their interaction with clients. They are thus an important source of information about the predicament of both the worker and the client. In the case outlined above, projective identifications[1] were stimulated in which the workers unconsciously adopted and enacted the split roles Mr and Mrs B had assigned to them. Their personal insecurities and uncertainties were amplified by an organisational culture that was becoming fractious and mistrustful under the strain of wider political pressures. This made them all the more receptive to the projections of their clients and liable, as the organisation was doing, to look for external sources of blame. Note that this analysis does not attribute priority to one or other level of explanation; the problem is to identify the relationship between internal psychic states and interpersonal behaviour and the ways in which they conjoin with organisational and political factors to produce particular emotional patterns and events.

Equality and inequality

The choice of the equality/inequality axis in Figure 1 will hardly be contentious. From its inception the welfare state has been regarded as a response to social inequalities. Since the Second World War its impact on overall distribution of wealth and social goods has ensured it a place of central importance on any government agenda. Even Margaret Thatcher identified a role for services that would mask capitalism's 'unacceptable face'. However, it will become clear that I do not refer to issues of equality in an exclusively material sense. Over the last 20 years the widening of income inequalities has put Britain near to the top of the European league tables for child poverty. These disparities have far-reaching effects – not least on health and life expectancy. As Wilkinson's (1996) epidemiological research has demonstrated, the impact of inequality on health can only be properly understood in psychosocial terms. It is not merely that low income is associated with material deprivation such as poor nutrition, inferior housing and unsafe neighbourhoods. Widening inequalities also have a corrosive effect on the social fabric and therefore on the psychosocial pathways – the sense of belonging, agency and solidarity - through which well-being is established and maintained. Although inescapably dependent on material resources, health and welfare are profoundly influenced by other considerations such as people's attachments to social collectivities.

While this axis invokes themes of wealth distribution and social solidarity, it also brings into play inequalities in caring relationships within families and between the users of services and professionals. It therefore bears on the issue of dependency, which we tend to see as natural and inevitable in children but a source of shame in adults. There appears to have been an unquestioned assumption on the part of successive governments since 1979 that the inequalities of economic exploitation can have a bracing effect on the entrepreneurial spirit while those implicit in relations of dependency are corrosive of character.

Attempts to address the perceived deficiencies of paternalism have led to a reframing of relationships of care in the public sector within the formally egalitarian terms of contract and partnership. However, this can amount to a denial of the inevitability of some inequalities where the use of state-sanctioned professional authority underpins systems of monitoring, protection and coercion. People subject to child protection procedures or the statutory provisions of mental health legislation have few illusions as to the locus of power. In these cases, talk of 'partnership' can seem like an instance of bad faith. More benignly, perhaps, the asymmetries of the therapeutic 'partnership' may be purposely used to promote forms of regression which re-enact unconscious familial dynamics within the helping relationship. A return to primitive states of dependency within a transference[2] may then be a prerequisite for the emotional learning which grows out of a re-establishment of trust in the world. While themes of partnership will be explored more fully in Chapter Five on the mixed economy of welfare, dependency, which stands in a complex relationship to separation and attachment, is a pivotal concept throughout the book.

The politicisation of dependency has arisen not just from the neo-liberal drive to excise so-called dependency cultures, but also through the challenges of disabled people – some of whom have suggested that the very concept of 'care' is now tainted and inescapably demeaning to its recipients. The direct payments lobby has argued, with a degree of success, that financial resources should be given directly to disabled people themselves, thus placing them in a position to employ personal assistants. While material resources are by no means easy to attain, they are comparatively simple to understand and argue for, and this has been an important and innovative gain for some people with physical impairments. However, it begs the question of how best to ensure that those who are vulnerable on account of their mental capacities – whether through illness, learning difficulties, emotional trauma or simply extreme youth or old age – can also find a voice within the formal and informal systems that must address their needs. The emotional resources that are mobilised within the helping process are elusive and resistant to political representation. There is a risk that when attention is shifted to the deceptive transparency of contractual rights to material help, the complexity and necessity of caring relationships may be obscured. The discourse of rights cannot encompass the emotional realities of intimacy, trust and compassion. The principle of equity carries a strong normative value – it would be hard to defend a welfare ethic that did not assume equality of moral worth. However, equity has many dimensions, not all of which can be straightforwardly realised within a contract-based emancipatory project.

Attachment and separation

The second axis in Figure 1 allows us to consider the ways in which social inequalities intersect with experiences of attachment and separation for both the individual and the collective. The experience of separation and differentiation through which individuals are formed depends on the quality of personal attachments. They provide the templates on which later abilities to negotiate connection and distance with others are patterned. Hence they can be understood as the psychosocial foundations of political individualism and collectivism which have informed conceptions of social welfare. The capacity to form personal attachments with distinct others is the basis for later experiences of social solidarity. The process of relating inner and outer reality depends on the nature of these attachments that influence our ability to understand the minds and feelings of other people. Without this there can be no giving or receiving of care.

Recognition of the importance of social and personal attachments for human welfare lies at the heart of the welfare project. In the West this has been explicitly conceived as a counterweight to the tendencies to individualism and social fragmentation inherent in advanced capitalist societies. However, an understanding of attachment-disordered children (Stroufe, 1988) alerts us to the fact that attachment can take disorganised forms which disrupt the processes of individuation on which the development of subjectivity depends. The insecure and avoidant relationships formed by such children extend in adult life into the social sphere, leading to problematic dynamics between individuals and social groups (Holmes, 1996). Collective attachment patterns can be no less problematic: for example, in some strains of communitarianism the community tends to be idealised and romanticised as a place where differences between people are annulled in the face of the common interest. Alternatively it becomes an arena whose boundaries determine the parameters of beleaguered inclusion and pejorative exclusion (Pahl, 1996). As with equality then, we need to develop a complex view of attachment and separation in interpersonal relationships and also as they come to be reflected in solidary or fragmented social relations.

The welfare configurations to which these axes give rise can be read in terms of face-to-face relationships that arise in the experiences of caring, being cared for and being cared about. They are expressed in families, in friendships, between lovers, as well as in informal and organised systems of helping. They are embedded in the discourses that reproduce cultural life – such as justice, morality and exchange. However, they also represent alternative articulations of the main principles around which the formation of the welfare state has revolved. These relate, first, to the proper balance between collective and individual responsibilities and hence between universalism and particularism in public service provision; second, to the role of publicly funded welfare in relation to inequalities of wealth and opportunity. In intimate and personal relationships and in our access to wider cultural forms, our separation and distinctiveness from others are inextricable from the power relations that arise from asymmetry and inequality. These are in tension with an impulse towards attachment and a sense of commonality, which presupposes a recognition of the equal moral worth of individuals. The grid produced by the intersection of the axes suggests the connections that organise the following chapters.

An overview suggests that the social relations of welfare can be characterised in three main typologies (quadrants 1 to 3) with the discernible outlines of an emergent fourth alternative. However, it is important once again to stress that each quadrant represents an ideal type and that the dominant configuration at any given moment is overlaid with features from each of the others. The reason for this has as much to do with fluctuations in our psychic investment in welfare as with the conflicted nature of public policy. Historically, in each of the four types, the underlying assumptions and principles that have driven reform have reflected different coalitions of class and interest. The institutional forms that subsequently emerged were always the outcome of compromise. All four quadrants imply a type of relationship – between the socio-political order, institutional cultures and interpersonal relations, and each of these relationships invoke our capacities for different states of mind. As such they should be regarded as 'positions'[3] rather than phases in the development of the welfare state. It is easy enough to discern successive moves from the universalist and collectivist tendencies implicit in the post-war settlement, through the neo-liberal inspired restructuring, to the emergence of the version of a mixed economy of welfare represented by Blair's 'Third Way'. To say this much, however, is to observe historical contingencies in post-war Britain, rather than make claims about the logic of development or any telos of progress. There is nothing inevitable about an anticlockwise circuit that travels from post-war welfarism, via the Thatcher–Major restructuring, to a consumerised mixed economy of care in tension with a newly emerging participatory paradigm. We could just as easily reverse direction and return to a post-Thatcherite dystopia of unrestrained competition in which care for the other is perceived as an unfortunate constraint on the acquisitive propensities of the self. As I have already said, the model does not in any case aim to provide a blueprint for the future. That would be incompatible with my argument that any enhanced capacity for the recognition of subjectivity in a highly pluralistic society will have to be based on new participatory democratic structures which, by definition, can only be created through social action.

The purpose of this book is not to trace the lines of development between stages of welfare. This has been done exhaustively within political economic histories of the welfare state. I do not intend to produce another one by simply filling in the psychological dimensions. The post-Kleinian psychoanalytic tradition on which I shall often draw is in any case careful not to suggest that the psychological development of human individuals can be read in terms of the sequential relationships between cause and effect that can be discerned in changing social institutions. These may have complex lines of development but there is a sense in which past events precede those in the present and future. In atemporal primary processes of the unconscious the influence of events in real time is often oblique to say the least. Dream images, for example, have a spatial 'here' or 'gone' quality. The distinction becomes clear enough when one witnesses a conversation between a philosopher and a psychoanalyst. The latter is comfortable with the everyday circularity of thought and experience, while the former is more likely to find it an offence against reason. In contrast to

Freud, who proposed a linear approach to the infant's working-through of oral, anal and genital stages, and where fixation is a failure of development, Klein directed her attention to emotional capacities for loving and hating that arise in primitive form in the very first months of life. The occupation of these mental 'positions' is influenced as much by an inner 'phantasy'[4] life as by external environment. Psychic life takes place through the interplay of these positions, even as the child matures and grows.

In Chapter Two I shall expand on this emphasis of Klein's. I shall then explore its implications for a psychosocial politics of welfare as the book unfolds and suggest some indications of future directions in Part 2. In Part 1 I depict the psychological possibilities in four ideal-typical models. While each of these has risen to prominence at one time or another through the process of political and ideological contest, they all continue to be simultaneously enacted in parts of the welfare system. The study of the particular mix of institutional forms in any national settlement is the province of comparative social policy within as well as between welfare states. Esping-Andersen (1990), for example, develops his typology of social democratic, conservative, and liberal welfare formations by assigning indices to features of key symbolic significance such as the proportion of private pensions, or health plans, or the significance of poor relief in relation to total social expenditure. Inevitably, given the large scale of his macro-economic canvass (which takes in 18 welfare states), this is a 'mapping' exercise, where any historical dimension is provided by comparing the institutional mix at different given points in time. Thus the UK scores high on 'de-commodifying' effects in 1950, but fails to progress, so that by 1980 it is at the bottom of the European league-table. While I am working on a much smaller scale with a focus on personal, micro-social and organisational dynamics within one particular welfare state, this too is a form of 'mapping' and I shall refer in more detail to the psychological correlatives of commodification.

My project, then, is to explore four alternative dimensions of welfare and ask how we might begin to understand their social relations, cultural meanings and institutional structures from the perspective of mental states or 'positions'. A close scrutiny of legislation and policy yields contradictory and overlapping lines of development which to some extent obscure the distinctiveness of each configuration. However, the clear definition lost in the practical implementation of policy is compensated by the sharp relief of accompanying ideological justifications. For example, the fact that the Thatcherite project was never realised in its pure form in no way diminishes its success in stimulating fundamental shifts in public sensibility. In particular, this affects perceptions of the proper balance between public and private responsibility; forms of altruism; the legitimacy of redistributive mechanisms; the attribution of moral worth and denigration; and the locus of persecutory anxieties.

I must confess to some nervousness in trying to represent reality in concentric circles. I will be open to the charge that this is far too tidy. Furthermore, it is out of step with the postmodern preference for the fluid play of multiplicity and irony (all of which I find as entertaining as the next woman). However, I do not think my approach ignores the insights that would follow from challenging the notion of a unitary subject. Postmodernism itself becomes a form of intellectual tyranny when it denies the need to organise our perceptions in order to think about the complexity of social relationships. Schemes like the one developed here act as containers for thinking processes. They should not be seen as the rigid determinants of the content of thought itself. A series of lectures to post-graduate students on postmodernism and welfare confirmed the usefulness of the grid – not in order to achieve a closure or resolve what had gone before. We had all enjoyed the permissiveness of the theme, along with the movies, architecture and the street style, too much for that. It was rather the realisation that play without structure – however transiently and loosely inhabited – quickly exhausts itself. My book is intended as a modest exercise in psychosocial bridge-building between domains which, for all our exhortations to interdisciplinarity and interprofessionalism, still tend to be dealt with separately.

The lines of debate

In diagrammatic terms, the evolution of welfare so far can be represented along a diagonal line drawn between quadrants 1 and 3. That is from universalistic 'old welfare' towards a consumerised 'mixed welfare' that will probably continue to evolve for some time to come. A line drawn between quadrants 1 and 2 represents the sharply polarised views of neo-liberal evangelism versus old welfarism; the unfettered market versus collectivist state provision; individualism versus universalism; and individual preference versus the paternalism of bureau-professionals. The opposition between the two pits the taxpayer against the needy and reached its peak with the inauguration of market-oriented welfare reforms under successive Conservative governments in the eighties and early nineties. It contrasts Thatcher's famous declaration that 'there is no such thing as society' with the principle of largely enforced collective responsibility. It represents the lines of political debate between the Old Left and the New Right. Although a pure market was perhaps never a political possibility, and the more radical versions of this vision are for the time being subdued, the restructuring of welfare around quasi-markets is still widely seen as synonymous with efficiency and cost-containment. I shall explore the psychological and institutional consequences of these two configurations in Chapters Three and Four.

If the 'no welfare' alternative (quadrant 2), were to be realised in pure form, public welfare work would not survive. However, even at the height of their radicalism, Conservative governments only succeeded in tilting the balance a little more towards the private sector. The Blair government by its second term of office was clearly prepared to push private sector involvement in public services further than the Conservatives had been able to do. This was in the face of considerable trades union opposition and public disquiet about the failure of rail privatisation and the future of the National Health Service. The public–private mix under New Labour can therefore be regarded as different in proportion rather than kind to that of its predecessors. For this reason some analysts may be inclined to develop a three-stage model highlighting the continuity between New Labour and Conservative versions of the mixed economy of care. Barnes and Prior's typology (2000) is a case in point where the social democratic welfare state is succeeded by the mixed economy of care, and new developments point to the emergence of an 'ecological' paradigm. Seen purely from the point of view of public policy this is a perfectly coherent approach in which Blair's Third Way for welfare is a compromise that seeks to arrive pragmatically at a liberal and social democratic blend. However, I will try to show that, from the perspective of mental states and relationships that find expression in welfare arrangements, it is essential to keep quadrants 2 and 3 apart. Quadrant 2 depicts a state of anti-welfare that has exerted, and continues to exert, a powerful psychological pull which finds tangible expression in the limits to collective responsibility – what we will *not* pay for, who we will *blame* for their own misfortunes and who we will *scapegoat* for ours. It gives rise to a vision of individualism in which the therapeutic, monitoring and coercive roles of public service professionals are reoriented towards the assessment and management of risk, and in which the provision of social care is privatised and driven by commercial considerations.

In Britain the influence of the neo-liberal turn was mitigated in practice by the relative strength of the public sector. Even after the prunings and confrontations of the Thatcher–Major years, the greater part of individual financial contributions towards welfare is invested in pensions. The continuing expansion of insurance for personal and nursing care affects only a minority of the population and this limits the scope for a vigorous American-style 'managed care' market. Nevertheless, the shifting of responsibility back onto families was a significant reversal of direction in welfare policy and one that New Labour was in no great hurry to undo. The first Blair government inherited the architecture of the mixed economy of care and thus far the infrastructure remains intact. A commitment to consumerism continues to inform conceptions of rights and social justice. However, there are significant differences in its interpretation of individualism and in its (moderate) denunciation of the inequality and inefficiency of unregulated markets. The modernisation programme combines more generous funding for health and welfare with an emphasis on regulation and accountability. Rights to welfare have been grafted onto obligations to participate in the labour market. Responsibility has thus acquired a new inflection as a mark of citizenship in a youthful 'modern' Britain where social support is linked to paid employment while 'old' dependency continues to be denigrated.

Within the Labour Party the 'Third Way' modernisers in quadrant 3 tend to depict the Left as a recalcitrant 'old guard' firmly located in quadrant 1. They lay claim to agendas of participation and empowerment that at first sight seem to belong in quadrant 4. Only a close examination of the meanings and intentions behind such concepts as empowerment, participation and partnership can reveal whether or not these claims are justified. Empowerment may mean nothing more than a 'choice' between limited predetermined options, and the language of partnership can mask new forms of coercion. The 'pull' of quadrant 4, though often marginalised, has always been present within grass-roots movements and as a democratic tendency ensuring an ongoing critical dialogue with the 'old welfarists' in quadrant 1.

The fourth quadrant necessitates a shift in focus and level of analysis. It represents not so much a model as a number of perspectives that are emergent and sporadically realised as an alternative democratising impulse within the welfare system. It finds expression more often as critique than as reconstruction. I shall argue that it is implicit in caring relations as such, and is suggestive of an ethic of care. I have called it 'beyond welfare' because it is an arena of suggestion and imagination or of creative 'illusion' as Hoggett (2000) would have it. There are always local politics, projects and practices that attempt to enhance individual and collective well-being. It is often among these that we find new ways of doing things. The perspectives that might take us beyond the welfare models in quadrants 1, 2 and 3 have disparate origins: feminism, the disability movement, some user and self-help groups, voluntary organisations and the often muted contributions of carers and the people they care for. They have historical roots in organisations for community regeneration which have assumed that democracy in welfare services needs to be anchored in group structures promoting affiliation and interdependency. Where they arise within mainstream and statutory provision, they tend to be vulnerable to wider political and economic agendas and, at a local level, to processes of rationalisation and restructuring. These perspectives serve as an insistent reminder of the abstract formality of discourses of rights and choice that constitute the mixed welfare model.

There is an obvious temptation to map the principles of individualism and collectivism onto the grid in such a way that the individual subject emerges as the prime focus of concern above the horizontal axis and collectives below it. This would be misleading if it were to be assumed that the individual and the social remain locked in eternal opposition such that one must always be privileged at the expense of the other. Although there is a sense in which tension between the two is inevitable, I shall suggest that an ethically acceptable welfare system must allow individuality, as opposed to individualism, to flourish to the maximum. The challenge then is to create the conditions for full recognition of the equal moral worth of persons, together with the inextricable attachments that individuals have to groups, whether these be families, associations or communities. In this way the submergence of the individual, along with the spectre of 'dependency culture' that so terrifies the individualists, can be avoided.

The task, in other words, is to help group members individuate themselves from the group, so that they may come to live freely and critically, while knowing themselves to be social creatures, bound in relationships with others

> from birth to death. In many ways an impossible task, some ways of failing at it are better than others. (Alford, 1994, p 7)

The recovery of the submerged and often subjugated knowledge that would allow a clearer view of more democratic and participatory social relations of care involves placing at the centre of the project an ethic of care and a fuller, more nuanced and more compassionate conception of justice than is to be found in quadrant 3. This involves response and recognition, understood as something different from professionalised models of responsibility and the reciprocity of contractual and consumer relations. In particular, it involves a transition to a set of relations in which the other is positioned as subject rather than as object. This is hardly a new project. A number of concepts which have gained currency in social welfare – particularly those derived from therapeutic discourses – have implied the dilemmas that arise from systems that reduce people to the status of objects. The concepts of respect for others, of self-determination, of non-judgementalism, as well as calls for greater user participation and ownership, have all been developed out of an assertion of the importance of subjectivity. They are recognised by many practitioners as worthy principles that are hard to ground in existing practices. Philp (1979) pointed to it in his paradox of 'creating a subject in objective knowledge'. The terms of this ingenious formulation could equally, however, have been reversed to encompass the other side of the problem – that of creating the object in subjective knowledge – in this context directing attention to the ways in which the external relations of domination and discrimination, that all too often exclude and marginalise those who receive welfare services, are internalised and represented.

The recovery of this in the context of a more acute political critique of the oppressive potential of welfarism is overdue. It would also help to bring the issue of compassion into the public domain, which is where it needs to be if welfare reform is to transcend the instrumental logic of modernisation and consumerism.

Notes

[1] Projective identification (see Hinschelwood, 1989 for summary explanation) arises when parts of the self are split off and attributed to another object – who is then induced to feel them and act them out. In its benign forms it leads to unconscious communication and possibly empathy. However, in more problematic forms it is implicated in omnipotent defences and involves the forceful evacuation of parts of the self which is then left in a depleted state. Effectively it leads to a confusion between self and other.

[2] Transference has been a pivotal and evolving concept within psychoanalysis (Hinschelwood, 1989). Broadly speaking, it now refers to the process whereby modes and patterns of relating that developed with earlier significant others are unconsciously re-enacted within the therapeutic relationship. It therefore offers an interpretive key to

unconscious conflicts and the possibility of their working-through, and resolution within, the context of the analytic situation.

[3] This is consistent with a Kleinian frame of reference in which mental life develops not so much through sequential stages as through the extension of the individual's capacity to handle the anxiety provoked by threat and the complexity of existence, without resorting to defensive simplifications. The ability to exercise this capacity is always provisional and reversion to primitive strategies of splitting is an ever-present possibility under stress. The different defensive modes and their consequences for thinking and relating to others will be explained in Chapter Two.

[4] Distinguished from 'fantasy' by its wholly unconscious origins.

TWO

Psychosocial welfare

I sought my death and found it in my womb;
I looked for life and saw it was a shade;
I trod the earth and knew it was my tomb;
And now I die and now I was but made....

Chidiock Tichborne, *Verses of Praise and Joy*
(1586, cited in Sackville-West and Nicolson, 1945, p 209)

The story of the welfare state – our institutional form of publicly sponsored compassion – is intertwined with the official story of post-war reconstruction. The repetition, elaboration, reworking and critique of that story in social policy and sociology is so well known that it needs little repetition here. According to postmodern sensibilities it reads, in the broadest of outlines, as a tale of hubris – a great misguided experiment of social engineering in the service of the common weal; a project which carried the seeds of its own corruption in its grandiose universalistic assumptions about our ability to understand and eradicate those levels of need which stood between the nation which had triumphed over fascism, and the good life it deserved. The key to its failings is to be found in an unrealistic faith in the state as a vehicle for compassion and a unitary and distinctly 'waspish' view of the citizen who was to become the beneficiary of its largesse.

Alternatively, a more nostalgic version gives the narrative a different twist: the welfare state is a tale of benign intentions thwarted by the logic of capitalist accumulation – ultimately hostile to the expansion of public expenditure. Itself an outcome of the struggles of the labour movement for distributive and social justice, it becomes another arena within which these demands and the conflicts they provoke are pursued. In this version the fragile compassionate values of human welfare are pitted against titanic forces of capitalist globalisation.

Yet another and distinctly less sympathetic account sees the entire project and its underpinning collectivist values as fundamentally flawed – an indefensible constraint on the pursuit of private interests which is to be held responsible for the degradation of the entrepreneurial spirit. Dependent on a modern version of state of nature theory, this view concedes to the state only the power to regulate the unacceptable costs of social competition and relegates compassion to intimate and private relations.

These are only the bare outlines of the available plots: they acquire depth and variation as the characters are written into them and as the action develops through their conflicts and fellow feelings. The focus of my interest is on these relationships between welfare professionals and the people they work with. I have argued that the most persuasive and rounded stories are psychosocial. They move between the intimate, local and particular and the wider culture and institutions. We need more than sociology to develop these accounts and in the final chapter I will take a closer look at the way in which the narrative form itself enables us to make links that might otherwise elude us.

Attachment and solidarity

This chapter draws primarily on the work of Melanie Klein and Donald Winnicott to explain the intra-psychic and interpersonal processes of attachment and separation. I do not, however, wish to downplay the significance of the tradition that has grown out of the work of Bowlby (1969, 1973, 1980). This may be better known to readers who are familiar with subsequent empirical research programmes on forms of attachment in children and adults, and their impact on personality development and social relationships (for example Ainsworth, 1982, 1989; Fonagy et al, 1994). This work has made an important contribution to the assessment of attachment behaviour within natural and substitute families.

Howe (1995) has pursued an empirical and theoretical research programme which attempts to develop the diagnostic and clinical implications of attachment theory. On the basis of this he has put forward a powerful argument for a return to relationship-based practice (1998), which has been jeopardised by the current preference for measurement of need and external behaviour. He points out (1996) that this shift is in line with a postmodern trend towards a preoccupation with surface at the expense of depth. This abandons any attempt to trace the underlying connections between motivation, personality, meaning and the social environment:

> The individual is seen as a psychologically discrete isolated entity without a psycho-social history.... The result is a here-and-now world in which work is episodic – cases are opened and closed according to agreements set, time allowed, immediate needs met. Each new case episode is unrelated to either the past or the future. (Howe, 1998, p 48)

It is no accident that in the post-war period psychoanalytically informed thinking influenced the helping professions via theories of attachment and child development. Rustin (1996) considered this within the context of a welfare state based on the ideal of a moral community and remarked on the resurgence of interest as the 'New Conservatism' began to show signs of having run its course. He asked if a 'politics of attachment' could provide a viable alternative to the individualism of the preceding 20 years or whether it signified a regressive and nostalgic longing for a world that is lost. The main impact of attachment theory has been to furnish an account of the micro-social processes in the early years of life whereby the basis of a secure personality and the capacity for relatedness is formed. The question that must be asked is what, if anything, can it contribute to an understanding of the ways in which these qualities and capacities inform our sense of connectedness to others in adult life? This requires levels of analysis that extend beyond the foundations of attachment in the early nurturing relationship to the conditions of belonging to communities and other social networks. Rustin suggested that in order to do this we should consider the importance of symbolic attachment within highly mobile and flexible modern societies where the media of communication have expanded the possibilities of identification with virtual or imaginary collectivities.

Rustin points out that new dimensions of social relationship become available to discussion once symbolic representation is taken into consideration. Attachment can be understood as the basis for a state of mind which allows us to trust and connect with others, including communities of value which can exist 'at a distance' in both space and time, and can change over the life-course. He also emphasises the importance of analysing the macro-social and economic preconditions for both secure face-to-face and symbolic attachments that need to be identified and pursued as political objectives. Margaret Thatcher's vision of economic liberty entailed the promotion of individualism with inequality as a necessary spur to competition. Whatever the achievements of 'New Conservatism', community development was not among them.

'Disin-klein-ed' to psychoanalysis

Melanie Klein (1975) regarded herself primarily as a clinician and references to wider culture and politics are sparse in her work. There are few social theorists who have reflected on the wider implications of Klein's views on mental development, but in recent years there has been a resurgence of interest in her ideas and in analysts such as Winnicott and Bion who responded to them in distinctive ways. Her influence among health and welfare practitioners has declined since the fifties and early sixties, probably because it was seen as predominantly clinical in its applications at a time when professionals were turning to sociology for explanations of the relationships between individuals and their environments. The assault on psychoanalysis in the late sixties and early seventies was inclined to parody the earlier work of psychiatric social workers and child guidance specialists as exclusively concerned with the inner life to the exclusion of material considerations, however overwhelming (Pearson et al, 1988).

Another line of attack came from advocates of scientific social work (Fischer, 1976; Sheldon, 1978; Brewer and Lait, 1980) with their insistence on behaviourist psychology, empirical research findings and the experimental method. According to Howe (1998) the overall effect was to strengthen the research community relative to practitioners – ironically without much demonstrable gain in effectiveness. Despite this, behaviourist interventions and empirical evaluation are enjoying something of a second coming via the evidence-based practice movement. This time around they draw strength from a stronger alliance – between public sector managerialists in league with academic institutions hungry for research grants, and powerful funding bodies with a historical preference for quantitative methodologies.

A third influence has come from the legal profession and a shift towards the management of risk (Parton, 1998). A series of public enquiries into child deaths exposed what were perceived to be the evidential and forensic shortcomings of the child protection apparatus in relation to an adversarial legal system. While proceduralisation has been a response to public demands for greater accountability and assertive management, practitioners may feel ambivalent about trading professional discretion for standardised protocols, whatever their defensive utility.

> The true winners of these battles against psychosocial casework have been lawyers, managers and proceduralists; the writers of manuals, the authors of guidelines, the advocates of defensive practices, and those who believe that human misery is best treated by trained functionaries working in highly structured organisations and not by educated professionals practising reflectively in organic free-thinking teams. (Howe, 1998, p, 48)

The development of psychoanalytic ideas continued in the therapeutic strongholds such as the Tavistock Clinic and benefited from contributions of feminism and cultural studies. However, it became increasingly difficult to sustain an overt commitment to the extension of psychodynamic practice within statutory organisations. This was neither the first nor last time that the direction of thinking within social work had run counter to surrounding intellectual trends. The restructuring and retraction of welfare provision in the eighties was to further the decline. Social services organisations were obliged to adopt increasingly rigid neo-Taylorist approaches to performance just as these were being abandoned in the private sector. Psychodynamic approaches were once again vulnerable to caricature – this time for being expensive and interminable. By the beginning of the nineties there had been a severe deskilling in this type of work. The Diploma in Social Work was thus founded on the functional analysis of a profession whose therapeutic repertoire had already been depleted. Competency-led models of assessment that rely on behavioural indicators may be in tune with wider tendencies to rely on reductive economic criteria of effectiveness, but they do not lend themselves readily to the reflective teaching and learning processes that relationship-based work demands (Froggett, 1997).

These combined influences have ensured that the development of Kleinian and post-Kleinian thought has been neglected in social work over the last three decades despite its increasing social application elsewhere. Dismay at the managerialisation of the profession and the loss of relational perspectives appears to be widespread. A short article in *Professional Social Work* (Froggett, 1998) calling for 'a revitalised social casework' elicited an unanticipated volume of mail. Many students still enrol on the Diploma in Social Work with the hope of doing relationship-based work and have their expectations abruptly confounded. Meanwhile continued demand for therapeutic services is reflected in buoyant recruitment to counselling courses. Many of these are based on humanistic psychology, which as I pointed out in Chapter One, does not necessarily extend to critical thinking.

A first encounter with Klein's conceptual framework is puzzling precisely because of her insistence on rooting her account of human development in the internal world of the pre-social child who has as yet acquired little in the way of culture. Other object relations theorists such as Winnicott have laid greater emphasis on the interplay between the internal and external world and on the interpersonal experience of 'real relationships'. Klein's approach appears to be in contradiction with views, which emphasise the socially constructed nature of reality. Indeed a radical social constructionism would be at odds with that part of Kleinian theory which appears to insist on a drive-related account of mental life based on the conflict between creativity and aggression. Later writers, however, have interpreted these drives less as instincts than as a passionate conflict in the development of the infant's mind – the interplay between love and hate (Alford, 1989).

Klein is notorious for her grim view of the centrality of hate and aggression in mental development, of our propensity for envy and paranoia, and of guilt as the foundation of the capacity for love. It is this that has made her work unpopular in the US particularly among ego psychologists, who share with humanistic counselling a central concern with processes of adaptation. In mainstream British social work, in much of counselling, and also to an extent in nursing, this interest in adaptation dominates the therapeutic agenda. It offers a very different perspective on personal integration to that of Klein's depth psychology and while some have expressed unease at its conformist implications (Rojek et al, 1988), it has furnished a relatively accessible, if romantically incoherent, mantra of helping relationship: the famous 'unconditional positive regard'.

Even when feminists put parenting and family relationships at the forefront of their agenda, Klein's work failed to attract much attention. This may have been because her account of the development of morality, love and knowledge, so firmly located in the context of babies' earliest relationships with their mothers, still appeared to focus one-sidedly on the infant. Dinnerstein's (1976) *The mermaid and the minotaur* was an exception. However, this book which connected psychosexual oppression, and the rigidity and deformation of the sexual division of labour, with the gendered nature of parenting, was probably less influential than Chodorow's (1978) *The reproduction of mothering*. The latter also mounted a critique of parenting arrangements from an object relations perspective, but one which seems to have been more digestible – probably because of its readier compatibility with familiar sociological accounts of family relations. In addition, while feminists such as Chodorow (1978) and Benjamin (1990) have creatively appropriated other forms of object relations theory, they have found Klein's apparent reliance on drive theory difficult to incorporate into a vision of human relations in which subjectivity is not entirely determined by gender. Within the welfare professions, belief in people's capacity to change in sympathetic environments is an article of faith leading to an understandable reluctance to acknowledge the existence of limits determined by nature, and unease at the implicit universalism of the passions. However, faith is a poor substitute for theory – a fact that becomes apparent as it collapses into a 'nothing works' pessimism, in which hope of change is abandoned in favour of 'damage limitation'.

At first sight, then, Klein's work seems unpromising as a basis for models of welfare which seem to require a degree of optimism regarding our ability to care for one another. It is, after all, optimism that allows us to imagine a better future and it is difficult to find its justification in a view of the mind that identifies a persistent potential for destruction; in which split 'paranoid–schizoid' states are a part of normal functioning; in which the propensity for gratitude and love is described in terms of the achievement of a 'depressive position', and even this is to be regarded as unstable. Yet despite, or perhaps because of, the fact that we are condemned to an ongoing struggle between our love and our hate, there is in Klein an account of love in which it is possible to discover not only our capacity for destruction but also our ability to make good the damage that we do. It is the reparative impulse born of guilt and gratitude that forms the basis of ethical life. This lends itself to an understanding of compassion – love directed to recognition of and care for the other.

Rustin (1996) draws attention to the impact of wartime disruption in turning public attention to the problem of how to restore and sustain social bonds. In addition, the experience of animosity and barbarity on such a scale gave rise to a need to understand and reflect on the psychic potential for destructiveness. It may well be that declining interest in Klein's work in the sixties reflected the shifting agenda of an increasingly individualist society while its recovery in the context of rampant consumerism and social fragmentation could offer a critical alternative to the social conservatism that advocates a return to traditional families and communities.

Love, knowledge and morality

Klein's observation of infants led her to identify a process of splitting as the first and most fundamental of the defences. Her starting point is the newborn baby who inhabits a chaotic sensual environment in which boundaries between self and not-self have yet to be established and in which there is no sense of mother as a separate person. This unbounded world can either be dominated by the warm, milky plenitude of satisfaction – the 'good' breast that answers to the baby's need, or the misery and frustration of the empty, absent 'bad' breast. Because the child has as yet no sense of spatial limits or the durability of things in time, these sensations seem overwhelming. The experience is one of being either completely loved and cared for, or persecuted by cold, hunger and pain. At this stage the baby creates its own internal reality through 'phantasy' which arises from an innate capacity to organise bodily perceptions according to a primitive sense of danger and fear, or safety and comfort. The sense of an 'I' that can think about and interpret the world is yet to develop, and in its absence complexity is unbearable. The splitting protects the fragile developing ego by keeping the phantasy of the good apart from, and uncontaminated by, the bad. Although processes of psychic differentiation and integration will eventually allow the developing child to develop the capacity for ambivalence and the ability to relate to whole objects, splitting remains as an integral part of the defensive repertoire – always the first to be mobilised when under threat. Welfare agencies, hospitals and schools are very familiar with splitting in clients who rage against a particular worker while idealising another. This allows identification with an individual who is protected from negative projections and becomes the bearer of hope for change; however, it also defends against the need to come to terms with an imperfect and contradictory reality.

By keeping the good sensations apart from the bad, the baby can build up an internal sense of goodness. This is the basis of the trust that will allow it eventually to overcome anxiety and fear, repair the split and develop a realistic ambivalence towards a world which is neither wholly good, nor wholly bad. In the meantime, it projects its internal sense of persecution onto 'bad' objects outside of the self (spitting, kicking, biting) where they can be safely attacked and annihilated. It also projects a sense of an ideal onto 'good' objects which it re-introjects (sucking, nuzzling), thus building up a store of internal, protective objects which can be loved and valued. We see the consequences of a failure to develop this inner bulwark against danger in paranoid adults who interpret life as full of menace despite all evidence to the contrary. It is futile to try to argue a hypochondriac out of his conviction that he is ill by pointing to his appearance of health, since this will merely be reinterpreted as symptomatic of pathology.

Besides helping to control primitive anxiety, splitting helps the baby to develop a capacity to make distinctions, initially between part-objects – loving and hating bits of experience in relation to the phantasised good and bad breast. Every object to which the child relates has an internal representation and therefore the active splitting always involves a splitting of emotional states between the loving and hating parts of the self. This is characteristic of 'the paranoid–schizoid' position and it is this that creates a predisposition to dualistic responses towards internal and external objects. It is at the root of those states of mind which will later latch on to cultural material that reproduces polarised representations of reality: bad/good, black/white, male/female. Because the splitting of our perceptions arises as a defence against anxiety, it favours the distortions of thought which give rise to the negative discriminations typical of sexism, racism or homophobia in which despised characteristics are located in others who are different. It is for this reason that communities under pressure from poverty, crime and other forms of social dislocation, or whose cultural or national identities are threatened, will so readily resort to exclusionary practices. The fact that the other is created not just as a social category, but as an internal representation, a repository for the disowned 'badness' that threatens the self, means that it performs a very useful protective function. For this reason, racial attitudes are highly resistant to rational persuasion. Although the nature of the threat and content of the projections takes very different forms, a similar psychic defence operates in relation to sexism, homophobia, ageism and so on. The establishment of a basic level of security and trust in the environment seems to be a precondition for 'reasonable' objections to such attitudes to gain a purchase.

In infancy, where the splitting works as it should, and where the mother survives the attacks and continues to provide relatively consistent loving care, the child can eventually begin to integrate its internal phantasies. As it acquires a new capacity for whole object relatedness the quality of mental life is transformed. The tendency to split the self and the object, and the extreme loving and hating gives way to a more realistic ambivalence. The infant comes to recognise that the good and bad mother are one and the same – the mother on whom it depends. In learning to relate to whole objects outside of itself, it develops a sense of self as a person separate from others – a subject. Along with this, it recognises that its aggression towards mother was directed at the very person who is the source of goodness, to feel guilt at this aggression, and to wish to repair the damage done in phantasy. Hence the achievement of the 'depressive position' opens the way for a growth of love based on gratitude and the ability to care and be cared for by another. According to Alford (1989) this kind of love is compassionate rather than libidinal in that the other is not loved merely because she satisfies a need, but for her own distinctive qualities.

Recognition that others are loveable in their own right drives the infant to get closer to them and gain a knowledge based on a sense of connection. In small children it is easy to observe a tendency to attack, destroy and control toys, household objects and mother herself. This then alternates with a playful caring. Both dispositions: to break up and destroy and to repair and preserve, play an essential part in coming to know the world. Through these activities infants enact the internal mental states which allow them to manipulate their objects. Some feminists (Benjamin, 1990; Rose, 1994) have pointed out that the success of scientific enquiry is often couched in metaphors of penetrative aggression – nature must be *forced* to yield her secrets. However, there is another route to discovery premised on relatedness and a concern to preserve the integrity of the object. The development of a capacity to recognise others as whole and separate is also fundamental to the *desire* to know. It signifies the ability to tolerate frustration and overcome fearfulness at things outside of the self. The child's curiosity can then emerge in the playful process of linking inner and outer reality. The depressive position thus establishes a connection between love, knowledge and morality.

The historical subject

The paranoid–schizoid position is essentially a timeless one in which the present is split off from past and future alike and only the feelings that belong to the here-and-now can be entertained. When people function in this mode their emotional responses become one-dimensional. They deny past experience and rewrite history in terms of the present. They are incapable of imagining that any future might be different. Their moods: gloom, rage, boredom, elation may turn out to be transient, but so long as they maintain their grip they have a changeless quality – they just happen. The transition to the depressive position marks the birth of the reflective historical subject (Ogden, 1992) where it becomes possible not only to have a sensation but to think about it, create meaning and understand how one is changed by it. This is obviously central to the development of the narrative faculty to which I will return in the final chapter. Ogden would in fact prefer the term 'historical position' in that the reaction to a past that is lost is not 'depression' as we generally use the term, but mourning – the ability to acknowledge that our lost and loved objects are gone and to sustain our feelings for them over time.

There is not only a difference in the quality of love between the two positions, but also the quality of hate. Along with the development of an 'I' comes a sense of personal responsibility which informs the principal anxiety of the depressive position: that our love will not be strong enough to preserve the loved object and that our aggression will drive it away. The distinction between envy and jealousy provides a useful example. Envy is a classically paranoid–schizoid two-dimensional state arising from a wish to have what one wants for oneself and to destroy what one cannot have. I once knew a who woman had spent some time decorating her small flat. When she moved out of it she systematically tore the wallpaper off the walls and scratched the paintwork, saying, "why should someone else enjoy what I have done?". Jealousy, on the other hand, implies the ability to put oneself in the position of a third party and to feel ambivalence towards them – resenting yet identifying with them for enjoying what one loves and wants. When I left the house where my small children had spent their early years, the thought of the new owners inhabiting this intensely intimate personal space was unwelcome and disturbing. Nevertheless, part of me wanted them to enjoy the place for which I had felt such affection, and after our furniture was carried out, I cleaned it from top to bottom, fretting over the stains on the carpet.

Reality and ambivalence

There is more to say of this ability to put oneself in the place of another (I shall return to the psychodynamics of compassion in Chapter Six where I identify its importance for a politics of recognition). For the time being, it is worth noting that this concept creates difficulties in welfare discourse because of its overtones of charity and sentimentality (Shakespeare, 2000). However, it has wider significance and is overdue for rehabilitation both as a state of mind and a form of knowledge. It offers us a starting point for the critique of instrumentalism within modern welfare services, where the attempt to cost every aspect of provision corrodes the communicative relationships on which care-giving depends. The capacity for compassionate love is for Klein a developmental achievement that depends on the ability to move from the desired unity with the 'good' mother to a more ambivalent and realistic 'warts-and-all' attachment to another person. This involves overcoming the all-or-nothing type of love that cannot withstand disappointment. This latter tendency is recognised as a mark of immaturity in childhood friendships and in fantasy worlds populated by heroes and villains. It has often been said that it reverberates through cultural attitudes to femininity in which women are either seen as implausibly virtuous or unspeakably vicious. It is very much present in unstable adult erotic attachments. Depressive love, by contrast, avoids the extremes of idealisation and denigration and because it is tolerant of imperfection it is able to appreciate not only particular qualities but the relations between them.

Because artists have a peculiar ability to represent internal emotional states in their work, cultural material is particularly useful for evoking the differences. Punk Rock and more recently some forms of Rap extended the possibilities of the paranoid–schizoid as an art form, and we frequently find this state of mind represented transiently in narratively structured drama and opera. Music, however, is especially well adapted to the expression of the depressive. The pieces that resonate most strongly with any individual are, of course, highly personal. For myself, they would include Beethoven's Violin Concerto, much of the work of Van Morrison, John Coltrane Live at Birdland, Schubert's Quintet in C Major, all the great requiems and too many blues songs to mention. Wordsworth evokes this state of mind in a meditation on nature occasioned by the anniversary of his sister's death (for Klein, this 'depressive' love is linked to knowledge – the ability to perceive the world as whole):

> For I have learned to look on nature not as in the hour
> Of thoughtless youth; but hearing oftentimes
> The still, sad music of humanity,
> Nor harsh nor grating, though of ample power
> To chasten and subdue.
> (*Lines composed above Tintern Abbey*, 1798)

The point to note is that this is not merely the work of adaptation and judicious balancing which is at the heart of liberal individualism. That worldview was captured earlier by Alexander Pope. It is a view of humanity and society as formed in the juxtaposition of competing forces which hold each other in check for the good of the whole:

> Two principles in human nature reign;
> Self-love to urge and Reason to restrain...
> Self-love, the spring of motion acts the soul;
> Reason's comparing balance rules the whole,
> Man but for that no action could attend,
> And, but for this, were active to no end....
> (*Essay on Man*, 1733)

The implications of Klein's account are that while reason and self-centred love can indeed oppose and check one another, this is not all there is. Love and knowledge need not stand in eternal opposition because in a depressive relation to reality they are linked in an attempt to come closer to the object, while recognising and respecting its otherness, and allowing it to speak for itself. We have here the basis of an intersubjective knowledge which, unlike instrumental reason, is oriented not to prediction and control but to a closer, more particular, understanding. In this view, knowledge cannot be abstracted from values, for it establishes our connection to the world. The quality of attention paid to its object depends on the state of mind of the perceiver. Even our most dispassionate knowledge is emotional at its core. The implications of this for welfare will be explored further, particularly in Chapter Six in relation to the links between care, compassion and recognition, and in the final chapter on narrative.

Disappointment, containment and creativity

Later writers who responded to Klein, like Wilfred Bion (1961, 1967, 1970) and Donald Winnicott (1958, 1965, 1971) focused on the interactive component of the relationship between mother and baby in an attempt to understand better how the transition from paranoid–schizoid to depressive position can occur. In the process they turned their attention to the development of thinking – the child's capacity to form and manipulate symbols, and the conditions of creativity in both caring and imaginative play. Once again the connection between loving, hating and knowing comes to the fore.

Whereas Klein emphasises the conflict that lies at the root of emotional life, Winnicott's concern with the developing infant's use of its environment is affirmative. His account of creativity (1971) and his depiction of the facilitating environment has immediately practical consequences which, extended beyond the activity of childcare, provide an account of the conditions for cultural creativity, with implications for education, social welfare, leisure and organisational life. His concern to depict the 'transitional object' and the 'potential space' between the internal and external world offers fertile possibilities for the articulation of psychoanalytic and social theory. His concept of 'good-enough mothering' has become naturalised among childcare professionals as a benign and realistic acknowledgement of both the needs of the infant and the difficult compromises of child-rearing. Furthermore, Winnicott has found sympathy in recent years among writers of postmodernist persuasion such as Flax (1990). She argues that his distinction between the 'false self' (rigid, intellectualised, controlling) and 'true self' (relational, playful and fluid) comes very close to the distinction between the unitary self of the Enlightenment and the 'decentred' self of postmodernist critique. Finally, although Winnicott does not himself address the gendered nature of development, his understanding of mothering opens the way to a consideration of an area of experience that is of crucial importance in feminist work on the subject – the desire of the mother.

Winnicott sees the process of becoming a person in terms of a separation that requires a backdrop of a loving union with a primary caretaker. The growth of mind takes place through a process of integration and differentiation. This begins almost immediately as the infant encounters the frustrations of an environment that fails to meet its needs perfectly and therefore, inevitably, imposes pain and fear. It is in the mobilisation of defences against this suffering that mental organisation begins. The process of becoming a separate person is both active, in that the child must learn to negotiate internal and external reality, and reactive in that the external reality imposes itself with conditions and properties of its own. Mother, who in the early stages is the most important aspect of this reality, must be recognised as a subject in her own right with all the unpredictability that that implies. The baby's early sense of omnipotence is derived from experiences of being at one with the world at those times when its needs were anticipated.

The responsive mother facilitates the necessary illusion that her baby has created the object of its desire and this imparts a basic sense of agency. Omnipotence must then be gradually relinquished if the child is to relate to a world outside of itself. As this happens it encounters the terrors of dependency – an unequal relationship in which it perceives itself to be little and vulnerable while its caretakers are strong. In compensation, however, there are the pleasures of mutuality. The mother's recognition of the child's subjectivity is the basis on which its own sense of agency can develop. Thus the disillusion that comes from discovering the limits imposed by a world that cannot be predicted and controlled is bound up with the discovery of other people: initially mother, and later a wider world of separate selves. The disappointment needs to be gradual: the parent perceives the anxiety this arouses, 'holds' the child and lets go as and when it is ready. This responsive holding and graduated failure is the prototype of all future forms of containment that we find in families, communities and institutions. It allows us to tolerate the uncertainty and frustration of an imperfect world. It is for this reason that Winnicott's notion of 'good-enough mothering' has entered the language of welfare professionals as a powerful metaphor for compassionate realism.

The concept of intra-psychic maternal containment was developed by Bion (1967) as an explanation of the ways in which the mother receives and processes the fearful and fragmented projections of her baby. He observed the capacity of nursing mothers to enter a state of dreamy attentiveness called 'reverie' where they appear to be able to process their babies' disorganised mental contents, to 'detoxify' these and make them available to the child in a less threatening form. Without this work of psychic 'metabolism' the child would be unable to make sense of this material and transform it into thoughts. Containment here is both an intra-psychic and an interpersonal phenomenon.

Winnicott's (1965) model for the latter was initially the way in which the mother 'holds' the baby both physically and emotionally and generates the first sense of a world that can be trusted sufficiently for the process of separation to occur. As the child begins to explore the surrounding environment, a 'potential space' opens between the infant and mother where the imaginative exploration of inner and outer experience can begin. The importance of containing anxiety in order to allow imaginative thought has been widely recognised in therapeutic and institutional settings. In a diffuse way it is a principle underlying much professional practice enabling social workers to work with distressed and disorganised clients, medical personnel to reassure the sick and dying, and teachers to create the conditions of effective learning. It is very specifically a function of professional supervision and also a mark of effective leadership. The experience of working in departments where anxiety is uncontained – for example where managers follow a 'divide and rule' – strategy is generally one of conflict and paranoia which severely limits the creative output of its members.

Recognition and response

One of Winnicott's most suggestive contributions to an understanding of the child's process of individuation comes from his account of the dynamic of recognition between infant and mother. As subsequent authors have pointed out (Benjamin, 1990; Honneth, 1995), he effectively gives a psychoanalytic account of the dialectic of recognition which was philosophically elaborated by Hegel (1969) in his attempt to account for the development of subjectivity. This preoccupation with recognition is of interest because it enacts the primary interdependence that gives rise to the possibility of social life. I can only recognise myself as a subject, capable of independent interaction with another to the extent that I can see myself from the other's point of view. For this the other must be able to do likewise. The first experience of recognition is in the context of the love relationship between mother and baby and leads to the mutual confirmation that each party needs the other. Benjamin (1990) combines a reading of Winnicott with the findings of research on early parent–child interactions to examine the role of these dynamics in establishing the basis for responsiveness in subsequent relationships.

In order to experience itself as a subject, the infant needs to find itself first reflected in the maternal gaze, but passive reflection would be insufficient. Only the answering regard of another subject who is distinct from, and yet like the infant, can begin to confer this sense of subjectivity. Mother herself must be recognised. The ability to recognise and be recognised by another raises the possibility of later relationships of equality and mutuality. However, reciprocal recognition demands that a tension be maintained between the assertion and abnegation of the self. If mother privileges her needs above those of the infant she creates an unresponsive and hostile environment If she becomes wholly submerged in its care she ceases to appear as a subject with needs and desires of her own. In either case the child loses the encounter with the reality of another person who represents both a limit and a possibility. In resisting the annihilating demands of the infant and becoming a significant other, the mother opens up both the promise of independence and a world of shared but differentiated feelings, meanings and complex emotion. For the infant the process is one in which the experience of care in the context of recognition leads to the growth of love based not so much on identification (with another who is loveable because she is like me), as on concern for the other (who is loveable in her own right). Benjamin suggests (1990, 1995) that a capacity for realistic interdependence may involve both of these simultaneously or in tension.

Winnicott's often quoted aphorism, 'There is no such thing as a baby', expresses his conviction that individuation and separation depart from a state of oneness or 'primary intersubjectivity'. Furthermore, it is not only the infant who is dependent. The mother's identification with her child, even prior to its birth means that in the early phases of symbiotic nurturing she experiences its neediness as her own insufficiency. Differentiation therefore requires the active engagement of both parties. The mother must move from the initial sense of being cocooned with her baby to re-engage with the social world, while the child makes use of the holding environment to move towards a sense of physical and psychic integrity. Crucially, however, this involves the mobilisation of destructive aggression. Winnicott showed the necessity of the toddler's annihilating rages where the fantasised destruction of the mother becomes a creative testing of the limits of its own omnipotence. The mother's task is to survive and recognise that the child's attacks arise out of its attempts to demarcate itself as a finite individual. This surviving mother then becomes the object of a love based on guilt and concern that Klein had formerly identified with the depressive position.

In his account of the dynamic between master and slave, Hegel (1969) showed how the successful exercise of absolute power tests their relationship to destruction. By refusing to recognise the slave, the master denies the latter's subjectivity, but in doing so destroys the agent of his own recognition as master. The breakdown of the tension between self-assertion and recognition leads to a dynamic of domination and submission that ultimately annihilates both parties.

> We might call this the dialectic of control: if I completely control the other, then the other ceases to exist, and if the other completely controls me, then I cease to exist. A condition of our own independent existence is recognising the other. True independence means sustaining the essential tension of these contradictory impulses; that is, both asserting the self and recognising the other. Domination is the consequence of refusing this condition. (Benjamin, 1990, p 53)

Psychically speaking, maintenance of the tension involves movement between destructive and reparative states of mind – between annihilation and recognition of the other on whom the affirmation of the self depends. Benjamin's (1990, 1995) work inserts the power relations of the gender order into the dynamics of domination and recognition showing how the separation of public and private – effectively a split between the father of autonomy and the mother of dependency – is possible). While the breakdown of the tension between self-assertion and mutuality in personal relationships opens the way to domination and submission, this is replayed on a social scale as a struggle for rationalisation and control.

Understood thus, an ability to apprehend the dialectic of recognition and suspend the urge towards domination is a precondition for mutuality and communicative social relations premised on the equal moral worth of both parties. It must therefore be fundamental to the creation of non-oppressive social institutions. The prevailing tendency to exalt an ethic based exclusively on individuation may be seen as culturally grounded in Western individualism. Yet it is clear from the above that the dialectic of recognition is inaugurated by the dynamic interplay between a sense of separation and attachment that is continually developed as the child grows up through encounters with parents, siblings and an ever-wider network of people. Inevitably these are relationships in which inequalities contribute to the rearrangement of patterns of dependency and autonomy. The personality develops in relation to these experiences which recall, defend against and transform earlier patterns and it re-enacts them in the present. Thus interpersonal relationships come to reflect and modify a uniquely personal psychic organisation.

This account establishes in terms of the child's inner world and relations to others the possibility of concern and hence caring as an activity that arises from recognition and interdependence, and its development in the attachments of early nurturing and subsequently in interpersonal relationships and social institutions. This is important for my argument, because it traces the origin of a capacity for care not in some optimal form of socialisation but in the existing emotional repertoires of most people who have experienced good-enough parenting. However, the account is as yet incomplete in one important respect for which Benjamin herself has been taken to task (Burack, 1994), and for which closer attention to Klein can act as a corrective.

Destructiveness and hate

Thus far, the emphasis has been on the recognition achieved in early attachments as a basis for the capacity to love and care. This benign vision of human emotional response can lead to the exclusion of its other side: the aggression and hatred that we express through negative emotions such as anger, greed, and envy. All too frequently these can impede projects directed towards the welfare of others. In Klein's work there is a progressive view of development in which maturation implies the eventual transcendence of the passions associated with the splitting of the paranoid–schizoid position. This gives way to an altogether more selfless capacity to acknowledge other people for their unique qualities and moral worth. While accepting that this is indeed an achievement of the depressive position, later writers have stressed its instability – it is after all a 'position' rather than a phase. We do not have to look very far to see that in 'normal' adult life we oscillate between destructive and reparative, splitting and integration. A life devoid of gratitude would be impoverished but one devoid of envy would, for most of us, be impossible. Furthermore, public organisations are by no means immune from the mental states of the people who work in them. Menzies-Lyth's (1988) classic study of a teaching hospital illuminated the ways in which the organisational environment can either contain and process aggression and persecutory anxiety, offer defensive structures for it such as procedure and routine, or massively reinforce it through blaming systems. Her development of the notion of a socially structured defence system has been invaluable in analysing the ways in which staff in helping organisations can unconsciously 'lean' on organisational structures and conventions to collude in avoiding the anxiety-provoking task of caring for the sick and vulnerable (Obholzer and Zagier Roberts, 1994).

In both private and public life we continually encounter acts of selflessness and recognition alongside processes of overwhelming objectification in which personhood is manifestly denied. Feminists have been drawing our attention to the ways in which this has oppressed women for some considerable time, but the rise of user and advocacy groups, as well as the more politicised disability movement, has elaborated this critique in terms of its significance for populations with very specific histories of exclusion. If we identify in parts of our welfare system some reflection of our capacities for care, then we must equally expect to find a correspondence with our destructiveness towards others. Those who seek help only to find their status as subjects denied pay a high price for these shortcomings as many user groups have made clear.

This negative assumption also finds an echo in popular accounts of the subversion of well-intentioned reform because of the supposed selfishness of 'human nature'. Whereas the essentialist concept of 'human nature' can be easily deconstructed in academic social science, its persistence in conventional wisdom arises from the fact that it carries a commonsense ring of truth. Quite simply, our projects for the common good are often undermined and our best intentions corrupted by the failures of giving and receiving – a seeming inability to love our neighbour very much, or for very long.

The virtue of Klein's work is that she places the struggle between love and hate at the centre of psychic life. While we may hope that in overcoming depressive anxiety our love may prevail over our hate sufficiently to sustain our altruism, the conditions of existence in a divisive social order, that is inequality, injustice, competitiveness and exploitation, inevitably stimulate persecutory anxiety and rage. Indeed the combative state required to challenge injustice positively requires a capacity to mobilise our aggression. Klein's view, however, implies more than this: that depressive love, which expresses appreciation and concern for the other, arises from the impulse to reparation. It is constantly renewed in relation to our sense of the damage that we inflict and our gratitude to the other for survival.

I have dwelt in general terms on the question of hate and aggression in Kleinian thought, partly because I intend to try and trace its implications in four welfare configurations identified by the grid, but also because the institutional expression of these propensities justify a fourfold division where many social policy analysts have defined three. This will become clearer as I develop the theme of the anti-welfare sentiments suggested in quadrant 2. It follows from the point of view above that the diagram represents four *positions* rather than *phases* and there is no implication of inevitable progress. Not only could we revert in terms of policy to the 'no welfare' position depicted in 2 – the mental states represented therein are a continuing influence, surfacing in different ways in different institutional settings.

At this point, and with the reminder that it is ideal-typical and therefore by definition a schematic simplification, I will risk the scepticism of both social scientists and the clinically minded by depicting the innermost circle of the grid, characterising the quality of the dominant anxieties in each welfare 'position'. The justification will be developed in the chapters that follow.

Figure 2: Dominant mental positions implicit in and stimulated by successive welfare settlements

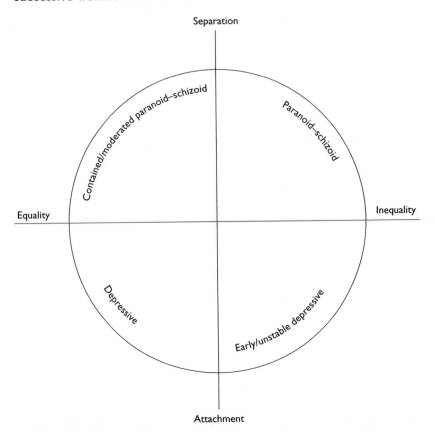

THREE

Old welfare: from warriors to citizens

> Did he therefore look backwards towards the past rather than forwards to the
> future? It's difficult to say. After all what else is our future made of if not our
> longings?

Amin Mahlouf, Ports of call (1999, p 35)

The profile of the ideal welfare subject constituted in the aftermath of war through the construction of the social democratic welfare state demonstrates the links between the concentric circles in the Old Welfare section of the grid (Figure 1). It reveals that he (the use of the male pronoun is apt here) was positioned as subordinate client within a welfare system increasingly reliant on the expertise of personnel within the rapidly professionalising public service occupations. These bureau-professionals articulated an essentially paternalistic relationship between state and welfare citizens who were in turn invested with paternal authority as heads of household within their family units.

The extension of social citizenship rights implied movement towards greater social equality, but was paradoxical in effect. It stimulated expectations of distributive justice while concealing the inegalitarian assumptions which justified the emergent social relations of welfare. Marshall's (1963) conception of expanding citizenship was presented to the welfare subject of the post-war period as an index of progress and a prized reward for the battles he and his compatriots had fought in defence of democratic freedoms. Scarred by memories of hardship and pre-war interclass conflict, the welfare subject's incorporation into a settlement of family, class and nation was a mark of identity in a reconstructed national community. The war had left its own legacy of social dislocation, but he looked to a benevolent state as an instrument of social integration and improvement. A universal but familialised system of health, education and income maintenance was to confer 'cradle-to-grave' social protection for himself and his kin. Citizenship, dependent on nationality, established eligibility for such support when required and determined who was to be excluded.

For the post-war welfare subject, the idea and reality of enhanced social citizenship transformed his relationship to state and community. Institutionalised welfare mediated between his individual rights and social obligations. Despite this extension of rights and the collectivism implied by the mildly redistributive effects of the new system, his citizenship was constructed in a field of tensions, notably those deriving from the continuing inequalities of class. In addition, welfare rights were closely tied to participation in the labour market, which ensured that most married women remained economically dependent. The entitlements of immigrants were circumscribed by residency and by progressively more exclusionary definitions of citizenship itself (Lewis, 1998). The egalitarian effects of the new provision were thus significantly qualified. Furthermore, the consequences of exercising social rights were not always benign. The new welfare subject enjoyed publicly funded education and healthcare free of stigma to the extent that his own interests and the public good were seen to coincide. However, other forms of welfare provision – especially those provided by social services – were conditional, a mark of degraded or at least unfortunate circumstance and provided by the collective as a moral duty of care. As Lewis points out, the objects of such institutionalised 'compassion' were by implication lesser citizens. Marshall (1981) was explicit in his view that the moral claims of 'the old' or 'mentally handicapped' should be respected but that they could in no real sense be said to accord with the interest of society as a whole.

The incorporation of the post-war welfare subject into a national reconstruction project, underwritten by political consensus, promised future stability and full employment. In return for this he willingly paid tax and National Insurance contributions in the knowledge that while all would pay, all would benefit. Hence he was motivated only in part by self-interest. His investment in comprehensive welfare provision was an act of solidarity signifying a state of belonging to a national community with the expectation that all would be cared for in times of need. In principle, therefore, he had no qualms about exercising his rights and his capacity and willingness to do so depended on the very education that the state provided. His contract with the state anticipated that the burden of care would be mediated, shared and delivered by public institutions guided by enlightened social policy, based on rational administration. Bellah (1988), writing of the US, points out that the most adept clients of 'welfarism' are likely to be middle class, skilled at negotiating complex systems and overcoming bureaucratic obstacles. The attitudes and approach of their low income counterparts could be better understood as a form of clientalism, characterised by an unquestioning acquiescence to professional authority and a passive acceptance of even the most unresponsive forms of provision. In Britain, class, along with race and gender, remained an indicator of differential access to health and education and, via work-related social insurance, to income maintenance. National assistance for the poorest was set at low enough levels to impel participation in the labour market.

As a responsible householder, the ideal subject of old welfare was the principal earner of a family wage supported by the services of a wife whose 'career' lay in marriage and homemaking. The paternalistic principles underlying the social relations of welfare within public organisations paralleled the distribution of authority within a patriarchal family, whose male members, along with the young, old and ill, were supported by the unremunerated and privatised caring activities of women. To the extent that women were enmeshed in extended families and traditional working-class communities they were able to draw on significant female support. Geographical and social mobility was eroding such communities but the sense of security they provided was partly compensated by the expectation of continued prosperity and economic growth. It was anticipated that this would lead to the reduction of income inequality, and a progressive improvement of prospects for all.

In sum, the post-war welfare citizen was positioned in a series of interlocking relationships expressed in the concentric circles of the 'old welfare' quadrant of the grid (Figure 1). At an interpersonal level (first circle, Figure 1) his authority within the family was upheld by the structural subordination of spouse and children. Health and welfare was delivered through a partnership between professionals and mothers, but this too was premised on paternalistic relations in which the working-class mother, re-educated in appropriate child-rearing techniques (Wilson, 1977), was to become the supervised conduit for middle-class values and habits. Her induction was to be overseen by a growing force of specialists (second circle, Figure 1). Their claims to bureau-professionalism were sanctioned by their location within government departments where they were able to mediate the relationship between welfare client and beneficent, tutelary, social democratic state. At the local level, occupational groups such as social workers were able to benefit from this organisational base and acquire a relatively privileged position within the labour market (Clarke, 1993). At the national level, the formerly generalist civil service, upholder of the public service ideal, was propelled towards increasing specialisation.

The drawbacks of 'old welfarism' and the dependency culture that it is said to have fostered have been invoked to justify both the neo-liberal restructuring of welfare institutions and their 'modernisation' under the Blair government. (These themes are addressed in the next two chapters.) It is increasingly difficult to question this within contemporary organisations (Froggett, 2000). Positive evaluations of past practices are taken as evidence of a morbid inability to come to terms with change. Yet while nostalgia signifies an affectionate relation to the past (Gabriel, 1993), it does not necessarily mean uncritical disavowal of shortcomings. In addition, Taylor-Gooby (2000) argues that any attempt to characterise public sector workers as recalcitrant and self-interested misunderstands their motives. His examination of their attitudes shows that they value the role of public welfare in ameliorating inequality, and mediating structural divisions based on social class. The reparative impulses underpinning the welfare state are integrally bound up with commitment to social justice.

Symbolic meanings of welfare

The critique of post-war social policy is well-travelled ground. Dissatisfaction has focused on the unresponsiveness of state bureaucracies with a stake in the development of service-led models. The bureau-professional model entailed a powerful alliance between the professional and the state in which claims to expertise were effectively inviolate. This had allowed a progressive penetration and regulation of private life by state-sponsored agencies and extended paternalistic intervention into communities, families and intimate relations – those areas of experience where selfhood is achieved. Rather less consideration has been given to the symbolic meanings of 'old welfarism', the states of mind it may have fostered, and the ways in which these could have been implicated in the experience of unequal power relations. In order to understand this better it is important to locate the construction of the welfare state in the aftermath of war and its particular emotional climate.

The paternalism directed towards adult clients had a counterpart in the focus of professional attention on children – especially the 'uncouth' urban children who had so taxed the patience of the provincial middle classes during the evacuation programme. The stereotype that emerged of the working-class child, offspring of a supposedly dysfunctional family, served to mobilise public opinion to incorporate the working classes into a settlement of family, citizenship and nation (Williams, 1989). Reparative impulses were part of the story but were offset by a distinctly controlling stance towards the people who were to be assimilated. In principle, welfare benefits accrued to the needy as a right of citizenship but their receipt entailed entry into a relationship with the institutions of the state and their representatives, which have been criticised as offering very little scope for self-determination, and which effectively debarred the poor and disadvantaged from adult status and responsible citizenship.

In part, the post-war settlement could be seen as founded on a collective experience of guilt for the fissures revealed by, and caused by, the destructiveness of the war. The projection of aggression onto an external enemy gave way, in the years immediately following, to an acknowledgement of a society deeply divided against itself in its class structure. The reparative impulse was directed towards the reconstruction of a more inclusive Britain in which pre-war levels of insecurity and poverty were no longer felt to be acceptable. The renunciation of reparation payments from Germany was represented to the generations of schoolchildren who, like myself, grew up in the fifties, as the victory of enlightened self-interest over a brooding vengeful longing for retribution. Equally, the ambition of the Marshall Plan, that of safeguarding peace by tying the erstwhile enemy into a reconstructed global economic order, was represented as liberalism's artful manoeuvre in defence of reason and freedom.

I was aware that war had shaped my parents' political landscape in a way that I would never entirely be able to understand. When the subject of Germans arose, the conflict between the new political obligations of inclusiveness and a deep and primitive hostility was palpable. If this were ever thought to warrant explanation it would be in terms of atavistic notions of 'national character' – the cold Teutonic killing machine. The fact that, on an emotional level, Germans were scarcely distinguishable from Russians confused me even more. Since the human spirit could scarcely survive the crushing weight of the Stalinist monolith, Russians had their personal characteristics systematically erased. I remember being thrilled when I saw a play on television about an affair between a cultural envoy and her Western lover and I began to understood the delectable perversion of 'sleeping with the enemy' that featured in the war movies that my mother watched on television.

It dawned on me as an adolescent that not taking reparation payments had a profound symbolic importance for my parents' generation. It provoked an emotional conflict between desires for revenge and repair, which underlay all their subsequent political vacillations and played itself out throughout the years of the Cold War. Just after the Second World War, it must have been vital in allowing the population to put aside the impulse to inflict humiliation on the vanquished and to turn its attention to the task of repairing the social fabric of the nation. The unity had been revealed as precarious enough in the inter-war years. During active hostilities it would have been possible to disavow knowledge of the injustices and deep divisions in British society. The exceptional cruelty and self-aggrandisement of the Nazi regime had made it a particularly appropriate receptacle for projection and provided a point of contrast in relation to which the content of national self-idealisations could be moulded around kindness, tolerance, decency and care for the vulnerable.

At the same time, a sense of gratitude towards the dead contributed to an urge to make good damage inflicted on those who had suffered bereavement, loss of property and physical and emotional injury. The impulse (at least until the Cold War once again transformed the psychic geography of the Western world) was towards a unity based on national reconciliation – and to some extent, however briefly, an ideal of a whole nation able to acknowledge and confront its blemishes. This new and more benign aspiration which contrasted with the triumphalism of victory informed the project of welfare construction, under the post-war Labour government and drew on a remarkable consensus around universal provision. To be sure, discriminatory tendencies were at work, which ensured that the basic architecture of the welfare state was racialised and gendered from its inception (Williams, 1989). Nevertheless, the integrative impulse was strong enough to install the principle of collective responsibility with the support of the middle classes. Despite being regarded at the time as a significant force for redistribution, it was formed in the face of professional and financial interests that did not obviously stand to gain in any immediate material sense.

Of particular importance were what Esping-Andersen (1990) termed the 'de-commodifying' effects of the new welfare settlement which aimed to guarantee citizens a degree of independence from the market in times of unemployment, sickness and old age. It is commodification, not only of labour but of wants and needs, that extends the reach of the market into personal and social life. In identifying the commodity form as the root of alienation both from others and the self, Marx (1965) had obliquely indicated a pathway between capitalist economic relations and the inner world. As commodities, people find their needs and capacities are abstracted from their being and subject to a pricing mechanism that is humanly created yet seemingly beyond anybody's control. Furthermore, they are positioned in an intrinsically competitive relation to one another and are ultimately expendable. Above all, human 'worth' is no longer a moral category but an economic one and dependency, without which there is no attachment, is weighed in a calculus of needs and costs.

The post-war settlement retained the social assistance principle with means testing and meagre benefits for those who had not paid insurance contributions and in this respect continued to underwrite people's subjection to the laws of the market. However, the principle of universality as it was realised in other parts of the welfare system, particularly in the National Health Service, established the expectation that there are areas of human experience – those where we are at our most vulnerable – which are properly beyond the reach of market operations. Market independence became, as it were, a measure of personal dignity and a moral foundation for the welfare state. In Scandinavian countries it has largely remained so, while in Britain it was to be contested by successive Conservative governments under Thatcher and Major, and later by Third Way modernisers. I shall return to the psychic consequences of commodification in the next chapter since it is with the installation of a cultural preference for privatisation that its effects become pervasive.

Whatever the limitations of the institutions that emerged, they represented from a Kleinian perspective an entry into a collective state of mind dominated by depressive rather than persecutory anxiety, which entailed an orientation to the collective good and a sense of responsibility for the disadvantaged. This represented a tentative and unstable achievement, which was reflected in the mobilisation of what might be seen as manic defences of omnipotence, arising from fears that it would not be possible to make reparation. Such fears typically provoke attempts to control and manipulate the object in order to ensure the desired outcome. The inflated rhetoric of building 'a land fit for heroes' and the elimination, no less, of the 'five giant evils'[1], set the tone and provided the political backcloth to the detailed process of social administration. Thus the humility implicit in the ideal of public service which invokes qualities of patience, curiosity, persistence and compromise was countermanded by the grandiosity of a political project which would brook no obstacle – least of all from those who were destined to be the objects of its generosity.

The experience of mourning, of acknowledging the loss of so much that had been loved, could hardly have failed to influence the real work of reparation – that of restoring a sense of goodness that might have been feared destroyed. Klein (1975) suggests that mourning involves entry into an emotional state which recalls the conflicts and anxieties of the early (infantile) depressive position and is therefore likely to call forth similar defensive strategies, of which omnipotence is one. However, there are even more problematic responses – most significantly triumphalism – an obvious danger in post-war Britain, under the circumstances.

The sense of triumph, if it is more than transitory, breeds contempt, and evokes the possibility that the defeated and despised enemy in turn seeks triumph. Distrust continues to pervade the relationship and internal persecutors are correspondingly strengthened. The state of mind thus created is one in which persecutory anxiety remains as an important filter to the external world which is perceived as containing elements that continue to threaten the destruction of all that is valued. The readiness with which people responded to the propaganda of the Cold War, so soon after victory, would seem to suggest that these fears were incompletely assuaged.

The scale of ambition represented by the avowed determination to eliminate the five giant evils was breathtaking. Omnipotence is based on the mechanism of denial, in the first instance of psychic reality and then to a greater or lesser extent of external reality. The denial of psychic reality follows from an overpowering anxiety and fear of the internalised enemy – in this case, finding an external counterpart in the persistence of a deprived and potentially subversive substratum of the poor, who could be seen to threaten both the social fabric and the longed-for sense of national reconciliation. In addition, the burden of guilt was amplified by the inescapable knowledge that the urban poor had borne the brunt of the destruction of cities through bombing campaigns, while the working classes in general suffered disproportionate disorganisation and loss through mobilisation. Yet these were the very people whose culture and family life were felt to be so inadequate for the task of producing the nation's labour force. The denial of the integrity and subjectivity of the poor was thus accompanied by disparagement. The impulse to mastery and control actually arises from a fear of dependency. This reverses the commonplace understanding of the one-way construction of dependency of the welfare client on the providers of welfare and locates its dynamic in the interaction between the two.

Benjamin (1990), referring to Hegel's master/slave relationship, describes the problem in terms of a reading of the intersubjective relations that drive the struggle between them:

> Since the subject cannot accept his dependency on someone he cannot control, the solution is to subjugate and enslave the other – to make him give that recognition without recognising him in return. The primary consequence of the inability to reconcile dependence with independence, then, is the transformation of need for the other into domination of him. (1990, p 54)

The disparagement that results takes the form of contempt and denial of the importance of the object. The fantasy of a nation of free and equal citizens, which includes the masses, is preserved at the price of denying the personhood of those who present themselves to the health and welfare systems as subjects with real embodied needs – there are, after all, so many of them and the task is so huge that only by diminishing them does it become manageable.

> 'Surely', argues the ego, 'it is not a matter of such great importance if this particular object is destroyed. There are so many others to be incorporated.' (Klein, 1935, in Mitchell, 1986, p 134)

Instead of a realistic appraisal of the difficulty of the task, particularly if it is to include recognition of subjectivity, it must be completed, as if by magic, in a great project of social engineering which assumes that the people are malleable, and by and large passive, instruments of social transformation.

In this way, the paternalism of the post-war welfare state is forged, combining its duty of care and concern for the people with parental omniscience. The professional–client relationship, informed by the wider relations of welfare, plays out a struggle for recognition in the context of a quasi-familial inequality in which the professional speaks for, to and about, but seldom with, the now infantilised client. The latter, placed in a position of enforced dependency and denied the status of adult subject, is unable to return due gratitude and recognition for the state's largesse. Hence the discomfort among the public at those who exploit services. Benefit fraud is notably greeted with polarised reactions ranging from apologia that sees it as the last resort of the desperate, to moral indignation at the corruption of the gift relationship. Either reaction grasps only part of a story, which may well include retaliation for the denial of the status of subject. This also explains the peculiar preoccupation of welfare professionals with clients who are denigrated as 'manipulative' or 'attention seeking'. The ascription of moral deficit to the individuals concerned conveniently obscures the more difficult point: that the real incentive to retaliation arises from the unequal and dependent nature of the relationship itself.

The casework paradigm

In the post-war context, social casework became the paradigmatic model for social welfare as practised in the community. Historically, though not inevitably, it has become linked with a residential counterpart: institutional care in the long-stay psychiatric, 'mental handicap' or geriatric facility. Although the theory and practice of social casework extends back to the work of the Charity Organisation Society in the 19th century, it proved to be an adaptable model which, despite criticism from both radicals and neo-liberals, continued to dominate work in the personal social services until the implementation of the 1990 NHS and Community Care Act. Despite the fact that a fair amount of casework continues in contemporary statutory and voluntary organisations, its relative importance has declined as care management has developed along increasingly administrative/managerial lines.

Casework is an individuated approach used by a range of helping professionals in health and social care but most extensively articulated and theorised within social work. It assumes that where individuals or families are unable to draw on personal resources to cope with their problems, change can occur in a relational context with a trusted professional. While social work may emphasise this more than other occupations, partly because of the past influence of psychoanalysis, it remains crucial for health visitors, community nurses, occupational therapists and midwives among others. The shared premise is that any help that is offered must start from the uniqueness of the individual case, and that the person should always be understood in a biographical and situational context. Since work on any particular case has its own rhythms and boundaries, it is likely to be open-ended and may be long term. Recognition of the importance of continuity and persistence, and negotiated rather than imposed timetables, allows for the meaning of change to be integrated into personal narratives. I shall return to the question of narrative in Chapter Nine.

With casework as a dominant methodology, social work was not obviously located within any particular academic discipline. It was able to accommodate a variety of theoretical perspectives primarily from the social and psychological sciences. It was extended to cover a wide range of person/situation possibilities, and over a period of a hundred years or more incorporated some very diverse forms of practice. From elasticity, it was often a short step to eclecticism, viewed by some as a virtue and by others as a sign of intellectual laxity. However, despite its vagueness, the 'person-situation' formulation succeeded in marking out the territory on which social work operated. It was against this backdrop that care management emerged in the nineties as a methodological break with an entire professional tradition.

Payne (1996) identifies three major, and by no means mutually exclusive, orientations, which he describes as 'reflexive-therapeutic', 'individualist-reformist' and 'socialist-collectivist'. He provides a useful summary of the history and evolution of casework, illustrating its ability to incorporate all three of these strands, despite their seeming opposition. He shows, for example, how the charges levelled in the seventies at the therapeutically-inclined, by Marxist-inspired radicals: that they ignored poverty, pathologised distress and produced deviants in the process, were an echo of earlier dualisms that preoccupied people working in the welfare arena – between maladaption and adjustment, practical aid and emotional support. These tensions were clearly present from the twenties and thirties, if not earlier, and were rearticulated and revisited in the closing years of the 20th century in the conflict between managerialism and professionalism.

It is for this reason that Philp's (1979) approach, referred to in Chapter One, remains particularly helpful. In seeking to define social work not in terms of the content of its theoretical or practical formulations, but in terms of the nature of its discourse, he drew attention to the fact that it is continually obliged to cross boundaries, between the individual and the environment and between subjective and objective knowledge. This knowledge, which he describes as 'uncertain in the extreme' does, nevertheless, arise within a recognisable 'regime of truth' which determines the categories that are and are not admissible. 'Evil', for example, is nowadays excluded as an essentially theological construct, 'inferiority' for its patrician overtones, 'fecklessness' for its moral condemnation. More positively one might identify, as others have done, the overwhelmingly humanist tenor of the discourse:

> The basis of all casework is the natural human response of one individual to another in some need which he cannot meet alone. (Cormack and McDougall, 1950, pp 16-17)

It is in the context of the flexibility and humanism of social work that its potential and its shortcomings can be found. Flexibility has enabled it, for better or ill, to be remoulded by the changing social relations of care expressed in the different sectors of Figure 1. It remains to be seen whether it has contorted itself beyond recovery. Humanism has at times lent it a blithe sense of certainty in its mission to improve lives and an untroubled disregard for difference. The voices of users have insisted that this error can eclipse all others in its importance.

Barbara Wootton's critique was scathing:

> ...modern definitions of 'social casework', if taken at their face value, involve claims to powers which verge upon omniscience and omnipotence....

> It might well be thought that the social worker's best, indeed perhaps her only, chance of achieving aims at once so intimate and so ambitious would be to marry her client. (Wootton, 1959, p 296)

In the 20 years following the Second World War, casework continued to generate claims to expertise and authority that are characteristic of all professional groups. In itself, and providing it is open to scrutiny and contest, specialised knowledge is the least that the users of social work services deserve – and this knowledge, when produced in dialogue, carries its own authority. The ability to speak for, with and about disadvantaged people demands no less. However, all knowledge bears the imprint of the circumstances under which it emerges. In the postwar welfare state, an ideology of universalism, with its abstract claims to equality, took shape in the context of quasi-parental relationships between clients and professionals. Social work was explicitly conceived as restoring distressed or deviant individuals to normal social functioning, and for a variety of reasons, including the state-sponsored nature of welfare and a climate of social conformism, there was little room for individuals to negotiate around those norms. Not only are they generally unquestioned in the texts of the period, the continuing use of institutional care for different client groups acted as a powerful constraint on challenges from below. In addition, the explicitly diagnostic and therapeutic orientation of social casework in the fifties allowed social workers the option of modelling their working relationships on those of clinician and patient. The critique of medical mystique and the power relations it preserves came somewhat later and inspired the anti-psychiatry movement (Cooper, 1967) and polemics such as Illich's *Limits to medicine* (1977). The skirmishes provoked by these attacks on the power of institutionalised medicine and its fellow-travellers in social work appear to have put psychodynamic practitioners on the defensive. Systemic, task-centred and behaviourist methods, if not exactly egalitarian, were seen as less invasive and implicitly less corruptible than approaches which were tainted by their proximity to medical models. In all of this, there was a blurring of different dimensions of the problem. The question too often left aside was whether the therapeutic ideal itself was flawed, or whether the problem lay within the social relations of welfare in which it had been pursued.

A relationship-based model of work has the potential to respond to the complex and highly individual ways in which people negotiate their relations with the outside world. It also establishes, far more effectively than approaches that seek to manage behaviour or produce care plans, the conditions in which fragmented inner states can be contained and thought about. However, it has its attendant risks. The helping relationship that arouses unconscious phantasies of omnipotence and dependence is a particularly sensitive vehicle for the transmission of wider institutional and social dynamics. It becomes a point of articulation between social and individual defence systems. The helping professional is a powerful figure in a model that positions the client as doubly subordinate to paternalistic and expert-based authority. A focus on power reveals the structural dimension of social relations but tells us little about the nature of the experience for either party. Social defence systems are context specific and operate by allowing individuals to unconsciously make use of institutional structures or modes of work organisation to assuage anxiety (Menzies-Lyth, 1988).

Professionalism itself can be used in this way. It may allow the individual worker, faced with the unfathomability of a client's disturbance, or the responsibility of removing a child from its family, to disavow the emotional impact of the work and retreat into an omniscience which appears to be sanctioned by a rigid adherence to role. All pain and confusion becomes lodged in the client while the helper takes refuge in a delusional certitude. Hinschelwood (1998) describes institutionalisation processes in psychiatric hospitals, where staff and patients collude in becoming 'creatures of each other'. The patients lose all their 'healthy' characteristics – which are enacted for them by the staff – while negative aspects of the staff group surface in the patients. The legitimate purpose of institutional care – the holding environment – fails.

It is the role and task of the institution that determines the specific content of anxiety within it and the social defences that respond to that anxiety. The post-war welfare state was organised around pervasive worries about internal division and destructiveness and the hope that a model of care based on unquestioned quasi-parental authority might heal and protect. The task of the parent is to withstand the inevitable attacks of the child, ceding power to dialogue. Whereas the good-enough family will be able to evolve towards democratic relationships as children mature, the larger social institutions of the welfare state struggled to overcome internal rigidities, eventually inviting a more radical restructuring from a government hostile to its founding principles. A sense of the importance and therapeutic potential of relationship was then lost as managerialised processes supplanted casework.

Angela Foster (1998), drawing on a model developed at the Tavistock Centre, referred to the tendency inherent in welfare arrangements to focus on binary relationships and the difficulty of maintaining a perspective from a third position (Britton, 1989). It is the existence of this third position that creates the space for thinking about the tensions and polarities that are sometimes so difficult to resolve and that push professionals/clients, managers/staff, agency/state into irreconcilable oppositions. Paternalistic relationships are particularly disposed to this since power and authority are linear, passing from parent to child in such a way as to all but eclipse the outside world. Growth and development take place when the awareness of a third position allows the outside world to set limits to parental authority without destroying it. If welfare relationships are conceived in triangular rather than binary formation they are less likely to become stuck or oppressive. Foster considers the case of community mental health work where the triangle requires a simultaneous focus on the clients who are mentally ill, the professionals who care for them, and the surrounding community. Where the social relations of care lead to a privileging of the relationship between the first two at the expense of community, the result is the institutionalisation that retarded the development of community care until the nineties. If, on the other hand, the perspective of professionals is lost, as was to happen with the ascendancy of care management, the model is one of rationalisation. Where clients themselves are excluded, it is marginalisation (see Figure 3).

Figure 3: A theoretical framework representing the potential difficulties between the three elements involved in community care

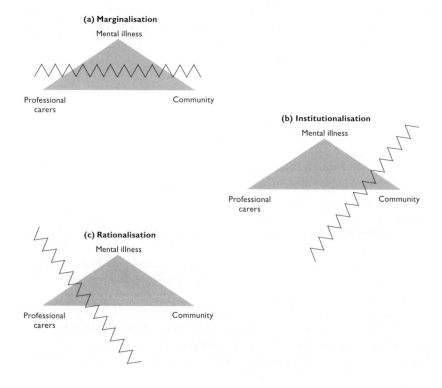

The ability to sustain third-position thinking might be thought of as a test of the adequacy of the welfare environment. Casework certainly extends beyond the walls of the institution but if it does so in a context where the reality of the outside world (in the form of community networks and resources) is not allowed to intrude into the professional/client pair, it will itself become a mini institution prone to pathological forms of dependency. This is the sort where the active self of the client is progressively eroded. Within any welfare system at a local level there is a potential for any of these three dysfunctional models to occur. Dyadic relationships in the public sphere are always seductive because they avoid complexity. They are seldom egalitarian and, to they extent that they become self-enclosed and immune to influence, they are vulnerable to degeneration into disrespect and contempt. The more rigidly the third is excluded, the greater the potential for abuse and hence the recurring scandals that have marred the reputation of institutional care. While the community-based caseworker was always more likely to reckon with an external reality, anxieties about the lack of accountability in the model have led to systems of monitoring which substitute technical checks for a true third position and the reflective faculty that it stimulates.

The fracture of consensus

My analysis of the symbolic meanings assigned to public welfare in the post-war period has emphasised both its reparative nature and the socially structured defences which, in hindsight, can account for some of the features for which it has been criticised. A period of consensus and social cohesion was underpinned by the welfare rights of family units headed by male breadwinners, but was nevertheless *symbolically* inclusive. According to Marshall (1971) this extension of 'social rights' qualitatively transformed conceptions of social justice to include access to healthcare, education and social insurance, all of which were implicated in widening conceptions of social equality. While Marshall's work exemplifies the argument for greater fairness through democratic reform, the importance of affiliative and altruistic motives was perhaps most eloquently expressed by Titmuss (1970) in *The gift relationship*, in which he extolled the British system of blood donation over American and European systems of blood selling. I do not, in the light of what came later, wish to either eulogise or downgrade these achievements. They gave a far from perfect collective expression to a generalised broadening of conceptions of rights and obligations and an enriched understanding of the social concomitants of citizenship. Paradoxically, the progressive intent was tempered by the self-congratulation it induced, and by denial of the continuing economic disadvantage for which it was intended to compensate. Acknowledgement of the real and symbolic virtues of generosity embedded in parts of the British welfare system did not entail for Titmuss disavowal of its limitations, either in terms of the transfer of social capital to the poor or its ideological role in obscuring the unpalatable reality of continuing 'diswelfare'. He was inclined to be scathing about the complacency that had been fostered:

> Generalised slogans rarely induce concentration of thought; more often they prevent us asking significant questions about reality. Morally satisfied and intellectually dulled, we sink back into our presumptive cosy world of British welfare.... (Titmuss, 1968, in Butterworth and Holman, 1975, p 25)

Titmuss went on to penetrate the obfuscation that permitted this illusion:

> ... the services used are not essentially benefits or increments to welfare at all; they represent partial compensations for disservices, for social costs and social insecurities which are the product of a rapidly changing industrial–urban society. They are part of the price we pay to some people for bearing part of the costs of other people's progress; the obsolescence of skills, redundancies, premature retirements, accidents, many categories of disease and handicap, urban blight and slum clearance and a hundred-and-one other socially generated disservices. (in Butterworth and Holman, 1975, pp 34-5)

We find in the writing of Titmuss, Marshall, and other analysts of the sixties who were operating within a climate of social reform, an endorsement of universalistic values in social welfare and a commitment to rational critique based on social scientific enquiry. The extracts above are written in a spirit of honest evaluation and humility – a welcome corrective to the earlier strains of triumphalism. It is noteworthy for maintaining this stance while refusing to mince words on the shortcomings of welfare policy. The work of Abel-Smith and Townsend (1965) in the 'rediscovery of poverty' was influential in promoting a phase of reassessment. There was some ground for hope at the beginning of the seventies that this work, combined with a Marxist-inspired climate of social activism, admittedly more concerned with labour relations than the future of the welfare state, might have been a basis for reorienting welfare towards more inclusive conceptions of justice and recognition. In the event, the seventies saw a progressive loss of optimism especially among the middle classes who became increasingly restive about the tax burden of public services, which had become the occasion of so much disappointment.

Perhaps too much had been expected from welfare bureaucracies – idealisation set them up for failure and the unifying values that motivated post-war reconstruction gradually fell foul of processes of fragmentation, rooted in a rapidly diversifying social and economic base. The welfare state had promised the rationalisation and organisation of responses to vulnerability, dependency and the wilder shores of emotional chaos. It supported what Berger et al (1974) described as a bureaucratic model of the self: anonymous, meritocratic, consistent, controlled and predictable – a self lacking in internalised authority and therefore amenable to external regulation, inclined to conformity and somewhat restricted in its imaginative range (Craib, 1994).

This became less and less sustainable in the sixties and seventies. Class divisions, partially obscured during the economic growth of the fifties, came more sharply into focus with a shift towards longer, more intransigent and more politicised industrial disputes. The cultural history of the period follows the growth of a consumer society with its diversified lifestyles and identifications. Rock and Roll had already put the writing on the wall in the fifties when Elvis voiced the fetishistic sensibilities of the stylist-consumer in bestowing his worship, not on the girl, but on his blue suede shoes. Jackson Pollock had turned expressionism into a form of excrementalism. In the years that followed, other ruptures charted the disintegration of a moral order premised on paternalistic authority and the containment of desire. High art went to court in defence of fantasies of interclass animalistic sexual transgression (D.H. Lawrence's *Lady Chatterley's Lover*). Paedophilic anxieties were aroused through the literary scandal of a 14-year-old 'seductress' and her teacher (Nabakov's *Lolita*). The very beaches that had been spared from invasionary landing became weekend battlegrounds between yesterday's rebels (Rockers) and tomorrow's consumers (Mods). The Union Jack became a fashion accessory and appeared on underpants. By 1979, the year of Thatcher's ascension, Dick Hebdige, subcultural sociologist, remarked on Punk's exposure of the vacuousness of commodified artistic 'style in revolt' through 'revolting style'. Vivienne Westwood founded a fashion house on her 'confrontation dressing' and earned an OBE, which she collected without wearing her knickers. Economically, culturally and politically the scene was set for change.

The very grandiosity of the welfare bureaucracies prepared the ground for the disillusion and rejection that followed exposure of their shortcomings. Effectively, manic defences impede the process of coming to terms with the imperfections of reality. The demise of the collectivist welfare ideal generated different responses. Among certain user groups and ethnic minorities it opened up spaces in which to promote new forms of advocacy and democratic participation. Some of these found shelter in Labour local authorities throughout the eighties. A degree of public sector union activism through minority forums and equal opportunities policies lent vitality to their internal politics. Most noteworthy, or notorious, until their abolition, were the Greater London Council and the Inner London Education Authority. These developments, which afforded opportunities for imagining a more participatory and differentiated welfare system, were submerged, however, by the onslaught of Thatcherism.

Note

[1] Beveridge's post-war 'five giant evils' were want, disease, ignorance, squalor and idleness (Beveridge, 1942, p 170).

FOUR

No welfare: privatisation of concern

It is a contradiction in terms to depict the ideal welfare subject of the New Right, whose programme was premised on his abolition. In the second sector of the grid (Figure 1) there is no true counterpart of the expert–client relation since privatised welfare is a commodity like any other, sought by autonomous and competitive individuals who strive to satisfy wants in the context of market-led private provision. Relations between them are governed by the pursuit of self-interest within a reinforced ethos of possessive individualism. This ethos, which links the labour of individuals to entitlement and property, positions the working taxpayer at the centre of the New Conservative project, while inheritors of wealth and privilege subside in importance.

The New Right subject seeks to maximise his personal well-being within a circumscribed sphere of private, family-based attachments, but faces his peers as an atomised individual driven to defend his own interests and maximise his opportunities in a competitive environment. In ideal form, he provides for himself and his family without recourse to public aid of any kind since this would expose him to unwarranted interference from professionals inclined to their own advancement. He pays for private health insurance, education and pension insofar as he is able, and in the absence of sufficient means, prefers fiscal transfers such as voucher schemes or tax rebates, which preserve his status as consumer. As a taxpayer he is impatient of the needs claims of those who depend on the public purse, and requires of government continued financial stringency for whatever residual provision is needed to preserve public decency and order.

He is entrepreneurial, competitive and achievement-oriented by inclination, and conceives of his rights in primarily negative terms as the freedom to pursue his economic interests within a deregulated environment. While his principal goal is the maximisation of personal wealth and property, he is not averse to charitable giving to support those genuinely unable to enter the labour market. This form of assistance is freely chosen, conditional and altogether preferable to uniform, unresponsive and expensive state services. However, he is convinced that the deserving poor are few. Generosity is ever open to abuse and may contribute to the formation of dependency cultures, particularly if donations are perceived and framed as a response to welfare rights. In particular, he is opposed to universal benefits and would hope to see the eventual abolition of the welfare state in favour of compulsory private insurance. He accepts both the inevitability and the necessity of an unequal distribution of talents, resources and outcomes – which foster the acquisitive self and sustain market behaviour.

The New Right subject identifies his family as the legitimate site of mutuality and cornerstone of a stable moral order. Privatised altruism is inherently discriminatory – the 'natural' preference for those who are similar to oneself begins in identification with kin, and passes via communities who share cultural and racial attributes to a sense of national identity and patriotic fellow-feeling. Within the family, patriarchal relations of authority ensure that 'natural' gender roles are respected and children are raised in a socially conservative milieu. They are inculcated with traditional values of thrift, self-reliance and self-discipline. For the New Right subject this is an arena properly immune from outside intervention providing he discharges his responsibilities. Failing this, he would expect a legal rather than welfare-driven response from a lean but strong centralising state, which confines its operations to its proper sphere of interest. This includes upholding the social institutions of marriage and parenthood and maintaining a robust stance on law and order.

Beyond the family, the state's role is to create the optimum conditions for the New Right subject's performance as consumer. He supports, therefore, the introduction of quasi-markets; the encouragement of an expanded private and voluntary sector; and systems of inspection and regulation. Remaining public service professionals are to be subject to the discipline of a robust public sector managerialism with an emphasis on outputs in practice and observable competencies in training. Pseudo-markets and a contract culture are assumed to enhance performance and offer consumers choice in relation to a range of specified provision, mostly purchased from the private sector. If, as a user of such services, he is unsatisfied, he may complain through legitimate channels but his ultimate sanction is his right of exit in search of competing provision.

The Thatcherite compromise successfully brought together two contradictory strands of conservative opinion (Edgar, 1986): the neo-liberal economics developed by Hayek (1944) and Friedman (1962) and strands of socially authoritarian Conservatism represented in America by the likes of Kristol (1978), Rusher (1975) and Senator Jesse Helms. In Britain they included Roger Scruton (1980), Maurice Cowling (1978) and the journalist Peregrine Worsthorne, who politically defined themselves in opposition to the moderate, centre-Right, Europhile Conservatism of Edward Heath, and identified with the controversial nationalist and anti-immigration stance formerly adopted by Enoch Powell. They were united in an assault on the social libertarianism of the sixties, which seemed to represent nothing less than the collapse of a collective superego and a regression into an infantile world of limitless gratification. The spoilt children of affluence, turned public sector professionals, had turned to bite the nurturing bourgeois breast. However, an attack on their unbridled appetites could hardly critique the very consumerism that the liberalised economy demanded. This was an offensive against the demons of boundless hedonism for whom market liberalism had no adequate riposte. "It could refute Marx effectively, but never thought it would be called upon to refute the Marquis de Sade" (Kristol, 1978, p 68).

In their lust for power, the irredeemably regressed sixties' generation had assumed a new guise of teachers, social workers and administrators in unholy alliance with the feckless poor. Urban disorder, feminism, gay rights, affirmative action, rising street crime, anti-nuclear protests, all came to be seen as a failure to internalise parental authority. Above all they exposed as hollow the civilising claims of the paternalistic welfare state. Two decades later David Marsland (1996) summed up this enduring perspective:

> The Welfare State and its army of tenured servants is the prime source of the parroted emphasis on rights without commensurate responsibilities which has increasingly made of the British people an ungovernable, unemployable mob, bereft of values and scornful of rules. (Marsland, 1996, p 29)

Apart from the discipline of the market, the antidote to this decadence was the radical restructuring of public sector organisations, which were thought to be responsible in large measure for the erosion of national moral fibre. The reforms that followed can be regarded as the durable achievements of the Thatcher/Major era. Charged with the task of instilling the business principles of efficiency, effectiveness and economy into public sector organisations, these have deflected professional resistance and have emphasised performance and delivery. The shift in the locus of power to managers has entailed a re-ordering of priorities and administrative scrutiny of professional decision making.

Technical–rational assumptions have since been reinforced by the evidence-based practice movement, which has accented methodologies based on quantitative measurement and behavioural indicators. The guidelines for researchers wanting support from the Association of Directors of Social Services Research Group (1996) were telling: they cited as "negatives" factors intrinsic to much qualitative methodology, including "over-generalised" questions "leaving staff not knowing how to answer" and "questions that need lengthy narrative answers". In social work there has been critique of this trend by academics with a number of different viewpoints (Kilty et al, 1995; Everitt and Hardiker, 1996; Turney, 1997; White, 1997). They have pointed to the unstructured, situated and interpretative basis of much professional knowledge and its dependence on face-to-face relationships and capacity for emotionally grounded reflection. However, their voices have been muffled in agencies where there has been a general unease at the hostile climate of the times but little apprehension of the ideological uses of the new methodologies. This would recognise the inextricable connections between a possessive individualism that best finds expression in free markets and a methodological individualism in the understanding of human behaviour. The underlying assumptions differ radically from those of post-war welfarism which was founded on a view of human beings as fundamentally social and as likely to be motivated by concern for the other as by self-interest.

Since the focus of this book is on the relationships between people involved in managing, providing and receiving services, I shall try to account for Thatcherism's success in terms of how it induced not only structural and cultural changes but altered states of mind. Rather than providing a systematic overview, I shall focus on the interrelationship of key aspects of these reforms.

Thatcherism's radical assault on perceived vested professional interests was pursued through the programmatic introduction of market and consumerist principles. In hindsight, it seems surprising that such a dramatic break from public service values should have met with muted resistance. My own experiences in interviewing staff in one department were hardly unique (Froggett, 1999). Some people still referred to professional values, but almost apologetically, fearful of seeming old-fashioned. Others, mostly in purchasing teams, had embraced the reforms enthusiastically and spoke the language of contracts and audit with ease. A significant number seemed demoralised or in a state of cynical disengagement. Whatever the reaction, the ethos of public service and therapeutic attention was regarded as a thing of the past. Individuals who endeavoured to preserve these were likely to suffer considerable role strain. In one highly managerialised authority they cast themselves as subversives, producing a satirical 'samizdat' newspaper – the scurrilously witty *Sammy's Dad*.

Within the local authority sector, managerialism offered some a new career route. Personal success and qualities of leadership were now to be evaluated more for their contribution to corporate performance than their ability to sustain viable working teams. The primacy of business principles, together with increased emphasis on consumer choice, introduced a new vocabulary and way of thinking. The reinterpretation of accountability revealed this most clearly.

Levitas (1986) identifies accountability as a defining motif of the New Right, although she points out that the question of 'accountability to whom' was seldom addressed. When I trained as a social worker in the early eighties, accountability was explicitly situated within a system of humanist professional values but was understood to entail conflicts of power and responsibility. It invoked a constellation of people, at the centre of which was the client, with whom, and on whose behalf, one was obliged to negotiate. To the question "to whom are you accountable?" we would have replied "the client in the first instance, but within the constraints imposed by agency function". Considered thus, accountability represented a requirement to keep the client in mind; awareness of the agency 'third position'; and a recognition that these always set limits to professional omnipotence. Accountability invoked at one and the same time a relationship internal to the work process, a defence against abuse of power, a principle that guided professional transactions and a means of locating oneself within a set of institutions. Recently, a group of my own students construed it in predominantly economic terms: "We are accountable to the agency and the taxpayer". The political dimensions were only obliquely recognised and the client or service user was now marginalised. Accountability was perceived as a constraint wholly external to the work itself and oriented to the public interest as distinct from that of clients. It had effectively been disembedded from personal relationships and had come to describe an abstract relation to a remote and generalised other, in need of protection from the very people who required services.

These students had a sound, if uncritical, grasp of the meanings that the term now carries and with which it came to be imbued during the eighties. Above all it is interpreted in terms of competing interests and financial limits. It is not that resource constraints have become a central concern where once they were ignored. Rather, they have been removed from the field of negotiation. They stand as limits imposed by an unyielding reality, an inevitable constraint on those who make demands on social welfare provision. This implicitly sets up a conflict that forces professionals to position themselves either as advocates for the service user or protectors of the public purse. At the same time the abstract nature of audit which removes accountability from the arena of interaction conceals a very concrete power relation, in which the professional is obliged to cover their back – if necessary at the expense of the client. Such oppositions, if unmediated, would carry the risk of adversarial and potentially politicised relationships. The injunction to 'manage' dissent is a requirement to smooth over energy-consuming antagonisms within the system. Eligibility criteria and procedural approaches to work formalise and rationalise the process of negotiation, bypassing the communicative content of the encounter and the potential for conflict within it.

In defence of this version of accountability it might be argued that if the meaning is now more restricted, it is at least clearer, cuts through the potential for ambiguity and obfuscation and acts as a more effective curb on professional discretion, producing more accountability, not less. Deakin and Walsh (1996), reviewing evidence on the effects of the introduction of contracts, argued that there was some evidence of enhanced accountability to the public in the case of simpler services, such as refuse collection, but there was little to suggest it in the more complex delivery of health and social care. The move towards formal setting of standards and specification of outputs had resulted in an increasing reliance on measurement at the expense of qualitative evaluation, dialogue and judgement. Between organisations a narrower definition of accountability had led to greater transparency – at a price:

> Since current definitions of service are usually based on budget categories, a service that isn't costed, isn't counted and doesn't count. (Kearney, 1996, p 16)

From the point of view of professionals this reflects a reinterpretation of the nature of risk. There are two far-reaching and interlinked consequences on which I wish to focus: the development of an actuarial consciousness and loss of trust.

From clients to consumers

The recasting of users of services as consumers or customers is part and parcel of the attempt to impose market discipline on public services. The client model which drew on an imagery of the citizen voluntarily seeking help in the form of professional expertise was, as Clarke (1996) argues, at best an over-simplification: first, because it concealed substantive inequalities which do not automatically characterise relations between users and providers in other professions; second, because it obscured the fact that many welfare clients were unwilling recipients of the attention they received. Nevertheless, this representation preserved the public service model of accountability. Clarke argues that in deconstructing the notion of the citizen, neo-liberalism opened the way for split representations of subject positions in relation to public services. His account reveals the fissionary nature of this process and the aggressive and persecutory tenor of the anxieties released. He notes the pre-eminence of the taxpayer 'robbed' and 'diminished' by the burden of taxation directed to the sustenance of the 'scrounger':

> This exploitative individual exacerbates the problems of the tax-payer's already troubled life by taking advantage of the state's liberality in order to avoid work and procreate wildly. (Clarke, 1996, p 3)

He observes that the counterpart of the taxpayer is the consumer and that repositioning the client as consumer provides a solution to the problem of empowering the deserving (those who choose wisely and thriftily) while foreclosing potential for abuse of the system by the feckless. The marketisation of relationships in health and welfare promotes efficiency among providers by subjecting them to bracing competition, and increased choice for users who are expected to exercise responsible and rational discretion on their own behalf. The assumption is that needs are transparent and obvious to the consumer, requiring no interpretation by professionals, and that welfare is merely a commodity. All this rather begs the question as to why people need services in the first place – they are already, by definition, 'failed' consumers.

Clearly this eliminates any notion of public welfare as an expression of interdependence and pitches the rational, calculating, self-interested individual into an environment of similar individuals. Equality of citizenship, which derives from a political relationship to the state, is replaced by an abstract contractual equality at the point of exchange and the right to pursue interests in the marketplace. Thatcher's dictum, 'there is no such thing as society', was an accurate, if polemical, expression of the point of view that a 'collective good' is a contradiction in terms. Economic man seeks to maximise his individual benefits – knowing that in so doing he contributes to the maximisation of aggregate 'goods' and therefore need not concern himself with the needs of others, or the impact of his actions upon them. The loss of connection to others is a small price to pay, and in any case is compensated within the family in a privatised sphere of intimacy, beyond the reach of the interfering 'nannyish' state.

Eric Miller (1993) reviewed the findings of a number of group conferences run by OPUS [1] in the early Thatcher years. These relatively unstructured events establish a reflective space from which participants can think about society from the perspective of their citizen roles. Departing from the well-tested principle that societal dynamics find a reflection in those of the group, they draw on the conference itself as a source of information about processes and concerns in the surrounding environment. During 1980-81 the conferences registered a complex of social defences which Miller identifies with 'failed dependency'. This transitional state is analogous to that experienced by the abandoned infant and is characterised by fear and disorientation at the departure of parental caretakers, a severe loss of trust in the environment and terrible anxieties about survival. The themes that dominated the OPUS events of the early Thatcher years were of withdrawal and retreat; impotence in the face of potential nuclear annihilation; the displacement of aggression into sub-groups and the creation of an external enemy. The first of these, psychological withdrawal, had a material counterpart in the massive loss of jobs as the economy moved into recession and employers, encouraged by a combative climate of government, adopted a more confrontational stance towards the trades unions. For those who remained in work, the temptation was to keep one's head down. Miller observes that these survivors were unlikely to maintain contact with their redundant ex-colleagues and the trades union movement as a whole proved an ineffectual source of advocacy for the unemployed.

In the OPUS conferences, deterioration in international relations was palpably linked to a sense of personal powerlessness. After the attenuation of the nuclear threat during the latter part of the sixties and early seventies, the Soviet Bloc re-emerged as the implacable enemy – to be designated by Ronald Reagan as the 'evil empire'. Survival was impossible in the face of such overwhelming destructive capacity, but retaliatory impulses found plenty of outlets in domestic politics, most dramatically in the 1981 race riots in Toxteth and Brixton. While street fighting was the most dramatic manifestation of internal division, split-off aggression found a pervasive and accessible target in the imagery of the underclass.

Splitting and demonisation

Clarke's (1996) emphasis on the fragmentation of the unifying idea of citizenship is apt. Thatcherism stimulated a very active form of splitting in which a composite of political, economic and social rights and obligations was dispersed into opposed components. Since even very residual and instrumental views of welfare (the technical safety net, for example) seem to invite judgement on moral desert, these oppositions took on the character of a struggle between virtue and vice: taxpayers versus scroungers, wet versus dry politicians, promiscuous underclass versus sexually continent families, nationals versus aliens, dependants versus entrepreneurs. Bell (1997) pointed to the seductions of this primitive form of morality, which resolves the strain of trying to achieve depth understanding of complex changing circumstances. A hospital, school or social services department must be either 'good' or 'bad' and these are categories which exist without history or context such as depleted resources or low staff morale. This feeds into a survivalist mentality whereby the 'good' will be saved and the 'bad' will be damned (or suffer the final humiliation of being handed over to the private sector). While Thatcher appeared to enjoy phallic imagery of the unbending 'iron' thrust that was 'not for turning', John Major (*Sunday Express*, 18 May, 1995) summed up the spirit of evangelical discipline with the injunction to "understand a little less and condemn a little more". Bell suggests that this climate favoured a destructive narcissism – a specific personality organisation in which any form of vulnerability and dependency must be systematically expunged, while 'hardness' is idealised. Within organisations such individuals find their element in macho management cultures that reward authoritarian forms of direction, ruthlessness and personal ambition. Such environments are likely to foster harassment and bullying, leaving staff with a debilitating fear of victimisation if they step out of line, and of dismissal if they break the circle of corporate secrecy that allows such behaviour to flourish.

In this kind of environment, paranoid-schizoid anxieties undermine the ability of welfare professionals to maintain an eye to the third position (described in the previous chapter). This calls for tolerance of ambiguity, contradiction and complexity – a capacity for differentiation that requires careful listening and suspended judgement. From a psychoanalytic point of view, polarisations (unlike the capacity for differentiation) are defensive manoeuvres and a sign that unwanted attributes are being split off, disowned and projected onto others where they can be safely attacked. However, this arouses fears of retaliation. Retreat into the bunkers of self-righteous certainty is the understandable response of the embattled. On a societal plane the net effect of these polarisations was to increase the potential for persecutory anxiety on the part of those who stood to lose from the apparently insatiable demands of the poor. Thus a sense of insecurity that derived from the fact that large numbers of people *were* being expelled from employment was inflected with paranoia. The New Right views of the underclass which identified a pathological culture of dependency (for example, Murray 1984) promoted an imagery of a parasitic sub-stratum of humanity parented by single mothers on welfare, a seedbed of delinquency, duplicity and degeneration. Paradoxically, this group was seen as at once chaotic and disorganised – isolated over generations from the disciplines of the work ethic, and yet at the same time possessed of an evil genius with which it was able to maintain itself effectively by manipulating the benefits system. Thus it flourished as a source of moral corruption, a cancer within, aided by the ever-extending influence of the 'bleeding-heart do-gooders' of social welfare.

In this scenario, welfare became a symbolic node around which social relations with unproductive groups was reconceptualised. From a psychic point of view, it represented a splitting between good and bad aspects of selfhood. Representations of welfare drew upon a feminised and infantilised imagery of dependency counterposed to the entrepreneurial self: assertive, virile and risk-taking. The effect was to create an atmosphere in which despised attributes were deposited in a range of people who were characterised as unwilling to take on adult responsibilities of self-reliance. Although the delinquent underclass was most likely to be thought of as young, male (and probably black), this was a deformed and wayward masculinity undersocialised by licentious and ill-educated mothers and untamed by appropriate male role models. Of course the scourge of single-motherhood extended beyond the underclass and everywhere suffered guilt by association. Hence, it was entirely possible for the Child Support Agency, eventually introduced by John Major's government, to ensure that the proceeds of paternal financial responsibility benefited the Exchequer rather than mothers and children.

The underclass were by no means the only threat. Paranoid-schizoid states of mind may demonise any group that cannot be incorporated. The sixties' 'permissivists' have already been mentioned. Edgar (1986) makes the point that Conservatism was and is particularly perturbed by youthful idealism, which is seen as an unstable and irresponsible source of corruption. Blair, the champion of youth and renewal, was to be depicted in the Conservative Party propaganda prior to the 1997 election with 'demon eyes'.

It was the Enlightenment project and its faith in the goodness and perfectibility of human beings which banished the ubiquitous demons of pre-modernity. Thatcherism signified a loss of trust in the possibilities of a benign environment and a narrowing of the claims made for rational behaviour – now co-terminous with the pursuit of private economic interest. The demon in pre-modern iconography is a receptacle for the projection of illicit desires, expelled from the self into a site where they can be safely annihilated. It stands as a libertine mocking the constraints of the superego.

For the New Right the bad objects that cannot be owned are the morally perverted forms taken by untrammelled economic licence. Unrestrained market behaviour is premised on aggression towards the competitor and it is fear of one's own aggression rather than the adversary's response which, when moderated by the superego, leads to the development of conscience (something of an inconvenience in a pure market). If split off, it can return via the demons who forestall the painful realisation that one is the source of one's own persecution. A superego, properly speaking, is the property of an individual, allowing the development of self-regulated moral behaviour. It is gradually acquired as an internalised representation of the parent who both nurtures and admonishes. However, as the discussion in the last chapter made clear, the state too can be said to stand in symbolic relation to the citizen as parent, particularly insofar as it occupies itself with the people's welfare. The repudiation of a 'parental' state and the assertion of unconstrained economic licence may then appear to weaken the 'collective superego', eroding the capacity for moral regulation and necessitating a government of law and order. Thatcher was at pains to sustain this with a public persona of iron moral rectitude but her departure seemed to expose a party devoid of internalised authority. Demons have a habit of sadistically repossessing their former hosts. By the time of their defeat in 1997 the Conservatives had become irretrievably mired in sleaze and set on a course of schism and recrimination. From a Kleinian point of view, compulsively self-destructive behaviour would be the expected outcome of an inability to bear the burden of guilt that would be aroused by a phantasised killing of the parental state, particularly where the avenues for reparation had been foreclosed by the irreversible depredations of welfare cuts and privatisation. And if this were not enough, there remained the unresolved matricidal guilt of Thatcher's betrayal.

The construction of demonised categories in the population provided a focus for much publicised fears of breakdown of law and order. To the extent that crime rates actually were rising in the eighties, there appeared to be a realistic basis for anxiety, although debates around victimisation rates revolved around the question of whether expressed fear was proportionate to risk in different sectors of the population. Hollway and Jefferson (1997) consider that this is a somewhat superficial way of posing the problem and argue that fear of crime can in any case be understood as a displacement for other more diffuse anxieties stemming from pervasive uncertainty and the inability of either the applied social sciences or regulatory social institutions to order an increasingly unpredictable reality. The preoccupation with risk assessment can be understood as a defence against this uncertainty which is sometimes extolled as opportunity, but unconsciously perceived as threat.

Since projection is an unconscious strategy for ridding the self of unwanted attributes, it invites aggressive attacks on the bad object in order to annihilate these undesirable parts. In environments that combine insecurities of risk and unemployment with the ideological denigration of other groups, exclusionary discourses identify the scapegoats and offer very potent vehicles for aggression. We would then expect to find a rise of overtly racist, homophobic and misogynist practices, depending on which group offered the most appropriate target for destructiveness at any given time. From a Kleinian perspective, the potential problems associated with massive projection are twofold. In the first instance, the evacuation of parts of the self into other groups leaves it depleted and divided, as parts of it are lodged elsewhere, where they appear to belong to another. In the second instance, projective identification induces the other to feel and act out the projected aggression or vulnerability. Feeling states thus get passed on rapidly and without any processing, leading to the emotional 'contagion' which results in moral panics and the creation of scapegoats.

Within the welfare sector, concern at the corrosive effects of racism and, to a lesser extent sexism, began in the mid-eighties to stimulate a range of equal opportunities policies and, overtly at least, some awareness of the need to develop anti-discriminatory initiatives. Homophobia proved an altogether more difficult issue in the climate of rising panic generated by child sexual abuse scandals. Long-established prejudices eliding homosexuality and paedophilia probably contributed to this. Gay couples wishing to put themselves forward as foster or adoptive parents continued to face enormous obstacles, even as the scarcity of candidates obliged authorities to consider other non-conventional applicants. I have argued elsewhere (Froggett and Sapey, 1997) that in the context of the increasingly instrumental cultures of social services departments, anti-discriminatory initiatives risked becoming yet another administrative requirement, items on a procedural checklist rather than full recognition and respect for otherness. This in turn laid the basis for some fairly mechanistic and formulaic thinking leading to polarised positions on complex and sensitive issues. For example, concerns that children's racial identity was being ignored or violated in mixed race fostering, led in some authorities to an effective moratorium. The human-interest value of rejected fostering applications provided part of the press already hostile to social workers with a basis for accusations of facile political correctness while little children languished in care. In the event, the argument that racial identity had an automatic priority over all other needs, including those of secure attachments in young children, proved politically unsustainable and this most delicate of balancing processes became an arena of polemical and often ill-informed contest.

The image of the underclass succeeded in providing something of a catch-all category by incorporating a whole range of truanting, unmarried, unemployable, homeless, itinerant, delinquent and deranged, which, together with the denigrated middle-class public sector professionals, captured many facets of projected anxiety. Politically this created a basis for the alliance between the government and the 'people' through which Thatcher's 'authoritarian populism' (Hall, 1983) was forged. In a society of widening income division, diminishing trades union rights, and rising insecurity, this distinction between the employed and increasingly home-owning working class and the deviant flotsam and jetsam of the 'sink estates' was a vital legitimating factor for a politics which claimed the authority of the people for the erosion of public institutions. By drawing a boundary around those who deserved to share in the eventual benefits of national thrift and economic growth, and those who were to become candidates for regulation and repression, the danger of social conflict along traditional class lines could be averted. The welfare sector, cast in this regulatory role, was to ascertain through its ever more vigorous gate-keeping activities who was worthy of rehabilitation. This changed role has entailed a profound shift away from preventive, therapeutic and maintenance activities, towards the management of risk (Parton, 1998).

Welfare, risk and the public

In what sense does the risk society promote the splitting, fragmentation and paranoia that derive from paranoid–schizoid states of mind? And where is the potential for a depressive response? Beck (1992) identifies a number of concomitants of escalating uncertainty. In the first instance, a risk society is one in which threats of an unknown future begin to outweigh sources of optimism. Hence the overall decline of a faith in the progress characteristic of the post-modern consciousness. Attention turns to problems of damage-limitation – how to regulate, moderate and make safe a future perceived as dangerous in unspecifiable ways. Both the natural and the man-made environment become sources of menace and attempts to control and manipulate them raise anxieties of catastrophic and unforeseen destabilisation: pollution, global warming, BSE, genetic engineering, the millennium bug, HIV, international terrorism, the return of tuberculosis and malaria, and most significantly, the global economy itself.

As if this were not sufficient, the decline of group affiliations to family, community, class, and the mobility and fragmentation of increasingly urbanised populations, leave the individual substantially alone to face these terrors. There are no automatically available reference points or sources of meaning. To be sure, people in the advanced industrial societies have their entitlements to the protection of health and welfare systems, but these are increasingly penetrated by quasi-market principles and methodological individualism which weaken their former symbolic function as institutional expressions of the common good.

In one sense, the insecurity and anxiety in the face of a reality that can only provisionally be deciphered, and that threatens to overwhelm the individual with unanticipated misfortune at every turn, describe the state of uncertainty that many disorganised and marginalised people chronically suffer. Contrary to the entrepreneurial ideology that identifies risk as a stimulus to creativity, this condition only too often leaves people with a grinding sense of helplessness rather than stimulating the internal resources that sustain initiative:

> The decisive point ... is that the horizon dims as risks grow. For risks tell us what should not be done but not what should be done. With risks avoidance imperatives dominate. Someone who depicts the world as risk will ultimately become incapable of action. (Beck, 1994, p 9)

One of the important concomitants of a risk society is that whereas industrial society, which thrives on a belief in progress, struggles with the problem of how to distribute the 'goods' that it produces, risk societies are preoccupied with the distribution of 'bads': the negative consequences, whether in terms of environmental, health or social dislocation, of its system of production. Titmuss's (1968) charge, quoted in Chapter Three, that the ideology of state welfare systems obscured their own purpose as a compensation for the 'diswelfares' of industrial production, was nevertheless consistent with a defensible role for public welfare as a distributor of genuine social 'goods'. The risk society implicitly shifts the blame for ill-health and diswelfare onto individuals themselves, undermining the argument for public services as a redistributive force in the interests of social justice. If health and welfare are a predominantly personal responsibility, those who believe themselves to be making fewer demands on the system, largely the middle classes, are likely to perceive an interest in restricting public expenditure.

The welfarism of the post-war period was based on the principle of social insurance whose symbolic function was to bind the individual citizen into a system of scientifically administered collective responsibility. Although assumptions relating to its viability as a financial underpinning of an expanding welfare state proved to be wide of the mark, the principle itself was integrative. It implicitly accepted the fact that the poor and vulnerable would make disproportionate claims on health and welfare services and that these costs would be borne by the wider community in recognition of the higher goals of mutuality and social cohesion. Privately financed insurance based on actuarial principles, which calculates risk on the basis of probability, operates to quite different effect. Although the rise of private medical insurance, followed by insurance against loss of employment, private pensions and continuing care, has been significant during the eighties and nineties, its symbolic importance has been greater than the size of the private sector itself would imply. The model has in any case been adopted as a means of instilling calculability into finance-led public services.

Figlio (1989) argues that the actuarial thinking of private insurance, which divides the population into categories of risk and attempts to predict the likely incidence and costs of accident and illness on this basis, signifies a change in ways of thinking that can degrade the very notion of the 'public'. He explores the influence of private medical insurance on the National Health Service insofar as it has adopted actuarial methods of projecting future demand for treatment. The effect of statistics on income-related incidence of illness has been to demonstrate the correlation between high risk and low social class, with the result that the latter come to be seen by the low–risk middle classes as reservoirs of disease within the body politic. In a culture stressing self-reliance, the causes of this pathology are likely to be located in behavioural traits such as irresponsible dietary habits – the legendary deep-fried Mars Bars of Northern cuisine. The 'goodness' represented by the health of the low–risk groups, who must suffer the financial consequences of others' heedless lifestyles, is then seen as the just reward for temperate habits. Meanwhile the underclass comes to represent split–off desires that oppose the work ethic: hedonism, intoxication and a general disrespect for discipline. Such simplistic explanations are made all the more likely by the disinterest that a society dominated by contractual relations shows for causes, and hence a disregard for any epidemiology which traces the complex psychosocial roots of health and illness. Western models of objective science have tended to see disease as an alien pathogenic attacker. Actuarial thinking is divisive in that it facilitates fantasies of certain social groups as the vehicle for this aggression. The ultimate logic in institutional terms would be the solution favoured by New Right thinkers in which private health insurance guarantees access to privileged health services for those who have been selected by the industry as low risk (and by implication, virtuous) and to open the way for the residualisation of the public health sector. The destructiveness that leads us to project unwanted propensities of the self such as impurity and vulnerability onto other groups, would then become reified in separate institutional arrangements. The force of this analysis is that it identifies the potentially protective effect of universalist public services. Robust public institutions act as symbolic containers for the destructive envy that expresses itself in anxiety that the poor might misuse and thrive on welfare systems, exploiting the generosity of those who pay for them. More than this, they present institutional models of interdependency where fragile and fluctuating reparative impulses can find durable organised expression.

> Public is not the same as state, class or culture. Health is a public word; disease is a private one, which stands as a challenge to it, and relies on mastering anxiety by externalisation. Public and health provide reservoirs of group phantasy of a particular sort, in that they are removed from contributing to the projective loops that I have described. They receive and supply phantasies that cannot be absorbed into cycles of idealisation and contempt. (Figlio, 1989, p 96)

The risk society may maintain formal rights and entitlements to welfare but entails a destruction of 'welfarism' insofar as the rational self-interested and calculated choices of consumers replace bureaucratic planning of public services. Individuals are expected to weigh up the costs and consequences of their actions and those who do so successfully, in that their behaviour, parenting or self-care remains within socially acceptable parameters, will largely evade scrutiny and interference. The role of professionals is reoriented towards the assessment and management of risk in those imprudent sectors of the population who fail to manage it on their own behalf. Social welfare then becomes central to the process of drawing the lines of division and defining the boundaries beyond which regulation occurs. Parton (1998) points out that since children are all potentially imprudent, attention devolves on those who bear responsibility for them. He points out the divisive consequences:

> This art of the management of risk to children is key to understanding the sphere of operation for child welfare at the junction of the self-managed world of the affiliated and the twilight world of the socially and economically marginalised and excluded, particularly those sections of the poor who make up the biggest proportion of the 'clients' of child welfare services, such as single-parent households, substance misusers, homeless families and certain ethnic groups. (Parton, 1998, p 20)

Worries during the Thatcher and Major years about the enemy within coalesced around the spectre of the dependency culture. Although thought to be manifest in its most toxic form among the various groups that made up the underclass, it came to signify a fatal weakening of the moral fabric of the nation – a legacy of the profligate years of 'old welfarism' that had contaminated the national character, where it remained like a dormant virus constantly threatening to irrupt and infect the new entrepreneurial culture. Constant monitoring and salutary habits were required in order to keep this pestilence in abeyance. Within organisations it seemed that its breeding ground was stability. Cultures of constant change, once thought to be wasteful of human energy, were now reframed as invigorating. Scepticism was itself symptomatic of an underlying malaise, inviting the derisory diagnostic label of 'old guard'. In one longitudinal study (Froggett, 1999) of a well-intentioned attempt to introduce a process of cultural change which could sustain a reflective professionalism, the attribution of 'old guardism' proved so divisive that it threatened to subvert the whole process. Staff also complained of a back-watching, blame culture. Even when they recognised senior management's good intentions, they still felt obliged to 'dodge and weave' to stay ahead of the 'game'. In interviews with over 40 members of staff across different sections of the organisation and at different levels in the hierarchy, over half expressed persecutory anxieties at some point in the interview – even though few had ever felt personally victimised.

Douglas (1992) argues that refined blaming systems are a concomitant of the risk society in which nothing is allowed to go wrong without it being attributed to some party who can be held to account. The formalisation of institutional life, often justified in terms of the clarification of roles and relationships, is reflected in the growth of complaints procedures, graduated disciplinary mechanisms and litigation. Every organisational memo, document and procedure is a potential forensic resource in the event of mishap. Social workers can with some justification feel themselves to be placed in double jeopardy in that they are more than usually prone to attack from without by a society which feels ambivalent about the role it requires them to occupy, and from within organisations who attempt to protect themselves from censure by demonstrating themselves to be fully abreast of approved cultural trends in workforce discipline. As Parton (1998) has pointed out, the effect of this trend is to replace the trust formerly accorded to professionals by audit, thereby introducing new relations of regulation whereby every decision is referred to approved procedure, recorded and rendered visible. He concurs with Howe (1992) that 'the focus becomes, not making the *right* decision, but making a *defensible* decision' (Parton, 1998, p 21).

P held responsibility for a case where a woman with quite severe learning disabilities became pregnant and wanted to keep and raise her baby. None of the professionals involved thought that this would be possible without permanent 24-hour support. Even then it was unlikely that she could provide an environment where the baby's developmental or safety needs could be met. P knew that a case could be made for rapid removal of the child after birth, with the possibility of fostering arrangements where maternal contact could be maintained. In the event, she went along with the decision of a case conference that the mother be allowed to demonstrate her incapacity to care for her baby in the context of hospital surveillance. Afterwards she realised uneasily that the whole discussion had been framed in terms of building the case for care proceedings, although overtly it had been presented as allowing the mother time to accommodate the decision. The case for intervention was duly established at some risk to the child when the mother mishandled the baby. In hindsight, P felt that the evidential requirements of the case had overshadowed the interests of both mother and child. The casualty of the process was the possibility of establishing the conditions under which continued contact between them might have taken place.

Conclusion

The New Right promoted an uncompromising form of competitive individualism which derived from the extension of market relations and the retraction of public welfare provision. The purpose of this chapter has been to identify some of the ways in which this project reconfigured the social relations of welfare. The aim has been to trace the lines of connection between primitive states of mind and the 'primitive mind of state' (Bell, 1997). This expands our understanding of the practical impossibility of sustaining public welfare alongside the assumption that we are fundamentally asocial, self-seeking isolates out to do the best for ourselves in the competitive environment of unrestrained markets. As this will hardly be news to most people employed in public services, it is important to explain the success of the neo-liberal movement in overwhelming resistance and penetrating and transforming the working relations between managers, professionals and clients. Clearly, any process of social transformation is likely to be successful to the extent that it realigns feelings, meanings, relationships and social structures in ways that reflect and reinforce one another.

From a Kleinian point of view, the period favoured the splitting characteristic of paranoid–schizoid anxieties and the polarised thinking which they foster. This is characterised by a primitive talion morality in which right survives and thrives and wrong is blamed and punished. Justice tends to be conceived in terms of reward or retribution. The defences are oriented to keeping apart the bad from the good in both inner and outer worlds in case what is good is corrupted and destroyed. The social effects of this are idealisation of the good (nation, family, entrepreneurial man) and the scapegoating, exclusion and aggressive attacks on the bad (aliens, dependants), particularly where this represents an attempt to excise a feared and despised vulnerability which threatens to weaken the subject.

Such states of mind are likely to project anxiety, which finds expression in an imagery of internal corruption and external threat. The linking of welfare dependency to the supposed underclass implicated the welfare system itself in the wholesale construction of social exclusion. This is something qualitatively different from the stigmatisation that was produced by welfare bureaucracies. The person who is stigmatised is marked out for attention. The attention may be relatively benign or patronising, controlling and distorting of individuality, but the effect of stigma is to render the person visible. The significance of underclass imagery is that it agglomerates and excludes whole categories rendering them unworthy and ineligible for individual consideration:

> An individualist culture finds ways of making its disadvantaged members
> disappear from sight. To stop stigmatising would be another way of making
> them invisible. (Douglas, 1992, p 36)

I described the second quadrant of the grid (Figure 1) where relations are characterised by inequality and separation as the 'no welfare' position. This seems apt, although not because Thatcher and Major succeeded in dismantling the structures of the welfare state. They demonstrated that it was possible to dispel 'welfarism' as a principle that rests on the sense of attachment between people, that begins in the sphere of the private and intimate but finds expression in mediated form in the lived relations of the 'social' and in the idea of the 'public'. An important part of their strategy was to direct their critique at those professions which mediate between private distress and public institutions, between the socially excluded and the socially included. The ensuing transformation of the organisational cultures in which health and welfare professionals worked involved a reorientation towards the management of risk, systematic proceduralisation and incorporation of accountability within corporate blaming systems as a refined mechanism of control. Less refined mechanisms included bullying management styles and denigration of all opposition as out of tune and out of touch.

These changes were experienced as profoundly destructive on the part of many of those working within public services. Managerialism allows people to distance themselves from the emotional impact of their work, watch their backs, and mind their careers. However, the costs in terms of lost creativity, or simply ability to establish a realistic relation to reality, are immeasurable. Elsewhere (Froggett, 1997), I have argued that mediative professionals (pre-eminently social workers, but also others in the human services) are obliged to engage in linking activities which require as their condition forms of intellectual and emotional containment which are likely to be eroded in high performance, high anxiety, blame cultures. The question of whether a greater commitment to equality expressed as 'fairness' within contractual guarantees of rights can generate such containers will be explored in the next chapter.

Note

[1] OPUS, the Organisation for Promoting the Understanding of Society, reflects the Tavistock Group relations tradition of organisational consultancy and study of group behaviour.

FIVE

Mixed welfare: from consumption to compassion?

... if we could experience the irresistible rush of the new unaffected by anything else, if the old did not cast its shadow on the new, our life would be a ceaseless wonder; every moment between day and night, between birth and death, would be a thrilling miracle; we couldn't distinguish between pain and pleasure, hot and cold, sweet and sour; there would be no boundaries, no borderlines between our most extreme sensations, because there would be no in between, and thus we'd have no word for the moment, no division between day and night, and out of the wet warmth of our mother's womb we wouldn't come wailing into this cold, dry world; and in death we'd only crumble like stones scorched by the sun and lashed by the icy rain, for there would be no slow decay, and no dread, and no language either, for words can name only recurring phenomena; in the absence of recurrence we wouldn't have what we like to call intelligent discourse, only the divine gift, the ineffable joy of permanent impermanence.

Peter Nadas, *A book of memories* (1998, p 571)

The ideal welfare subject of New Labour in the 'mixed welfare' quadrant of the grid (Figure 1) understands that his or her stakeholding in the welfare state is upheld by a series of rights that imply reciprocal obligations. These rights, defined predominantly as the rights of the consumer, are underwritten by contract and guarantee his or her ability to exercise choice in any sector of the mixed economy of care. A more detailed consideration of the profile of this welfare subject reveals the connection between the key terms represented on the grid. Since 'he or she' is cumbersome, I shall switch to the use of the female pronoun here in recognition of the fact that the gendered disparities in welfare provision and participation in the labour force, although not eliminated, have considerably diminished.

The New Labour welfare subject appears to us in ideal form as the informed, rationally choosing, welfare-maximising consumer able to access a range of service options without prejudice as to whether they are provided by the public, private or voluntary sector. Freed from dogmatic and dated allegiances to institutions from whom her antecedents might have expected 'handouts', she is a socially responsible and engaged individualist – keen to ensure that debts incurred are repaid by her contribution to the community. Most importantly, this contribution takes the form of participation in the labour market. She understands the proper role of welfare in terms of social investment and the building of social infrastructure to ensure that she can maximise her opportunities within a world of paid employment. She expects that those who are reluctant to shoulder this responsibility will be impelled to do so for their own benefit and that of others.

She is concerned with the ethical standing of welfare institutions, requiring them to be free of corruption and adequately, though not lavishly, funded. When in employment she expects that her tax contribution will be prudently spent on fully monitored, accountable and efficient organisations whose disbursements and service provision will be allocated in accordance with the dictates of fairness. These organisations mediate her stakeholding in society, guaranteeing a series of rights and imposing reciprocal obligations. She conceives of her relationship to them in terms of partnership governed by a contract to which she is an equal party. She is an active participant in upholding this contract and is keen and competent to ensure that its terms are respected. She will not exceed her entitlement but will expect it to be fulfilled in terms of range and quality of provision in education, health, or social care.

There will be no stigma attached to use of benefits such as Income Support, for although she will probably explore options for private insurance against the vagaries of the flexible labour market in which she is obliged to seek work, she accepts that she must embrace the risk society with all its uncertainties and learn to live as independently as possible within it. Her contract with the state ensures that she is protected against misfortune for which she could not herself reasonably be expected to have provided. Retraining opportunities will always be available within the lifelong learning culture of which she is a part – if her skills become obsolete or she suffers from disabling illness or accident she can take advantage of an educational infrastructure that will re-equip her to make a useful contribution to her local and national community.

The welfare subject of New Labour upholds 'family values' but may not live in a traditional heterosexual two-person family and is reasonably tolerant of non-traditional family forms. She expects a range of good quality childcare and education options for any offspring who will be raised in a disciplined household committed to the work ethic. Her children will not become unduly attached to a chosen course of life but will be educated for adaptability and well versed in the all-important arts of consumption and information seeking. The family will be united in its understanding of the virtues of the market and the competition that it imposes. They will be sanguine about the inevitable inequalities that ensue, provided that they have a sense of competing on a level playing field. They are involved as individuals in a project of continual self-renewal to meet the need for an ever-changing complement of skills. The love of all that is modern and new may leave them somewhat ambivalent towards ageing members. Certainly they are unimpressed by nostalgia, impatient of tradition, and uncomfortable with states of dependency. As moral citizens they accept a duty of care, but they are concerned about levels of expenditure and services for unproductive groups. On the other hand their busy working lifestyles ensure that they have little personal time available for them.

Beyond the family, whatever its particular formation, the New Labour welfare subject may develop a range of strategies for coping with the uncertainties of the new world order and the inevitable strains of a pluralistic society. In her search for a stable identity she develops affiliations to groups of people who share her interests. Pre-eminently these will reflect lifestyle and leisure activities, reflecting her status as discerning consumer. Hence, while she is encouraged to participate actively in a community, her allegiance is probably to a 'community' of choice. She is nevertheless a patriot who identifies weakly, if at all, with a particular social class and is even less likely to belong to a trade union or political party. If she happens to be from an ethnic minority, religious or cultural affiliations may assume great importance and she will expect this to be reflected in services that respect her differences from the majority culture. These may involve appropriately recruited and trained personnel or dedicated facilities such as day centres or faith-based schools. It is through the representation and consultation of such group-based interests that her 'stakeholder' identity is consolidated.

The organisations through which New Labour welfare subjects access their services are expected to be customer-focused. There are clear and open procedures for complaint, should the service fall short of legitimate expectations. Within the public sector at least, they remain subject to tight financial control. They are regularly inspected and audited and operate within a highly regulated environment. The ethos simulates business-style efficiency where activity is measured by outcome and value for money. They continue to be led by a command-style management and a corporate identity is encouraged with much importance attached to mission and self-presentation. Manual staff wear uniforms in the corporate colours, blending tastefully with the office furniture. In some areas this is required for quasi-professionals — at a minimum a discrete badge bearing the logo signifies appropriate commitment. Scope for dissent among staff is limited and individual performance carefully appraised. In all these respects there are significant continuities with the New Conservative project. Indeed it would seem that any differences are of degree rather than kind — the changes in corporate cultures having been more fully worked through in the intervening years. Although the main public service professions: teachers, nurses and social service personnel are all suffering recruitment crises, there have now been several cohorts of newly qualified staff whose early professional experience has been within highly managerialised environments. They have been trained in accordance with an outcome-led, competence-based culture and are increasingly literate users of information technology, and within certain established conventions, research. Their professional formation has emphasised practicality, relevance and the needs of employers and they may have rather little experience in critical reflection. On the whole they form a docile and well-disciplined workforce. Claims that they are correspondingly unimaginative abound but imagination, of course, is a quality resistant to audit.

Despite the structural similarities between welfare organisations in the neo-liberal and mixed welfare models, there may be significant differences in how they feel as places to work. The themes of partnership and participation have become the pre-eminent routes to social inclusion and these carry the egalitarian thrust, such as it is, of New Labour social policy.

Third Way – spin or substance?

A brief look at the broad canvass of New Labour policy indicates a coherence to the evolution of a 'Third Way', even though use of the term, lacking the sharpness of focus required of soundbite formulations, has gradually declined. Blair in any case is avowedly impatient of ideology. Initially, the conceptualisation of a Third Way helped to distinguish a significant difference of approach and leadership style from the Conservatives. The blurring of the very clear lines of division between the values of welfare and the values of the market signified an altered state of mind, a renunciation of the adversarial politics of possessive individualism in favour of more workable forms of mediation between competing interests. It was perhaps most immediately understood as a new set of political attitudes, a politics that invoked the new-found maturity of 'joined-up' government. As such it could have been expected to foster changes in those areas of public life where actors engage in conflict resolution. Mo Mowlam's refusal to be sucked into sectarian polarisation in Northern Ireland established an early example of communicative realism, although not one that ultimately endeared her to the leadership.

What seemed to have been envisaged in the 'beyond Left and Right' politics (Giddens, 1994) was a pain-free process in which conflicts were skilfully managed and smoothed by appropriately designated personalities. Such a politics would be 'grown-up' but definitely not old, 'creative' without a hint of subversion, 'responsible' but biddable, 'compassionate' within the dictates of prudence, deliberative but consensus-oriented, woman-friendly but not too feminist, green-tinged but enchanted by commercial technologies: in short, moved by Blairite 'ideals' but strictly within the 'realistic' limits imposed by global capitalism.

There seemed to be some difficulty in delineating a Third Way which was anything other than a middle way, effectively a politics of compromise, seen not so much as the art of the possible but as an elevated form of consciousness. As Hall remarked:

> It has no enemies. Everyone can belong. The 'Third Way' speaks as if there are no longer any conflicting interests which cannot be reconciled. It therefore envisages a 'politics without adversaries'. This suggests that, by some miracle of transcendence, the interests represented by, say, the ban on tobacco advertising and 'Formula One', the private car lobby and John Prescott's White Paper, an ethical foreign policy and the sale of arms to Indonesia, media diversity and the concentrated drive-to-global power of Rupert Murdoch's media empire

have been effortlessly 'harmonised' on a Higher Plane above politics. (*Marxism Today*, November/December 1998, p 10)

What Hall captured so acutely were the mystical overtones of Blair's self-presentation with its evocation of vision, values and vigour in compensation for a certain programmatic vagueness. The party machine that promoted him had learnt well the lessons of presentation and performance developed previously by the Conservatives, and sought to combine these in a new inspirational leadership of the political centre. In adopting a manner sympathetic to established conventions within the business culture, Blair achieved a reassuring identification with the methods and style of a sector that presents itself as modernising and wealth creating, while at the same time welding them to a new politics of consensus. Furthermore, Park (2000) points out that the development of hortatory emotional rhetoric of 'passion', 'creativity', 'commitment', 'innovation', 'resourcefulness' and 'leadership' is related to the increasing conviction that ability of corporations and nations to respond to the flexibility required by the new global order for technological, social and personal change will only be achieved by mobilising new levels of responsiveness in employees and citizens. Within organisations this responsiveness can be 'harnessed' by managers and fed into both vertical and lateral information flows to feed the 'learning organisation'. The task of the modern manager is to empower the workforce and release creativity.

As in the private corporation, so in politics: henceforth with a carefully orchestrated use of the media and relentless behind-the-scenes organisation, the art of management could be seamlessly extended from private and public sector organisations into the whole of the social and cultural sphere. This revealed an authoritarian strand directed to the erasure of dissent within the political process. New Labour's obsession with image and opinion formation was rewarded with barely disguised public glee when the arch-spinner Peter Mandelson fell foul of his own methods at the close of 1998. The issue of spin continued to dog the party well into the second term and was emblematic of an obsession with control, pervasive deceitfulness, a shallowness pervading political life, and the low turnout in the 2001 election. Matters came to a head when the special adviser to the Secretary of State for Transport, sent an e-mail, subsequently leaked, urging that the destruction of the World Trade Center's twin towers, one hour previously, afforded an opportune moment to bury bad news. The story refused to die quickly despite apologies and stimulated debates in Parliament and throughout the media on the source of political cynicism.

Issues of presentation were always of the utmost importance to New Labour – indeed successful opposition to the political leadership was more likely to be put down to failure to transmit the message than to any flaws in the content of policy itself. It may be that the Third Way was never much more than a rhetorical device for repositioning the party between the Old Left and the New Right, while at the same time making a bid for intellectual respectability through an alliance with intellectuals such as Anthony Giddens (1998) and the work of think-tanks such as Demos. Freeden (1999) argued that New Labour policy-making was in any case eclectic and identified an ideological configuration which drew selectively from British and American traditions of socialism, liberalism and conservatism. Within this mix, welfare and work were counterposed as alternatives in which welfare was reduced to support for the marginalised.

The focus of the Socal Exclusion Unit was very firmly on groups such as the homeless and pregnant teenagers. The expansion of human potential or well-being, or even attention to the role of the excluders, was apparently beyond its remit. Third Way thinking was squeamish about the very concept of 'welfare' – considered less as a form of protection, than something from which the public should be protected. Justified spending on public services was characterised as 'social investment' to be rigorously controlled at ground level by the perpetuation of monitoring and blaming. To those on the receiving end, teachers for example, it felt more like scapegoating, designed to exorcise the spectre raised by Chris Woodhead, while still Chief Inspector of Schools, of an education system encumbered by thousands of incompetents. The Blair government was in fact prepared to go further than its predecessors in 'naming and shaming' and supporting privatisation as a solution to 'failing' schools and other services.

In contrast to Freeden, Buckler and Dolowitz (2000) put forward a persuasive case for a coherent emergent strategy, incrementally achieved. The Third Way, they suggest, is essentially a form of social liberalism in that it retains a commitment to principles of liberal individualism combined with a Rawlsian concern for a degree of distributive justice. This is to be understood in terms of the availability of opportunities and accepts that inequalities of outcome are necessary for the effective operation of markets. Equitable distribution of wealth and common ownership, associated with Old Labour, are clearly rejected in favour of policies which aim to create the so-called level playing field – hence the overwhelming emphasis on education and programmes designed to build social capital such as Sure Start. The New Deal for Communities programme is envisaged as part of a shift from short-term income maintenance to the maximisation of employment opportunity through the regeneration of the social infrastructure on which individuals can draw in terms of health, education and the local environment. This has allowed the party to address the concerns of traditionalists about social disadvantage while allying itself with the ambitious and successful. In addition, the emphasis on 'fairness' is aimed at a remoralisation of political practice, which at the same time avoids positioning the government as redistributionist. It does this because it stems from a recognition of the equal worth of persons, acknowledges that formal commitment to equal opportunity is insufficient and that justice demands that those who suffer arbitrary disadvantage should be compensated. Hence, rather than a concern for class inequality, there is a discourse of 'inclusion' reflected in attempts to address marginalisation, concerns over child poverty and anxieties over the effect of university tuition fees on the recruitment of working-class students.

Prior to the election of the first Blair government, the quest for a source of moral legitimacy, particularly for a renewed emphasis on social obligation beyond the private sphere, emphasised the importance of civic participation in the community and voluntary sector, which was seen as having a crucial role in the mixed economy of care. Blair's emphasis on the enhancement of citizenship within active communities (Home Office, 1998) leaned heavily on the claims of communitarians such as Etzioni (1994, 1997) to identify a social philosophy which finds in a sense of community commitment a possibility of charting a course between the old political divisions of Right and Left. In so doing it reasserts the importance of moral obligation, echoing earlier largely Conservative forms of organicism and moral authoritarianism. It is worth asking how such a commitment squares with social liberalism. Driver and Martell (1997), in an attempt to identify the different strands of communitarian influence, identified New Labour's version as consistent with a shift away from social democracy towards a prescriptive moral conservatism that finds expression in proposals such as sanctions against parents of school non-attenders, a mistrust of progressive teaching methods and an intolerance of community nuisances such as street-sleepers, 'squeegee merchants' and wayward juveniles. Despite the general conviction that community is 'a good thing' and a force for social cohesion, the revitalisation of community morality under New Labour appeared from the outset to be a rather top-down affair, driven by government and law, and covering a range of issues from children's homework to religious intolerance. This conformist drift has taken little interest in the power of communities to revitalise their own ethical life and there are therefore questions as to how deep a commitment to pluralist local democratic forms can be sustained. Jordan (2000) echoes these concerns, underlining the emblematic role of 'enforcement counsellors' (such as New Deal personal advisors). New Labour's crude Benthamite approach to policy implementation stems from a simplistic and rather mechanical view of social transactions as ideally governed by the self-interested choice of the 'responsible' (compliant) consumer – failing this, by surveillance and coercion. He points to a lack of understanding by New Labour of the need for identities worthy of respect and support, and despite the communitarian talk of 'belonging', of social bonds:

> The notions of 'promoting independence' and 'meeting individuals' needs' are in line with the achievement ethos of the whole reform package, and its emphasis on a targeted, focussed and individualised form of social intervention – replacing generalised safety nets by customised trampolines. (Jordan, 2000, p 84)

By way of example, Jordan contrasts New Labour's approach to homelessness, now trumpeted as one of its successes, with that of the growing movement, in this country and abroad, of Emmaus communities. Whereas the government's concern has been to develop a range of regulatory measures to propel individuals to move from the unemployment register into paid work, the Emmaus communities emphasise acceptance and membership, allowing people to use their facilities for temporary respite or life-long residence as they prefer and with no questions asked, on condition that they work for the good of the community, participate, and respect its democratic decision making.

I do not in what follows intend to develop a systematic review of the contradictions in New Labour policy. My central question is how far Blair's Third Way is able to moderate the very pronounced paranoid–schizoid splitting, projection, exclusion and denigration that characterised responses to welfare recipients after 1979. I have already highlighted the residual role foreseen for welfare as a form of support for those who are, for whatever reason, outside of the labour market. The receipt of this support is conditional on willingness to subscribe to the work ethic and, as Freeden (1999) points out, Labour has conspicuously refused to countenance the possibility that state welfare has a role to play in human flourishing. Most importantly the support of the marginalised and vulnerable is not linked in New Labour discourse with the sense of a public good. This is to be achieved through a revitalisation of civil society conceived in terms of social networks, voluntary associations and active communities, but very much under the guiding hand of government as the guardian of values in the national community of communities. It could be argued that the reparative impulse can achieve satisfactory expression in the networks of relationships thus formed, moderating the consequences of market competition in ways which maximise individual participation and avoid the so-called 'dependency culture' and the baleful economic effects of heavy state expenditure. The rest of this chapter will explore psychic dimensions of significant aspects of the New Labour mindset and ask how far this impedes the development of a reparative politics of welfare.

Community, partnership and participation

Partnership and participation had become increasingly pervasive themes in social policy throughout the nineties, well before the 1997 election. However, the Blair governments have attempted to develop them into a vision of a distinctive set of relationships at all levels of the political process. The extension of participation reinforces the democratic credentials of Blairism while partnership gives form to its relational sensibilities and community is a source of values and social cohesion.

These linked and rather diffuse concepts underpin a variety of initiatives: local consultation with the public on small scale projects, attempts to mobilise community activism, public/private finance initiatives, interagency service delivery, joint executive planning in relation to shared responsibilities as between health and social services. On a national scale, Blair was elected with promises of a new partnership between government and people. It is clear that, whatever the success of these relationships, the principle of partnership and the enhanced participation it is assumed to facilitate has become an important aspect of the government's claim that it is committed to local renewal of political processes. It also appealed to the sensibilities of user groups and professionals who, in seeking to develop non-oppressive relationships with the people they work with, have stressed the necessity of participation and partnership with the service user. However, at this point it may be useful to uncouple the terms and consider the difficulties of partnership. The notion carries the expectation of a degree of equality or at least symmetry between the partners, indeed this is what gives it its appeal. The terrain on which it is perhaps most widely used and tested is that of community regeneration. 'Community', while wider than partnership, depends on it within networks of lateral relations based on shared experience in which members participate more or less as equals. Yet many of these relationships are fraught with difficulty and founder.

The psychosocial model of partnership is built on our perception of the first partners we come to know – the parental couple which the child aspires to emulate in its generativity, but which is also the agent of her displacement and exclusion. The infant first desires to partner mother but is thwarted by the dawning realisation that she 'belongs' to another, and moreover that these two are united in a reproductive pairing that may compound the displacement by giving birth to another sibling. Their partnership therefore evokes not only the fear of exclusion but the mixed hope and dread that it might produce another child to take one's place. Mitchell (2000) has recently supplemented psychoanalysis' emphasis on the importance of vertical or Oedipal relations with parents, by elaborating the role of real or potential siblings in introducing another set of desires based on lateral relationships. These, of course, indicate to the child where she might eventually find creative partners of her own in peer relationships. Partnerships, then, are potent institutions without which there is no baby, but they stimulate extreme conflicts. The child must first come to terms with exclusion from the parental couple and then the painful realisation that she is not unique, in order to gain a new perspective on the world. This perspective is the position of the 'third' which in superseding the infant–mother binary opens up a new possibility of relationships beyond the family and poses a new problem: how to come to terms with the existence of others who are utterly like me, yet at the same time completely different. Hence the child begins to rehearse the dilemmas of recognition that will pervade friendships, work relations and social life.

Urban regeneration projects have been continually beset by problems caused by the competitive bias of the funding arrangements (Mayo, 1997) decreed by the governmental 'parent'. We can read the difficulties of viable partnerships partly in terms of the psychosocial patterns outlined above. The problem of short-term fascination with innovatory projects is reminiscent of delight in the new 'baby' without regard to what it will become and the fact that it must travel some of the same old developmental pathways. Then there is the setting of organisations or sections of the community against each other in bidding for limited resources at the expense of their longer term need to live together while accepting that each has a distinctive contribution. Preoccupations with 'flagship' projects such as new sports centres lead to the neglect of existing projects, which still need to be nurtured to achieve sustained development.

The persistence of top-down approaches is effectively an attempt to manage or bypass the sheer difficulty of getting the participants to work cooperatively together. There is also an emphasis on achievement (output) which selects some for reward without attending to the process by which they reached their position, and why others have encountered greater difficulties. The shortcomings of the government as 'parent' may interfere with the recognition relations of community organisations and groups as 'siblings', but even with 'good-enough' parents the dynamics pose significant problems of coexistence.

Within community organisations, partnership also raises difficulties that stem from the ways in which it can mobilise group defences. Bion (1961) identified three 'basic assumption' states that groups frequently use to defend against anxiety and avoid the task they have set themselves. The basic assumption of 'pairing' often works against the development of successful partnerships and the wider group's ability to make creative use of them. It occurs when the group (or team) looks for a partnering pair (for example a new combination of senior professional and manager) who will deliver its members from their difficulties by miraculously producing the solutions that they have failed to develop on their own. The desire for generative, reproductive partnerships is something like the romantic idealisation of the wedding (Gould, 2001), suffused with the hope that the pair will bring forth a miraculous child – a source of future salvation. After the heady romance – always a self-limiting phase – the relationship encounters the mundane problems of day-to-day difference and negotiation, and disillusion sets in. The interest and support of the wider community may be rapidly withdrawn. Short-term voluntary projects are rather prone to this.

Gould stresses that partnerships within and between organisations are notoriously prone to failure and suggests that the question might well be whether the basis for successful partnership is 'reproductive' desire, and whether the 'offspring' will be recognised, nurtured and valued by the wider group when it fails to live up to inflated expectations. The problem with health and social service partnerships is not only that they are to some extent 'forced marriages', but also that the characteristics of their offspring are prescribed in advance or imagined differently by the 'parents', each wishing to mould it to their own likeness. According to Mitchell (2000), the unwillingness to give up this fantasy leads to another – the parthenogenetic impulse characteristic of the hysteric: to replicate without the partner, or 'go it alone' and sabotage the possibility of joint working.

The problem with partnership is not that it is in itself a bad thing, but its uncritical acceptance as self-evidently 'good'. In part this faith in its virtue derives from its egalitarian connotations but this may be a mystification. Mayo (1997) points out that one of the most influential models of partnership throughout the nineties was invested with 'transformational' aspirations – at least by governments who urged the union. This is the public–private variety where the explicit expectation was that the public partner would be infused with the dynamism, culture and methods of the private sector. The transformation has been perceived as a one-way affair, an assumption which has contributed to the continued denigration of public sector organisations, fear within them of loss of identity and declining commitment of many who work for them.

Cooper and Lousada (2003, forthcoming) also make it clear that at the level of face-to-face interaction between professionals and the people who they work with, the egalitarian assumptions of partnership may reflect a laudably anti-paternalist politics which can, however, lead to a failure to exercise appropriate authority. They specifically refer to the difficulties and confusions that arise in negotiating the triangular relationships between health authorities, users and front-line service providers. In particular there is uncertainty as to whether any 'parental' authority remains to think about the needs of the user:

> It seems important, but very hard, to distinguish between the consumer and the partner. Is it possible to be both, without something important to the process of giving and receiving help becoming denied and distorted? Making of the user as a partner has many democratic attractions, but it may also obscure the difficulties associated with giving and receiving care. (Cooper and Lousada, 2003, forthcoming)

One of the neglected pitfalls of partnerships in the context of any kind of caring is the way in which they evoke, at an unconscious level, fantasies of fusion, struggles over personal boundaries, and unfulfilled dependency needs. In romantic relationships these are as much the source of tenderness, passion and vitality as they are of conflict and contempt, yet the current rhetoric seems to acknowledge only the rational, autonomous self-actualiser. The problem here is that current notions of partnership take their meaning from a wider culture that refuses to acknowledge the very vulnerability they are designed to overcome. Welfare professionals become implicated in a denial of dependency needs which is at odds with the very nature and purpose of their involvement.

Denial of dependency

There are good reasons to suggest that the evolution of social attitudes to dependency in the last 50 years or so has been regressive in important respects. Whereas old welfarism tends to institutionalise it, neo-liberalism problematises dependency and elaborates a vision of autonomy premised on a declining role for public institutions in sustaining social bonds. The centrist politics of New Labour involves an attempt to reinvigorate these social bonds while upholding the superordinate principles of the market by emphasising responsibility rather than self-interest. This somewhat attenuates the competitiveness of market relations and demands that they be conducted in an ethical manner. Distinguishing itself from the party of 'sleaze' allowed the first Blair government to distinguish itself from its four Conservative predecessors. It also allowed for an acknowledgement that there may be some public interests, those of healthcare for example, which are not best served by institutions structured as quasi-markets. However, dependency continues to be regarded as a problem. Neo-liberalism is characterised by a denial of dependency, which is regarded as an excuse for laziness and profligacy but a year after the 1997 election Paul Hoggett (1998) identified a positive 'hatred' of it in the modernising rhetoric of New Labour. The connotations of age, debility, impotence and incompetence came to the fore, explicitly contrasted with an idealisation of youthfulness and strength and, like the ideal consumer, an uncritical fascination with everything new. For all Blair's avowed intention to develop a politics of fairness and a welfare system able to care for those who cannot work, there were important ways in which the disavowal of dependency gained new force.

Hatred of dependency has complex psychosocial roots, but it is worth asking why it should be problematic for a government that set out to display its compassion and commitment to social responsibility as a distinguishing mark. Any viable culture must find ways of accommodating human vulnerability, and the need to rely on others for a large part of the natural life-cycle. Without this, children could not grow up and there would be no learning from experience. In modern capitalist societies a high value is placed on those members who are capable of productive work, compared to those who represent a net social cost to the community. Children, who represent the workforce of the future, to some extent escape the stigma of dependency. It seems, however, that there is difficulty in conceiving of dependent adulthood in terms other than degradation. Professionals such as geriatricians find themselves in high-skill but low-status specialisms. The social needs of older people are now most likely to be addressed at the face-to-face level by unqualified and low-paid care workers, coordinated by a care manager if multiple services are required. This is hardly surprising in a society where youth, strength and beauty are idealised and have become the means whereby all objects of desire are peddled. Is this part of an inexorable trend towards the supremacy of the commodity form and the fantasies that lubricate its progress, or a trans-historical denial of our imperfections?

While the potential for disavowal may be ever present, it is a defence more likely to be deployed in certain states of mind – particularly where social containers for the underlying anxieties provoked by weakness and debility are dispersed. Entrepreneurialism is good for business and unleashes some forms of creativity, but it places notable strains on the self. The emphasis on risk taking, personal responsibility and material success encourage people to measure their intrinsic worth in terms of income and accumulation. Added to this, the phenomenal demands of 'flexible labour' - that we continually renew and reinvent our skills, social networks, self-presentation and rhythms of life - poses severe challenges to our ability to form stable core identities. Calls for regeneration of localities and community are sometimes put forward with a romantic utopianism, which fails to take account of the forces of fragmentation that isolated people in the first place. The preoccupation of Thatcher, Major and Blair with marriage and two-parent families is an implicit recognition that the flexible labour markets which they enthusiastically embrace, risk leaving people economically and geographically adrift for significant parts of their lives. Without at least emotional anchors, the social costs in terms of poor child-rearing, mental health problems and anti-social behaviour could turn out to be extremely high. Yet as Sennett (1998) points out: the flexible working day, at first sight so convenient for people with dependent children and relatives, may only serve to further isolate workers and families from attachments to workplace collectivities. The burden placed on intimate relationships, as they are turned into privatised sites of care, can sometimes seem intolerable as they are expected to fulfil needs for self-realisation which could formerly have been deflected into social networks. There is a particular irony for women of all occupational groups: the 'second-wave' feminists of the seventies demanded the right to employment as an alternative to the isolation of the home but many now find that work returns them to a redoubled isolation – formerly the lot of only the most exploited home workers.

The importance of the debate that followed the death of the Princess of Wales in 1997 was in the attention given to cultural responses to vulnerability. Whether or not this was a collective or unifying response, numerous commentators remarked that a certain cultural sang-froid seemed to have been dispelled in the very public expressions of mourning. Blair moved skilfully to claim the princess for the people while maintaining an overt protectiveness towards the palace, but in doing so he underlined the opposition between them. For republicans a revaluation of compassion became the context of an attack on both the body and the institution of a monarchy that had shown itself to be deficient in that quality (Watson, 1997). This was powerful enough to draw in many people who had taken little interest in Diana's life and were astonished to find themselves moved both emotionally and politically. Blair's message of love, delivered via his reading from Corinthians, was scrutinised for duplicitous intent. Was this a performance or a genuinely reparative gesture? The importance of the question, so soon after the election, lay in the fact that this was still a young government, yet to confront the sensitive task of reforming welfare. It was a moment pregnant with clues as to Blair's inclinations, character and likely future direction. If even the young, beautiful and royal could be vulnerable, and invite identification on that account, could the government not mobilise a reawakened compassion into wider public support for collective responsibility and mutual care? Might this not have been a leadership able to sympathise with the weak and participate in more benign and generous aspirations than its predecessors?

In the event, the government steered true to its chosen path: fiscal rectitude combined with strong leadership and vigorous image maintenance. This required that the veneer of infallibility and youthful conviction be kept at a high gloss. The risk with this political style is that it can promote perceptions of politics as manipulative, inauthentic and very much the domain of the strong and ambitious – that is, of people who are likely to have little natural sympathy for those who need public support. In this context it was perceived 'attacks' on single mothers, on access to higher education, and on the benefits received by disabled people that became the test of the government's intentions towards the welfare state.

The facilitation of entry into employment was then understood more in terms of its potential to curb public expenditure than in its opening up of opportunities.

The message to be drawn is one of ambivalence towards those public organisations delegated with the 'management' of vulnerability, dependency and mortality (Armstrong, 1995). On the one hand, there is a dread of having to deal with all this ourselves and therefore a sense of our own reliance on the continued existence of these institutions. On the other hand, we feel guilty for the inadequacies of the social environment we have created and hope that welfare organisations will discharge our obligations of compassion and care. When they fail in this because they mirror the society that has produced them, we respond with censure and moral indignation.

If the death of Diana inserted compassion into the political profile of the first Blair government, the collapse of New York's twin towers set the tone for the second. In enthusiastically embracing Bush's declaration of war on terrorism, Blair, with a sure populist touch, transformed himself into a warrior prince and global diplomat. His presidential persona and distaste for the cumbersome machinery of cabinet government was already well known and it was nearly a month before a small war cabinet was formed. The 'Churchillian' style gave way to something even more ambitions when at the 2001 party conference he appeared to pledge nothing less than the elimination of injustice and poverty from the world. Older members might have recalled the consequences of such grandiosity – also occasioned by war – for the ability to put in place policies and institutions designed to care for the vulnerable.

The real danger, as elaborated Chapter Three, is that such speeches are designed to engender a state of mind intoxicated with a sense of limitless possibility, unable to admit ambivalence and ultimately unable to recognise and engage with the very vulnerability that is to be overcome. They exert a formidable and stultifying pressure towards consensus in which admission of opposition, or even doubt, appears as an act of psychic terrorism in its disruptive effect on the fundamentalist psychic order that has been established. In this state of mind 'you are either for us or against us' – ironically it fell to the Iranians to uphold a 'Third Way'. The danger is that there is no realistic apprehension of the other, no understanding that the enemy so easily characterised in terms of theological absolutism as 'evil', also has a claim on morality and conviction.

In both guises, as chief mourner and warlord, Blair demonstrated a certain skill in gauging and defining the emotional climate. In both, his instinct was to home in on fears and longings related to a sense of vulnerability rather than invincibility, appealing to enough of the nation to emerge as a (largely) unifying force. However, from a welfare perspective the question is whether there were the elements of a reparative leadership.

New Labour, new narcissism?

Blair could be seen as representing a move away from the destructive narcissism of the Thatcher years towards a more benign and reparative form. Volkan (1980) elaborated this distinction in terms of political leadership. In destructive narcissism he identified the tendency of those who project unwanted aspects of selfhood onto other groups in order to attack them and safeguard the ideal self. This can unleash extremes of destructiveness leading to a rampant politics of hate, where self-aggrandisement depends on the physical elimination of populations who exhibit despised characteristics (ethnic cleansing is only the most recent example). Although Thatcher was no Milosevic, the scapegoating and exclusionary politics of her period of office was the outward demonstration of those very qualities of hardness around which her public persona was elaborated. A more reparative form of narcissism (Volkan cites Kemal Ataturk as a paradigmatic example) allows the leader to project idealised aspects of selfhood onto his or her followers in order to identify with them – thereby further reinforcing the grandiosity and perfection of the leader's self-image. This can result in the forging of electorally successful alliances and open the way to a progressive reformist populism, but insofar as the leadership becomes enclosed in a self-idealising loop, it ultimately works against the development of a responsive democracy. The question of whether Blair could be considered as a genuinely reparative leader (able to carry forward a welfare politics based on an ethic of care, recognition of difference and acknowledgement of dependency) or a reparative narcissist (whose self-idealisation would preclude such recognition) always turned on his success in fulfilling at least one of his soundbite promises – the development of a genuinely 'listening' government.

The problem with a leadership style which transmits a dislike of dependency and an over-valuation of the personal qualities of the leaders themselves lies in the extent to which it promotes what Lasch (1979) has called a 'Culture of Narcissism'. Lasch attracted criticism from feminists where he appeared to regret the decline of patriarchal authority; nevertheless, his arguments have proved highly provocative. He attempts to show the links between fundamental features of contemporary American culture and the development of subjectivity. Specifically, he argues that the experience of modern life stimulates narcissistic aspects of selfhood. The original myth of Narcissus is well known: the exquisite youth fell so in love with his own reflection in the pond that he lost all sense of judgement. Echo's calls, the persistent voice of reality, failed to break the circle of his enchantment and leaning forwards to embrace his own image, he drowned. This drowning in an illusion of the self captures a state of absorption in which the boundaries between what is and is not the self are erased. In such a self-referential state there can be no influence from the other (since otherness depends on boundaries which no longer exist) and the world beyond the self is but a fading insubstantial backdrop.

For Freud, primary narcissism arose from that blissful state of unity which the infant experiences in the early feeding relationship. At this point the baby, because it has as yet no perception of a separate world, perceives itself as the source of goodness that comes from the maternal breast. The longing to return to this original phantasised state of oneness with the world, 'the oceanic feeling', was thought by Freud and later psychoanalysts to be at the root of religious and aesthetic experience. The way in which the infant eventually negotiates the loss of this sense of unity, as external reality imposes itself and disrupts the sensations of plenitude and omnipotence, is the most crucial developmental passage of all. Not only does it initiate the process of becoming a separate self, able to relate to others, but the way in which it is experienced patterns individualised responses to anxiety and loss.

Although Klein and Winnicott (see Chapter Two) reformulated the problem in terms of narcissistic object relations, the ability to perceive a reality outside of the self remained crucial. Winnicott identified the quality of 'holding' and the nurturing environment as of central importance since it is this that facilitates the acceptance of frustration brought about by a reality which does not immediately anticipate the child's needs or yield to its demands. If mother withdraws from her absorption with the baby's needs too much, too little, or too haphazardly, the ability to come to terms with the existence of people and things beyond the infant's mother/baby pair is impaired. Differentiation then becomes highly problematic, the baby is unlikely to develop basic trust and instead defends against the anxiety provoked by recognition of its own dependency on a powerful other. It continues to take refuge in a world that is perceived as an extension of the self. If this is reinforced by subsequent experience in familial and cultural relations, it will impact deeply on relationships. The result will be a reduced ability to recognise and tolerate difference in other people, who become important insofar as they help to shore up the self. This leads to superficial attachments to whatever is new or changing and an inability to mourn lost and loved objects – a tendency to discard people and things when they no longer serve immediately felt needs. It also leads to profound difficulties in accepting the dependency needs of either self or others, since these assert themselves as limits demanding a recognition of a world beyond our control.

Lasch's argument is that modern consumer cultures tend to draw out, reproduce and reinforce our latent potential for narcissism. Competitive individualism and the uncertainty of modern life create anxieties which we may be tempted to assuage by de-differentiating, attempting to recover the 'oceanic feeling' whether through drugs, food, alcohol, religion, dance music or other comforts of consumption. But the counterpart of this dissolution of self into environment is omniscience and self-aggrandisement. In search of success we are impelled to idealise ourselves and to present ourselves in the best possible light at the expense of others who we manipulate and use to our own advantage.

In consumer cultures, narcissistic individuals are well adapted to an environment in which the economy demands a rapid turnover of lifestyles and consumption patterns, built-in obsolescence, and flexible, mobile workers without enduring attachments to anchor them to localities and social networks.

Narcissistic individuals make good consumers because of their self-absorption – indeed some post-modernist ideals of the self take this to extremes in espousing an endless quest for self-assembly and reinvention which extends beyond work to personality, home, leisure and the body itself. Bauman (1988) critically identifies the sphere of consumption as the principal arena of freedom in late capitalist society. It is in the search for identity through lifestyle that the heroic consumer haunts the shopping malls in a bid to assemble a collection of objects that together signify status, taste and group belonging. The freedom to choose is the freedom to assemble oneself. It is, in a sense, the principal compensation for the loss of social cohesion and the ascribed identities of traditional societies. Consumption calls forth an ever more differentiated array of goods and services to meet needs which are continually remoulded as identities evolve. Our hero is an individualist who is able, by varying his patterns of acquisition, to redefine himself at will through an alternative set of symbols. Lacking in core identity and psychological depth, he is adept at impression management whereby he maximises his social and economic opportunities.

Admittedly, all this presupposes income and skill, and Bauman, in making a distinction between the 'seduced' and the 'repressed', was specifically concerned with those, who by virtue of their lack of resources, are effectively excluded from the consumer culture. It is these latter groups: the poor, the unemployed and the marginalised who are candidates for welfare and therefore for state regulation and control. Thus Bauman's vision of the effect of state welfare in a consumer society is pessimistic. Rather than successfully incorporating features of the consumer culture, it becomes a mechanism of exclusion. Insofar as they are deficient in commodities, the repressed are denied access to the means whereby identities worthy of recognition are constructed.

Craib (1994) argues that the control afforded by the project of self-assembly is in any case illusory – a 'paradoxical ideology' which conceals the increasing powerlessness of individuals, as public institutions and 'civil society' itself are weakened by the forces of globalisation:

> Late modernity takes us beyond the notion of self-control to a conception of the omnipotent, self-constructing self, but the descriptions of such a self and the way it aims at gratification indicate that it is in fact a very weak self employing an illusion of power and satisfaction, protecting its fragmented state because that seems to be the source of its power. (p 132)

Craib points out that some psychotherapeutic approaches, particularly those that aim to inhibit the emotions such as behaviourism and cognitive therapy, or else to 'manage' them as in humanistic forms of counselling, can be readily co-opted into this project. It is also a product of one-sidedly sociological accounts of emotions (for example, Giddens, 1992) which assume that they can be subsumed under, or constructed out of, social processes.

The accent laid on consumerist diversity within welfare in recent years can be understood in the light of all this to be a rather mixed blessing. It has been embraced as a welcome corrective to the paternalist universalism of the post-war period and, as with many principles abstracted from the context in which they are interpreted, appears to point to a democratisation of relationships or at the very least to more responsive and particularised services. However, the fact that they now appear in every organisational mission statement and equal opportunities policy should not in itself reassure us. The discourse of difference has arrived in welfare partly via a consumerist celebration of choice and partly via the influence of an identity politics whereby groups assert the specificity of their needs as a means of claiming resources and respect. While this is a necessary moment in finding a voice and establishing their coherence as a constituency, it does not of itself lead to the kind of dialogue which promotes recognition, or to a more complex and compassionate realism. The stakeholder model still assumes that inclusion depends on the assertion of interest as a mark of particularity and that the significant dimensions of distinctiveness and belonging can be expressed politically in these terms. It seeks to protect a certain kind of plurality, and even to allow for the expansion of needs claims. However, it does so in an abstract way, seeking to manage and evade issues, or arrive at simple, formally just solutions to rather one-dimensional problems, rather than allowing engagement and confrontation with otherness.

At the face-to-face level, there is a demand that welfare professionals employ technologies of assessment, which are designed to avoid judgement and discretion, for example by employing mechanistic schemes of eligibility criteria. At the level of the organisation there is a flattening out of communicative processes, routing them via technical–rational systems designed to record and measure outcome as the pre-eminent test of an effective organisation. In the rush to protect the status and interests of the other, the obligation to engage with the meaning of his or her predicament is bypassed because there is neither space nor language in which to explore it. Armstrong (1996) points out that the recovery of meaning, always an attempt to bridge loss or absence, is very different from its 'management' (in any case impossible) currently in vogue as organisational 'vision', 'mission' and 'core values'. The subjection of meaning to instrumental manipulation is more likely to lead to cynicism than belief, leading to the perception that values too are a matter of presentation rather than a source of moral agency. In welfare organisations this is particularly unfortunate because acting to promote another's welfare involves moral engagement and judgement. The effective defence against unwarranted imposition of such judgement is to ensure that professionals, while maintaining discretion, do so within a culture and organisational framework which requires them to negotiate. Negotiation implies the effort to get as close as possible to the meanings of the other while acknowledging the limits implied by agency function. This in turn requires that the anxieties to which such a process necessarily gives rise be effectively contained.

Entitlement

It is not hard to see how an orientation to the management of risk that gives rise to a preoccupation with predictability, calculability and damage limitation is unlikely to incline us towards trust. It is less evident that an emphasis on rights in a risk environment might compound the effect. The expansion of civil, political and social rights was regarded by Marshall as an index of the emancipatory potential of modernity. Rights to welfare embodied in the post-war settlement have been regarded as an extension of social citizenship. Their emancipatory importance has been repeatedly underlined by marginalised and excluded groups for whom they represent a publicly redeemable form of recognition which sustains basic self-respect (Honneth, 1995).

An emphasis on formal rights re-establishes relationships between service providers and users as a form of contractual exchange and eclipses or 'colonises' values (Smith, 2000). Yet it is values that bear on the equal worth of individuals and hence on the moral basis of welfare. 'Respect for persons' is not reducible to a right – although rights flow from it as universal guarantees of entitlement. However, it also carries an implied injunction to attend to the particular qualities and capacities of individuals. As a value-base it yields both generalisable rights and an ethic of care based on responsiveness and situated, person-centred knowledge. Smith argues that we would do well to retain an eye to the distinctiveness of each as the current tendency to assimilate values to rights can only prejudice an ethic of care. She highlights the 'powerful motivating influence' of belief in human worth:

> The service user does not constitute the object of understanding but the source of understanding. In this way, values promote those qualitative and experiential elements of social interaction which contribute to caring and helping. Rights on the other hand only motivate by demanding compliance. In essence, values insist on the practice of 'care-as-gift' (Fox, 1995) caring and helping which are prompted by a moral sensibility and do not impose a reciprocal obligation. This perspective stands in sharp contrast to something which is required as an entitlement and given as a duty; it is doubtful whether caring and helping can make sense within this framework. (Smith, 2000, p 72)

A sense of entitlement can be psychologically paradoxical. While its achievement is a necessary moment in becoming an active subject, an over-investment in entitlement leads to a sense of grievance and lack. For example, the bitterness generated in drawn-out disputes over compensation claims can be more damaging than the original injury. It is questionable whether, in a consumerist society, a framework of rights can in itself act as anything more than a source of social protection for the negative freedoms of individuals to pursue their interests free from interference. In themselves, rights guarantee only a talion morality and a retributive form of justice. Reparative justice, on the other hand, in aiming to restore and heal, demands an intersubjective context in which the assertion of rights precedes recognition. Drawing on Winnicott (1971), Flax (1993) argues that justice is neither a finite state nor set of rules but a complex of interrelated practices, which are best sustained within transitional spaces. The formal conception of equity on which liberal humanism is founded may promote equality at the cost of effacing differences. Rationalistic approaches block the capacity for empathy or appreciation of otherness. Justice involves creatively bridging gaps, bringing that activity into the public domain, maintaining proper boundaries between inner and outer, and reconciling or tolerating differences. It cannot do this if conceived in purely objective (transcendental) or subjective (value-laden or power-driven) terms. Justice is linked to citizenship, which entails the transformation of private need into public action. It involves not only judgement but reciprocity, reconciliation and recognition. The difference between retributive and reparative justice is clear in the following examples.

S described her efforts to gain redress through a tribunal after she had been sacked from a job when her history as a transsexual had come to light. Her aim had been to establish a principle and gain compensation for affront and loss of earnings. This was granted by the judge. Later she realised that the abstract principles of justice and the money received were of secondary importance to the way in which she had been helped by legal professionals. She felt gratitude for the way in which the verdict had been delivered with sensitivity and a personalised attention that conveyed, in public, a profound respect for her as a person. She affirmed, "it was not until then that I realised what justice was – it healed something in me". The process had enabled her to reclaim her status as a subject. The validation of rights in this restorative context amounted to an act of recognition that forged a link between self-respect and social esteem.

G pursued a grievance against his line manager when, a year after his appointment, he felt that his duties had consistently failed to conform to his job description. The process proved to be lengthy and rather acrimonious and the outcome turned on detailed matters of interpretation. He also argued that as he was being asked to perform duties outside of his remit he could not trust management to support him if things went wrong. In the end he was technically vindicated and work delegated to him changed accordingly. However, he described this as a hollow victory in view of the corrosive impact it had on relationships and the way in which communication had taken on a formal and legalistic tenor. He felt that the only tolerable option was to seek alternative employment at the earliest opportunity.

Conclusion

It might be thought that a 'Third Way' for welfare would naturally facilitate the kind of thinking from the third position that the casework model (outlined in Chapter Three) found difficult to sustain. The very notion of a Third Way implied the transcendence of dualisms, originally between the political Left and the Right. In Chapter Four, I argued that the competitive ethos of blaming and scapegoating aroused by the new conservatism was even more likely to lead to exclusionary polarisations. The promise of the Third Way was for a new 'grown up' and 'joined up' approach, an inclusive 'broad tent' which signified the ability to acknowledge and incorporate opposing points of view. It is ironic then that a party which came to power with an explicit mission of reforming the conduct of political life should have been so dogged by mistrust of its style and motives. The name of the headquarters of the Labour spin machine – Millbank – has become synonymous with manipulation and deceit. Blair's 'presidential' persona has been seen as a threat to democracy itself. Even the harnessing of the rich and famous through 'business' and 'celebrity' has backfired as the public notes their unseemly allure for the political classes. All this fosters narcissistic qualities in a leadership perfectly suited to the advanced consumer society of late modernity, but disliked for it nevertheless. Health and welfare organisations that mirror this style are severely hampered in their efforts to develop third position thinking. This calls for an ability to maintain an eye on what lies beyond immediately perceived interests and the present agenda. It also requires a renunciation of self-referential and self-aggrandising obsessions with presentation and is unlikely to be achieved through executive bodies which approximate ever more closely to the management of a corporate enterprise.

The ideal New Labour welfare subject suffers from similar limitations. Essentially, she could be conceived as a 'self-creating' subject (Finlayson, 2000) who relates to the state by drawing on a range of codified practices and techniques to foster her own self-governance. The role of the state has come to lie in facilitating appropriate training, regulation, inspection and quality insurance and encouraging the right kind of investment and moral climate for a citizenry able to withstand the challenges of rapid change. Blairism departs from a conviction that the task of political leadership is to equip its followers to withstand the challenge of the new global economy. It offers a blend of individualism and significantly weakened collectivism achieved at a rhetorical level by adding the 'social' to the slogans of the Right: encouraging 'social investment', and building 'social capital' – these are the guiding principles of the public service modernisation programme aimed at nothing less than the modernisation of the political subject herself and her transformation into a new kind of responsible, risk-taking social entrepreneur. Demos, very much implicated in the development of this mindset, is clear that the task of government is to enable citizens to take up position in the new knowledge economy – hence the absolute imperative of modernisation. The New Labour subject is obliged to appease this overriding force. As Finlayson points out, this is not the rational enlightened subject but an individual consumer who can manoeuvre within this autonomous world order and face up to it. Hence the centrality of education to the New Labour project because of its role in producing a workforce with the necessary proclivities to self-creation or, more accurately, self-presentation, which in this context amounts to the same thing. Despite a rhetoric of cultivating human potential, it is a shallow emphasis on a system geared entirely to the production of competencies and an ethical outlook required for survival rather than critical judgement.

The limits to self-creation become manifest in our relationships with real others: in partnerships, intimate and formal, and within families, communities and organisations. Denial of dependency needs, results in an inability to acknowledge vulnerability within ourselves and therefore an inability to recognise them in others and sustain an orientation to their welfare. The problem with the New Labour subject is that the depth of her emotional engagement within the political process is suspect and this has been reflected in Britain, as elsewhere in the West, in a declining willingness to affiliate to political parties. It must not be forgotten that despite Blair's return to a second term with a barely dented majority, the electoral turnout was at a historic low. Despite his periodic attempts to rouse hearts and minds with talk of justice and compassion, it would appear that he has succeeded in stimulating only a weak and conditional form of commitment. Orbach's comment remains apt:

> We are left with a sense of participation through superficially shared emotional expression rather than a linking of the political, economic, social and emotional issues.... We can be emotional as long as it is cut off from deeper social or structural considerations. We can be emotional as long as it isn't political. (*Marxism Today*, November/December 1998, p 62)

The instrumental attitude which increasingly drives social care policy and shapes the immediate context of practice is justified in terms of its perceived effectiveness in modernising services and also in terms of the strategies it appears to provide for the management of uncertainty. However, professionals and clients move in a world that is inherently more contradictory than this reductionist goal-oriented approach is able to grasp. The dissonance between an institutional culture that demands the illusory perfection of technical–rational methods and an operational culture that deals with intractable disorganisation and irrationality can be contained by ritual and procedure. However, the potential for proceduralisation to sediment into rigid defensive structures, is high. The strain can be exacerbated by the expectation of seamless, accomplished performance, which further erodes a sense of a truthful relation to reality. Practitioners do well if they are adept in the art of polishing a brittle outer shell of confident competence which becomes a substitute for assurance and authority, downgrading knowledge which is grounded in practice, and concealing a growing anxiety at the formulaic abstractions which substitute for it.

Under New Labour the amelioration of the very marked forms of splitting and projection that characterised the last Conservative era has depended on the containment offered by strong leadership and a reinforcement of rights, framed in terms of consumer choice and social inclusion. The question for people who use services and those who work within the public sector is whether this has led to a more benign welfare environment. The answer to this question at the time of writing must depend on precisely where one is located. Teachers' unions point to low morale and recruitment, which they attribute to the continuation of a blame culture. Strenuous efforts are having to be made to entice nurses who had left the profession back onto the wards. Recruitment to social work training has dropped alarmingly. In this chapter I have argued that significant tensions remain as a consequence of the individualist and consumerist logic of New Labour's policies on the welfare state, a narcissistic leadership style which is positively hostile to vulnerability and dependency, and institutions oriented to risk management. Congruent with this is the elevation of individual rights over values – whether they refer to the moral worth of individuals or to social solidarity. The effect is to allow the development of relationships and arrangements favouring a formal contractual equality and a model of reciprocity based on rights and entitlements in return for responsibilities and duties. Public support is supposedly sustained on the basis that expenditure can be curbed and safeguards are in place to prevent the ever-present danger of exploitation of the system by the unscrupulous. In contrast to the Conservative ideal, overall responsibility for care in the mixed economy of welfare remains securely in the public domain. However, it remains a commodity to be dispensed with efficiency and fairness – a form of social protection rather than reparation, a right rather than a value, a cost rather than a gift.

Part II:
Introduction

In this second part there is a change of focus, level and organisation to the argument. It is much more difficult to write about the present than about the past and more difficult still to imagine the future. Already, the previous chapter on 'mixed welfare' presented problems in that I was attempting to describe the impact on relationships and practice of an institutional configuration that is still evolving. However, the political–economic parameters of New Labour's vision of welfare were clear enough by the second term of office and will be familiar to readers. In the fourth quadrant, entitled 'Beyond welfare' (Figure 1; Figure 2, p 47), I move on to even less certain territory where I am dealing with emergent tendencies that first find expression in the third (or voluntary) sector, in the gaps between formal services and in oppositional or experimental projects. Many of these are small scale, locally based and do not have a very explicitly theorised rationale. Their durability is determined by their success in attracting and maintaining public support, and their ability to thrive in a climate that measures their value in terms often dictated by narrowly economic criteria. These have included grass-roots movements of marginalised groups such as tenants and welfare rights, some ethnic minority organisations, charities, user and community groups, women's groups, single issue campaigns and new social movements. Some have been short lived, others have endured and been partially co-opted into local government services, often a poisoned chalice where reliance on funding blunts their critical edge. There are a few, such as Women's Aid, that have prospered by combining participative principles with a strong campaigning profile. Whatever the compromises forced by the imperative of financial survival, such organisations make an essential contribution to developing, modelling and disseminating innovative and egalitarian methods of work. It is from this bottom-up perspective that it becomes possible to discern the outline of alternative social relations of welfare.

Before I advance, however, it may be useful to briefly summarise the argument so far. I am claiming that the welfare system will inevitably fail to help people in the ways they find acceptable and consistent with human dignity, unless it can facilitate relationships of recognition. On one level this is a disarmingly simple statement in that the experience of recognition is one we are all aware of – needing no elaborate theoretical justification. To be recognised requires mutual understanding and respect. It is the simultaneous experience of being beheld in the eyes of another as we imagine ourselves to be, yet at the same time allowing our definition of ourselves to be formed in the context of the other's recognition. I wrote of the psychosocial basis for this experience in Chapter Two, pointing out that it requires an emotional capacity – the ability to maintain a depressive relation to reality in which we can see ourselves and others as imperfect, but whole and worthy of regard. We commonly express this through concern, or compassion, and it is this that enables us to care for others and allow ourselves to be cared for. The capacity is developed through the experience of social attachments and sustained in adult life in relationships which are free from domination and therefore consistent with an equality of moral worth between people who recognise each other's difference from themselves.

In the three ideal-type models of welfare that I have so far outlined there are significant psychosocial barriers to the recognition-relations on which an emancipatory project of welfare could be founded. This is because welfare arrangements have a potent symbolic function and in themselves contribute to the formation of collective emotional responses to vulnerability and dependency. Each of the three models have in different ways and degrees offered insufficient containment to moderate paranoid–schizoid states of mind among either the public at large or the people who give and receive care. In some respects they have actively promoted them. None of the three have been consistently able to sustain organisational environments that can support stable depressive position functioning.

I have suggested that in the old welfare position the reparative impulses that were embodied in the Beveridgean welfare state fostered states of mind akin to the early experience of depressive anxiety in the infant, where concern for the (m)other is beset by fears that she has been damaged beyond repair by the child's own aggression and greed. This responsibility is too much to bear and in defence against guilt, the child is lured into omnipotent phantasies of magically doing away with the consequences of his or her actions and making the world anew. There is contempt for anything that appears to get in the way and a loss of contact with the suffering that provoked the guilt in the first place. I have tried to show how similar processes might have been re-enacted in the post-war welfare system – notably how the difficulty in maintaining concern found a reflection in the unstable reparative effort of constructing a welfare state in the aftermath of victory, and with a looming Cold War.

The collapse of grandiose dreams of solving all major problems brings despair in its wake. There is an impulse to give up, reverse all that one has tried to do and retire bruised and disillusioned to attend to one's own needs. After all, if my own concern fails, then how can I expect concern from others? I am pitched in to the fight for survival. The survivalist mentality finds an apt expression in the pure market, and this was the psycho-political foundation of the retreat from welfare represented by the Thatcherite New Right. The fight–flight dynamic of competition invokes and supports the paranoid–schizoid splitting of early infancy, where something good must be preserved, idealised and kept apart from an essentially persecutory outside world. Hence the family became, in the imagery of the New Right, the counterpart of the good breast or the good mother – the protected site of care where the well-being of the individual is protected from the 'dog-eat-dog' world without.

In the mixed welfare position this paranoid–schizoid tendency is still strong, but a search for more containing arrangements in the public sphere offsets damaging effects of unrestrained competition. However, the fundamental commitment to market dynamics constantly creates tensions in those parts of the welfare system and voluntary sector where the profit motive has not traditionally operated. The idealisation of partnership and especially public–private partnership evokes the wish to bring together difference and overcome splits, but this is a perilous course. Successful partnerships require recognition between self and other and a renunciation of the need to dominate and control. In the absence of an environment in which depressive anxieties can be acknowledged and worked through, there is a compulsive tendency to spin, manage and manipulate rather than encounter the other as whole, different and a limit to the narcissistic desires of the self.

In each of the three models characterised so far, the welfare system can be seen to fail people partly because of the ways in which it supports structural inequalities and the power relations that flow from them. This is a theme that has been thoroughly explored in the literature on poverty and empowerment. It is also a consequence of the ways in which the welfare state itself is implicated in cultures of individualisation and exclusion which have been the subject of a great deal of attention. I acknowledge the salience of both of these themes but do not intend to revisit them here. Without wishing to recapitulate the argument on whether or not 'exclusion' is a diversion from 'class', it seems that there is a common ground, which assumes that shortcomings can best be addressed by focusing on a mixture of rights and redistribution. The appropriate balance between them is thought of as a pragmatic or political issue. I do not wish to deny in any way the central importance of either rights or redistribution, but the purpose of this book is to bring psychosocial factors into the frame. These find expression in struggles for recognition that inspire participation in many social movements, voluntary associations and civic life.

It would be satisfying to move from critique to a well-synthesised reconstruction, delineating the contours of an alternative welfare society at all three levels: interpersonal, organisational and political–economic. However, that project must be grounded in experience and in the micro-methodologies of welfare work and will emerge little by little from the contribution of many people with different priorities both within and beyond the welfare domain. I do not intend to dwell speculatively on the shape of the macro-political or socio-economic order, which might allow the generalisation of such experiences, although I shall make comments on political process.

In Chapter Six I shall expand on the connection between compassion and recognition, and their relationship to rights and redistribution by considering theoretical contributions to the discussion. In Chapter Seven I highlight some recent ideas about new forms of practice and organisation. I then go on to an extended discussion of a particular voluntary organisation, which illustrates some of the difficulties and potentials of a reparative organisational culture. From practice and organisation I move in Chapter Eight to a consideration of the kind of political processes which might sustain them. In the final chapter

I conclude with a section on the recovery of the narrative tradition and sensibility which is an essential dimension of relationship-based practice and has been undermined by managerialism and by the technical–rational turn. Narrative has been lost from social work with the demise of biographical casework and elsewhere it is constantly disrupted by the methodologies currently favoured by the regulatory bodies of the helping professions. However, it represents an alternative tradition on which we can draw – submerged but not quite dead. I shall therefore end with a discussion on its affinity with a reparative welfare culture.

Essentially, then, I am writing of welfare-promoting activities which have not yet cohered into a recognisable large-scale model and I do not intend to supplant them with a utopian construction. To depict one would in any case be at odds with my argument that viable alternative forms of welfare depend on the policy making process incorporating influences from below. Nevertheless it is possible to discern in all these strands an emergent paradigm which might inform welfare reform based on greater attachment and equality.

In order to trace the connections suggested in the fourth quadrant of the grid (Figures 1 and 2), I shall return to the dream of equality and solidarity that the welfare project has stimulated. I shall ask whether the capacity for recognition and compassion might fare better under markedly more egalitarian welfare relations than we have so far experienced. Equality, however, is not a simple concept, it is not easily achieved and perhaps in some respects not even possible. However, a wish for equality has played an important part in all radical and emancipatory political movements and, in a more diluted form, in the construction of the welfare state. These same movements have prospered or failed in relation to their ability to sustain relationships of interdependence founded on a capacity for mature attachment in their members and a vision of new forms of social solidarity.

SIX

Beyond welfare: compassion, recognition and ethics of care

In languages that derive from Latin, 'compassion' means: we cannot look on coolly as others suffer; or, we sympathise with those who suffer. Another word with approximately the same meaning, 'pity', connotes a certain condescension towards the sufferer. 'To take pity on a woman' means that we are better off than she, that we stoop to her level, lower ourselves. That is why the word 'compassion' generally inspires suspicion; it designates what is considered an inferior, second-rate sentiment that has little to do with love. To love someone out of compassion means not really to love.

In languages that form the word 'compassion' not from the root 'suffering' but from the root 'feeling' the word is used in approximately the same way, but to contend that it designates a bad or inferior sentiment is difficult. The secret strength of its etymology floods the word with another light and gives it a broader meaning: to have compassion (co-feeling) means not only to be able to live with the other's misfortune but also to feel with him any emotion – joy, anxiety, happiness, pain. This kind of compassion ... signifies the maximal capacity of affective imagination, the art of emotional telepathy. In the hierarchy of the sentiments, then, it is supreme.

Milan Kundera *The unbearable lightness of being* (1984, p 20)

In welfare agencies in the UK the word compassion is used sparingly and rather gingerly – for the very reasons suggested by Kundera. Although it may remain part of a personal emotional repertoire that enables welfare professionals to tolerate the pain and rage of others, it sits uneasily within a discourse of contractual or procedural rights, or of performativity. Historically, compassion became progressively more suspect as help for the poor was professionalised. It was identified by Victorian male leaders of an emergent social work with the supposed 'over-involvement' of the female do-gooder. Bernard Bosenquet lamented this loss of boundaries among certain Charity Organisation Society workers. Rather than pursue the objective observation and enquiry which would enable the local district committee to assess potential for 'cure' and then withhold or dispense in judicious measure, some were wont to be "carried away by the first impression of unreasoned pity" (Bosenquet, cited in Jones, 1983, p 96). Henceforth expressions of compassion for the plight of the disadvantaged would maintain the proper distance afforded by professional discourses which defended against anxiety at the perils of identification and leant on split representations of deserving and undeserving poor. Policy makers and the public have recurrently invoked these in order to moderate and channel generosity.

By virtue of its association with philanthropic and professional paternalism, compassion came to be regarded as something bestowed on recipients of public munificence by the more fortunate and educated. After the Second World War the concept seldom surfaced in public service discourse, being at odds with both expert and radical repertoires. It was somewhat more in tune with the overtly moralising emphasis on reciprocity and obligation adopted by the first Blair government when it surfaced briefly in the New Labour lexicon for the Princess of Wales' funeral. However, it was not invoked as justification for public support of vulnerable groups such as asylum seekers, where the safer philosophical detachment of the 'humanitarian' position occupied the moral high ground. Compassion-talk certainly plays no part in the modernisation agenda and seems anachronistic in the climate of pragmatic economic 'realism' that is cultivated within managerialised public sector organisations[1]. Even the loosely related 'empathy' – once a mainstay of welfare discourse – resonates like a faintly embarrassing echo of a more therapeutically assertive age. I will return to the question of compassion in welfare services by linking it to the capacity for recognition and the states of mind and social relations necessary to achieve it. First, however, I shall explore another twist to the enduring tension between socio-economic and psychosocial approaches which finds expression in alternative political agendas oriented towards rights and redistribution. I will then show how these themes have been brought to bear on welfare ethics by considering the psychological and ethical basis for recognition and care and contrasting this with justice-based models of decision making.

Rights, redistribution and recognition

Although the purpose of this book is to deepen perspectives on welfare by inserting a psychosocial dimension, it would be foolish to ignore the fact that there are sometimes tensions between struggles for recognition and those oriented towards rights or redistribution. The redistribution agenda has remained relatively weak and politically low key since the decline of a mass class-based trades union movement and the demise of the Left within and outside of the Labour Party. A number of anti-poverty measures introduced by the Chancellor, Gordon Brown, during the first Blair administration, including the national minimum wage, stimulated some discussion as to whether the government was effectively redistributing by stealth. Nevertheless, by the end of the first term in office, income distribution in the UK had become even more unequal. Such measures were in any case justified within a discourse of social inclusion rather than distributive justice.

It has been argued that a focus on recognition effectively displaces redistribution struggles. Fraser (1995) suggests that by the late 20th century the struggle for recognition – directed against cultural domination rather than exploitation – had become the paradigmatic form of movement against injustice. This raises cause for concern at a time when an expanding global capitalism is sharpening inequalities. Fraser argues that justice requires both social equality and cultural respect and she examines the extent to which a politics of recognition can support or undermine a politics of redistribution. She points out that movements against injustice typically take one or other of these forms and, by way of example, contrasts struggles around gender or race or sexual orientation with those around class.

In both instances, recognition and redistribution demands are intertwined, though with differences in emphasis:

> In the case of the exploited proletariat the logic of the remedy is to put the group out of business as a group. In the case of the gay community it is to valorise the group's 'groupness' by recognising its specificity. (Fraser, 1995, p 78)

Anti-racist struggles also stem from the need to participate as a peer in social life. The importance of the Stephen Lawrence inquiry lay in the fact that it exposed a pervasive form of misrecognition sustained by institutional racism. However, the question remains as to whether the appropriate remedy might be found in the kind of affirmative strategies that support group differentiation, or in social transformation. Many affirmative strategies take communitarian forms and are articulated around issues of identity. This can only too easily lead to competition for resources and therefore resentment and misrecognition against groups who make demands for reallocations of goods and respect. Effectively such strategies intensify the tension between recognition and redistribution. Fraser argues that transformative strategies that move beyond identity towards a politics of social solidarity are more promising in that they address sources of injustice at a deeper level and can avoid fanning the flames of resentment. The problem is that these strategies are less likely to reflect immediate perceived interests.

Redistribution and recognition demands are not ultimately easy to separate. If the 'protective' function of the welfare state lies in its de-commodifying effects (Esping-Andersen, 1990) it is because it constitutes a public sphere which is partly freed from the alienated and exploitative social relations of competitive market systems. This is achieved by a real and symbolic redistributive function, which may be quite limited in terms of the size of transfers but has an extensive psychological reach in that it maintains a collectively supported arena of concern for both intimates and strangers. Certainly the rise of identity group politics has paralleled the decline of such a public arena.

Although Fraser does not venture into intra-psychic territory, her argument is suggestive of the ways in which identity politics can emerge from paranoid–schizoid feelings of persecution, which may be real enough, but in which the celebration of difference thrives on competitiveness, survivalism and a rigid separation between self and other. The dynamic of recognition breaks down since the survival of one group is always at the other's expense. In such scenarios, appeals to group solidarities obscure intra-group differences. However, absent from this analysis is an account of the nature of psychic investment in group identity and its role in motivating struggles for self-determination. It is not only demands for civic equity that propel such movements but also the active construction of solidarities through the elaboration of stories that reposition the group in relation to oppressive discourses and institutions. I shall return to this issue in the final chapter.

Kleinian and object relations traditions depict psychic aspects of attachment and individuation in dynamic relationship to the surrounding environment. They therefore allow us to understand the ways in which group solidarities and the politics of difference can be defensively constructed by splitting off despised attributes of the self and depositing them in others. In the case of anxieties surrounding identity stimulated by racial difference, this evacuation and depletion of parts of the self exacerbates fears of being engulfed or overwhelmed, hence the resonance of images of 'floods' and 'rivers' in relation to immigration. Protective social institutions which sustain dialogue can act as containers, allowing such projections to be retrieved. Anxieties surrounding identity can then be realigned with a sense of existential vulnerability, which has its source as much within personal dependency needs as in a hostile environment. The critical question is whether these institutions allow us to contain, acknowledge and think about this anxiety from a depressive position. I have argued that there are inherent flaws in each of the three welfare models described in Part I of this book which impair their ability to contain and to promote the realistic relationships to different others which are the basis of recognition. This is not to say that such relationships are never achieved by people within them. Since we are all constantly involved in the struggle to reconcile inner and outer worlds, the question for any individual is how factors in the environment 'bind' to inner material, generating fragmented and persecutory, or reparative, emotional states.

If the redistribution agenda is now relatively muted in welfare discourse, the same cannot be said for movements concerned with the extension of social rights. I have drawn attention to the limitations of exclusively rights-based demands for welfare in the preceding chapter, suggesting that these can in any case be ultimately reconciled with the contractual principles underlying most current social policy. This leaves problems of recognition unresolved and can lead to a one-sided emphasis on personal entitlement. Honneth's (1995) approach is useful in that he considers rights as just one dimension of the struggle for recognition, which is also stimulated by the quest for love and solidarity. First, on an interpersonal level, love and friendship are at the root of basic self-confidence and the ability to accept the integrity and distinctiveness of others to whom there is a personal sense of attachment. Here Honneth refers to Winnicott's account of the interplay (described in Chapter Two of this book) between the child's destructiveness and maternal holding in the development of this capacity to recognise others and be recognised in turn. The re-creation of containing relations within social institutions then continues to provide the psychic conditions for interpersonal recognition on a wider plane. Second, juridical rights are the basis of publicly redeemable claims for respect and therefore for self-esteem. One is able to respect oneself insofar as one recognises oneself as worthy of the respect of others. A framework of rights provides a standard against which discrepancies in the social attribution of worth can be measured. Furthermore, in Marshall's (1963) argument, rights to welfare which arise as a consequence of equalising pressures from below are intrinsic to fully fledged membership of a political community. Social rights allow civil and political rights to be exercised. Their denial therefore amounts to a failure of moral responsibility and social exclusion.

> The idea that self-respect is for legal relations what basic self-confidence was for the love relationship is already suggested by the conceptual appropriateness of viewing rights as depersonalised symbols of social respect in just the way that love can be conceived as the affectional expression of care retained over distance. (Honneth, 1995, p 118)

Finally, ethical life depends on communities of value in which solidarity is premised on the fact that fully individuated subjects esteem one another. Neither the affectionate, intimate care that characterises love–relations nor the universal rights of the legally recognisable subject can account for the collectively sponsored care of strangers that the modern welfare state achieves – at least not those forms of care which are responsive to the particularities of individual needs and desires, and therefore consistent with human dignity. The third dimension of solidarity, which arises from social esteem, is premised on both the capacity for concern that first arises in the context of loving parental attention, and on legal recognition. However, in the ethical life of communities of value there arises the possibility of a plurality of relations between self and others that are neither wholly particularistic nor universalistic. Strictly speaking these should be characterised as symmetrical rather than equal. The other is then recognised as one who is worthy of social esteem on account of membership of a human community, held together by mutual respect but this respect is activated precisely by those personal characteristics and accomplishments that make him or her different.

> Relationships of this sort can be said to be cases of 'solidarity', because they inspire not just passive tolerance but felt concern for what is individual and particular about the other person. For only to the degree to which I actively care about the development of the other's characteristics (which may seem foreign to me) can our shared goals be realised. (Honneth, 1995, p 129)

Care, compassion and recognition

Old welfarism lost much of the support on which it was founded precisely because it was unable to sustain institutions and practices which were able to maintain felt concern for what was particular about its clients. The critiques of welfare bureaucracies that took hold in the seventies and eighties were philosophically diverse but shared as a common ground the urge to respond to individual and cultural differences. In the context of globalisation and the demise of the collectivist politics of trade unionism and the Left, the solution which attracted most widespread electoral support was the programme of consumerisation inspired by the New Right. However, despite the fact that the consumer in this model is supposedly sovereign, the managerial restructuring of welfare responded only to a 'thin' conception of human need that is amenable to procedural management. Within the care management model, relationship-based work was marginalised as a therapeutic option within a package of care oriented to determinate timescales and economic efficiency. As a result it was less able to achieve a realistic knowledge of the user and his or her situation which accommodated subjective perceptions of need.

> Care management is in its own terms of reference, about promoting choice amongst the rational and promoting rationality amongst the irrational. There is therefore a close relationship between the concept of self-determination and the concept of need underlying care management. In so doing, in the last analysis, there is an objectivist core to care management, whatever the protestation in the official guidelines that need is a relative concept. (Sheppard, 1995, p 133)

A truly individuated response must avoid the polarities of objectivism and subjectivism, moving towards full recognition of particularity, while maintaining an eye to the social context of every individual's predicament. It does not exalt compassion at the expense of rationality or vice versa. However, the capacity for compassion, which depends on the ability to maintain the depressive position, both facilitates and flows from recognition. Furthermore, it allows for the remoralisation of knowledge that nourishes an ethic of care.

The idea of founding a social order on reason and love has a radical history in the work of the Frankfurt school and its successors. Alford (1989) poses the question of why this project seemed to run into a philosophical and practical cul-de-sac. He suggests that an adequate conception of love is essential in providing an alternative to a vision of a world in which even intimacy and care are penetrated by the logic of instrumental reason. It is here that the distinction between Klein's view and Freud's becomes important. What Klein's work provides is an understanding of another more inclusive form of love, founded on early nurturing relationships and yet with profound importance in the containment of aggression and the later development of the capacity to relate creatively to others. This love, represented not as *Eros* but as *Caritas*, understood as compassion, underpins the very possibility of human attachments and also of an equality that recognises difference. The distinction is best understood by referring to Marcuse's philosophical argument for the emancipatory potential of Eros in *Eros and civilisation* (1969).

This book, widely taken up during the student movements of the sixties, represented to the generation of intellectuals whose work formed in that period, an affirmation of the importance of erotic love in the project of human liberation. It captured the spirit of the so-called sexual revolution and welded it to a critique of the bourgeois moral order in its insistence on the role of repression in the imposition of labour discipline. This repression, of both aggression and the pleasure principle, subordinates human needs to the goals of capital accumulation. Because it is implicated in complex systems of control that operate at the level of both psyche and social structure, its dissipation would entail a reduction in psychic conflict and a corresponding release of energy and creativity of potentially revolutionary significance.

This work seems very much a product of its time in that it provided an important, if partial, justification for the reform of sexual conduct in an increasingly secularised society. In doing so it paved the way for subsequent social movements – particularly of women, gay and disabled people, who have opened up the question of how the manipulation and renunciation of desire is implicated in structures of oppression and exploitation. With the benefit of hindsight, it has become clearer that the relaxation of sexual mores has also allowed, to an extent that would hardly have seemed possible 30 years ago, the commodification of sexuality and the symbolic binding of desire to the socio-economic order. If the diverse possibilities of erotic love are now more easily, or at least more widely, explored, the limitations of its subversive potential are also more obvious. This realisation was a major catalyst for the second wave of 20th century feminism propelled by a generation of young women who bore the brunt of the sexual revolution, literally on their backs. From the critique of patriarchal sexual relations, they went on to develop a critique of the conditions of women's caring role (for example, Maclean and Groves, 1991), which is still slowly working its way into social policy. What now seems remarkable in the literature of the seventies and early eighties was the extent to which the question of love became divorced both from sexual gratification and the gendered nature of caring.

The problem, according to Alford, lies in the identification of love with Eros. From a Kleinian perspective, Eros represents love from a paranoid–schizoid position. Despite its passionate energy and romantic investment in an idealised other, it is fundamentally greedy, taking what it can from the object of its desire for its own use. In this position, narcissistic identifications come to the fore: we project something of ourselves into the other, delighting in the correspondences we then discover. It makes us feel good about ourselves, feeding a sense of exhilarating omnipotence. We try to share our feelings but become easily offended when we fail. We attempt to manipulate the other into being what we need them to be. At moments of passionate intensity we seem to have incorporated the other inside ourselves, dissolving boundaries via a process of introjection, hence the orality of the fantasies that so often accompany sex. The love represented by Eros is a love that uses the other to enhance the self and to assuage an appetite. For this reason it can easily evoke fears of having damaged the object of love by devouring it, sucking it dry, using it up. One response might be promiscuity in which the lover moves on, avoiding sustained attachment and anxiety at the damage that might be inflicted, a damage that could return from the beloved to poison the lover. Another is intense disillusion when idealisation clashes with the intransigent reality of another personality. Another is to be drawn into a struggle for domination in order to ward off the narcissistic injury of being thwarted.

By contrast, Caritas represents a form of love which arises only after achievement of a depressive relation to reality, in that recognition of the uniqueness and separateness of the other leads to concern that their integrity be respected and that they be loved – as the saying goes – for who they are. It also recognises implicitly the imperfection of both the lover and the beloved and therefore fears for damage that can be caused to the relationship by frustration and aggression. However, faith in the possibility of repairing this damage allows both expression of negativity and the integration of disappointment. Above all it is based on a sense of gratitude for the goodness that the beloved represents.

Both kinds of love have their origins in early nurturing and are probably implicated in most adult erotic relationships, where the interplay between greed, gratitude and generosity is a source of vitality. However, where Eros dominates to the exclusion of Caritas, love becomes fundamentally self-serving. It is also entirely compatible with a culture which places a high value on individual gratification and which demurs at collective expenditure on public services. This aligns the lover with the shopper whose 'consuming passions' (Williamson, 1995) become *the* sanctioned form of desire. The paradox of Eros – loving the other to enhance the self – drives the erotic relationship in a direction that is congruent with wider contemporary meanings of consumption. This can only further a project founded on the commodification of care. The altruistic principle is then subverted. If the primary purpose of care for the other is that of making the carer feel better, its significance is transformed. The potential for recognition is lost – with the risk of dehumanising both parties.

Caritas, compassion – or for Klein, the concept of depressive love – furthers a dynamic of recognition because it is based on apprehension of the integrity of the object which can then be preserved in both knowledge and in morality. In terms of knowledge it implies an attempt to get closer to the object and to let it reveal itself without imposing on it preconceived, distorting categories of thought. In terms of morality, it impels a relation to the other founded on care, and a concern to preserve particularity. Fittingly, the ailing Marcuse, himself, came to this conclusion. Habermas (1980) reports his comment at their last encounter: "I know wherein our most basic value judgements are rooted – in compassion, in our sense for the suffering of others" (p 12).

Allowing the object to take the lead in determining the way in which it comes to be known entails a reversal of the relations that dominate current institutional practices. It involves restoring and rethinking what used to be called client-centredness and finding credible methodologies which will allow us to do this. It means understanding the proper limits of positivist methods of assessment and evaluation with their promise of certainty and predictive power. This is not to suggest that the scientific paradigm and quantitative methods have no value, but that their usefulness as instruments of knowledge in welfare is circumscribed.

Care and justice

It is because compassion is the vital emotional link between care and recognition that organisational cultures that are instrumental and narcissistic cannot sustain and nourish relations of care. I suspect it is for this reason too that the very concept of 'care' has become corrupted and therefore rejected by the disability movement. Care without recognition is demeaning and obliterates subjectivity.

Paul Hoggett (2000) takes up the question of welfare ethics, affirming the importance of both an ethic of justice and an ethic of care. He argues that whereas an ethic of justice has been under sustained attack for the last 20 years, an ethic of care has never been securely developed within formal services in the UK. It is this that has opened the door for an attack on the so-called dependency culture. This offensive has been uniquely corrosive of both justice and care and yet has come to be reiterated by voices across the political spectrum. He gives an example of a project that achieved a practical expression of both: the Battersea Action and Counselling Centre in which he worked for a while in the mid-seventies. This was something of an inspiration to a generation of radical mental health workers because of the way in which it sought to combine a vigorous defence of welfare rights with practical initiatives such as a day-nursery and food co-op, while offering forms of psychotherapeutic help to individuals and couples in distress. It also maintained a strong campaigning profile on issues of importance to the local community. The Centre was very much the inspiration of Sue Holland and a group of people who were committed to this combination of personal support, therapy and political action. As in the case of so many initiatives that, for a time at least, manage to dissolve ossified boundaries, it was a small, locally-based community project swimming against the tide. It was active around questions of social justice while at the same time offering highly individuated care. Such a balance is considerably more difficult to achieve in statutory services, though it is constantly called for.

Sandra was given to outbursts of temper and impulsive behaviour when provoked. She came from a large family who had always rather regarded her as the 'runt' and she had been severely and persistently bullied by her sisters and brothers. Unfortunately this pattern of victimisation was the hallmark of her childhood and adolescence, repeating itself at school and in her few early and unsuccessful brushes with the world of work. In her late teens she suffered the first of a series of psychotic episodes, which, no doubt on account of her violent temper, were 'managed' by heavy medication over quite a prolonged period. By the time she was in her early thirties it was hard to identify which of life's bitter experiences had damaged her most: the years of victimisation or the heavy psychoactive medication, which had left her with the stiff, shambling gait, and the slow, wooden aspect of the institutionalised mental patient. At the age of 34 she became pregnant although she was unable to identify a father. The pregnancy brought about a change that was almost unbearably poignant for those involved in her care. Something seemed to light her up from inside, as she began to experience a new range of emotions and a longing for her child. However, her years in institutions had left her with few self-care skills, no social networks and a very short fuse. It seemed unlikely that she would ever be able to look after a baby.

But what were the grounds for removing it from her at birth? She had never harmed a child, indeed like many first-time mothers she had limited experience of children. In addition, her social worker felt that she was a casualty of the psychiatric system and that justice dictated that she be given every possible opportunity, and whatever support she required, to see if she might learn just enough to have a chance at motherhood. The conflict between the rights of the mother and the rights of the child to safety and an adequate level of care seemed to create an impasse in which one party might lose all. Tragically it seemed that Sandra would have to sacrifice the only thing that had ever really given her any hope. The needs of the child were paramount and the end seemed a forgone conclusion. Child protection and court proceedings would be initiated as soon as she lost her temper or mishandled the baby, and her history of mental illness invoked. The bet was that this would not take very long. In any event she would require continuous and intrusive surveillance.

This situation could have led to the withdrawal of precious resources from a woman who – it might have been argued – was unlikely ever to benefit from them. Although a justice perspective could not do anything other than pit the rights of the child against those of the mother, a care perspective could maintain an eye to both. The social workers involved resolved to deal with her 'as if' she might yet be able to mother her child in order to devise a process whereby she might come to understand for herself what stood in her way. It would have been cruel and futile to send her to antenatal classes where she would have been out of her depth, but a personalised programme was devised with the help of a sympathetic health visitor. The daily details of babycare were painstakingly role-played in such a way that the physical and emotional demands of parenthood could be understood and thought about. In this very protected space Sandra received a quality of attention which was new to her and experienced something close to parenting herself. She slowly began to question her own readiness and to realise that what she wanted and needed most in the world was care for herself. She was able, with desperate grief, to give up and mourn for her baby.

All this happened some time ago in a social work team that by today's standards was well resourced. How can such labour-intensive methods of work be justified in the current climate? Where was the end point of this intervention? How could its outputs be measured? Two years after the birth of the child Sandra still felt she had been a part of the decision and seemed at ease with it. She had made a decision to be sterilised, and – though admittedly with ups and downs – there were tentative signs that she was learning to care for herself.

Sustaining the capacity for good judgement in the face of the complex intersection of justice and care requires formidable ethical and emotional resources. The dilemma returns us to the need to seek out a third position in which neither is sacrificed though initial conceptions of both must be modified. It is the desire to preserve relationships which drives this process. The environment provided by statutory health and social service organisations often fails to support the kind of thinking required because an outcomes culture does not contain the anxiety generated by the fact that there are no easy solutions. Furthermore, it does not place a premium on human relationships. Nevertheless, individuals and teams who experience these tensions at first hand do sometimes manage it. Child protection is a field that arouses anxiety at a level perhaps unparalleled in any other area of welfare work. There are now institutional mechanisms to allay this by introducing elaborate guidelines and high degrees of accountability into the work. But nothing is without attendant dangers and there is a risk of creating overly defensive forms of practice. The ethical complexity of the territory means that predefined procedure and checklist approaches are of limited usefulness.

I do not intend to review in full the debate over an ethic of justice or care which has continued now for 20 years or so, stimulated by a series of feminist writers in psychology and moral and political philosophy (Gilligan, 1982, 1988; Ruddick, 1989; Held, 1993; Tronto, 1994; Sevenhuijsen, 1998). Nevertheless, a short summary is important for my argument since a proper balance between rights and care is crucial for the practical realisation of recognition-relations. Gilligan's controversial research into the gendered nature of moral reasoning initially raised the profile of the debate and proved highly suggestive for the caring professions whose front-line workforce remains overwhelmingly female. She argued neither that care should replace justice as the foundation of moral reasoning, nor that justice and care are incompatible, although they are frequently in tension in particular judgements. The cultural dominance of justice models of ethical reasoning within the West is understood to derive from over-valuation of individual autonomy which is articulated through the gendering of moral sensibilities that tend to be internalised differently by boys and girls from infancy onwards. This is not to make an essentialist claim for a gendered morality. Gilligan used the metaphor of the 'moral voice' to distinguish the development of sensibilities oriented to care and justice among her research subjects. In asking boys and girls to resolve moral dilemmas she identified, more strongly among girls, 'a different voice' which has been submerged in theories of development that place a sense of justice at the apex of moral reasoning (Kohlberg, 1981, 1984).

One of her simplest and most compelling examples (Gilligan, 1988) was of a small boy and girl discussing what game to play. Conforming to gendered stereotypes, the boy wanted 'pirates' while the girl chose 'neighbours'. Faced with a potential impasse, but with the urge to carry on playing together, each proposed a solution. While the little boy suggested that they take it in turns, the girl's response was "you be the pirate that lives next door". In either case there is a concern for a fair outcome, but while taking turns is informed by the ideal of reciprocity, the alternative proposal recognises the legitimate desires of each party within one game. The dilemma is transcended by maintaining the contested elements in relation with each other. It is recognition of the distinct position of the other together with the desire to preserve relatedness that leads to innovation and a third position.

Whereas detachment has been seen as the basis for dispassionate judgement, the alternative voice comes from the compassionate and relational self and depends on the capacity to engage with others and sustain attachments. Although this faculty has been well observed in studies of childhood (Bowlby, 1969, 1973, 1980) it has not been well represented in theories of human development where a masculinised model of the separate, autonomous self has provided the ideal standard of maturation. A compassionate morality departs less from our responsibilities *to* others than responsiveness in our relationships *with* them. In assuming a self that seeks connection and is changed through dialogue, it recasts the 'problem' of dependency:

> Being dependent, then, no longer means being helpless, powerless and without control; rather it signifies a conviction that one is able to have an effect on others, as well as the recognition that the interdependence of attachment empowers both the self and other, not one person at the other's expense. The activities of care – being there, listening, the willingness to help, and the ability to understand – take on a moral dimension, reflecting the injunction to pay attention and not to turn away from need. As the knowledge that others are capable of care renders them loveable rather than merely reliable, so the willingness and the ability to care becomes a standard of self-evaluation. In this active construction, dependence, rather than signifying a failure of individuation, denotes a decision on the part of the individual to enact a vision of love. (Gilligan, 1988, p 16)

The nursing profession, increasingly keen to demarcate the care/cure boundary in its attempt to theorise its distinctive contribution to healthcare, has long reflected on the nature of caring as an activity and an orientation to service delivery (Phillips and Benner, 1994). Rhodes (1985) pointed out that the distinction between care and justice in social work corresponds in part to a long-standing opposition between a rights perspective based on liberal individualism, and a needs perspective that has its origins in 19th-century visions of Christian virtue. Yet despite its enormous relevance to the debate on ethical dilemmas of practice, the implications of this distinction seem to have had a rather limited airing among the helping professions in the UK. This is largely a consequence of the dominance of the rights-based anti-oppressive practice agenda. It may also reflect the harsh realities of what has been a politically hostile climate for both the poor and socially excluded, and professionals who are only too easily caricatured as apologists for their supposed inadequacy. In these circumstances the radical voice within the profession has preferred to draw attention to the manifold forms of discrimination and disadvantage and has been raised in defence of social justice and anti-oppressive practice (for example, Jones 1983; Dominelli, 1988; Dalrymple and Burke, 1995). While these approaches are by no means antithetical to considerations of relationship and process, the accent has been heavily on structural disparities of power and resources. Dominelli (1998) argues that anti-oppressive practice is necessarily holistic but her discussion of relational work is couched almost entirely in terms of power relations – a vital dimension but one seldom elaborated in intra-psychic or even interpersonal terms. David Ward (1998), in discussing the 'demethoding' of social work and the disappearance of the 'how' from the social work curriculum, points out the irony of the fact that this has led to the almost complete demise of groupwork – a method which was grounded in the very principles of equity, self-directed action and non-elitist leadership which anti-oppressive approaches avowedly espouse.

In this context the by now substantial literature on caring, much of it inspired by feminists (for example, Ungerson 1987; Langan and Day, 1992), has focused on the structural and political issues of who cares, or is cared for, and under what circumstances. In general, it has highlighted the low pay and status accorded to an activity which is largely carried out by women, both informally and as part of the labour force. There has been some opposition between authors from the disability movement and those who have chosen to address the so-called 'burden' of caring (for example, Morris, 1993 versus Dalley, 1988). At the centre of this debate is a question about the nature of caring as a form of emotional labour in which the practical and affective dimensions of the activity are inextricably intertwined. This is the dimension that tends to be ignored in public policy making. Hence the ethical issues which surround it are cast principally in terms of rights and justice in respect of distribution of resources and responsibility.

The disability movement has been forceful in arguing that institutional public care has been oppressive to disabled people, infantilising them within paternalistic relationships which effectively deny them control over their own lives (Oliver and Sapey, 1999). Shakespeare (2000) argues that contemporary care practices can only be experienced as demeaning by disabled people themselves, positioning them as other, imprisoned in failed bodies, deficient in their neediness. Such a construction of caring as 'burdensome' is only too often implicated in internalisation of inadequacy by disabled people themselves. Furthermore, care is offered as a substitute for the demolition of the obstacles that impede their full participation in social life:

> The construction of the Other through the discourses of care and dependency effaces the particularity of Otherness. There is a need for disabled people and Other help recipients to establish themselves as subjects, each with a voice and rights which are rich enough to respect their individuality while recognising them as a member of the community. (Shakespeare, 2000, p 20)

This formulation is richer than the discourse of civil rights, individual autonomy, choice and control that has sometimes been embraced as an alternative to charity, paternalism and enforced dependency. Shakespeare acknowledges the individualist premise of an exclusive reliance on rights-based approaches and draws attention to the creative possibilities in other forms of low intensity support by networks and communities which offer flexible non-professional forms of help ranging from decorating and gardening to form-filling, transport and social support. Despite his reservation over the term 'care' he guardedly accepts the feminist argument that initiatives such as these do not in themselves counter the highly individualised presuppositions of Western notions of independence which valorise an atomistic self-sufficiency. This leads to a failure to acknowledge and sustain a value-system based on mutuality and connectedness and a practical breakdown of the fundamental interdependence that constitutes social life. A sense of the corruption that has degraded the notion of 'care' for disabled people seeps through Shakespeare's text. Not only is the book pointedly entitled *Help*, there is a palpable reluctance to allow the possibility of an ethical stance based on caring – often he refers simply to a 'feminist ethic'. Similarly in the autonomy/dependence binary, it is clear that dependence is the degraded term. He accepts the necessity of 'interdependence' as a basis for welfare but there seems to be little room in this construction for the dependent states that are an irreducible dimension of human experience. The reader is left wondering whether the problem lies in the socially constructed discourse of care and dependency or within fundamental modes of relatedness which mark our entry and exit from this world, our growing up and winding down and, for all of us, significant tracts of adult life.

According to psychoanalytic views of human relationships it is not only at the extremities of experience – being born and dying – that we need something more than 'help'. The inability to accept dependent emotional and physical states, the fantasy that we are or ought to be somehow self-generating and self-contained, is a pathology of personality, albeit a pervasive one in Western culture. There are times that we need from the other something that we are not able to return in accordance with the perfectly symmetrical reciprocity that characterises the liberal ideal of equity. We need and lack and love according to our capacities, at different times and in uneven measure. An ethical life based on recognition of a wider and more generalised interdependence cannot bypass this uncomfortable truth. It appears that care-based and rights-based approaches have in fact come to be viewed as a binary opposition so that the argument for civil rights entails a disavowal of care and dependency needs that we all share. It is in this context that the perceived dependency of others becomes a mark of social disapprobation and exclusion. None of this is to suggest for a moment that there is not a great deal to be done, as Morris (2001) argues, to extend rights to appropriate education and employment opportunities, income support and personal assistance – rather it is to ask what mindset would allow differential support for dependency needs without it becoming a marker of social exclusion.

The consequence of this acceptance is a re-evaluation of vulnerability as so much an essential part of human learning and living that far from evoking pity or contempt, it is respected as an ingredient in the glue of interpersonal solidarity. This potential becomes transiently visible in the aftermath of national disasters. I first drafted this passage two days after the destruction of the twin towers of the World Trade Center. In New York, that most mercenary city of individual striving and enterprise, the television screen revealed sharply opposed responses. On the one hand, desire for revenge – the determination to excise a new-found vulnerability and expunge self-doubt led to calls for a purgative retaliation on a shadow (no perpetrator had yet been named). There was little comfort in the revelation that the assertive phallic power of the twin towers had all along been inconceivably fragile. The admiration for the rescue workers reflected gratitude for real bravery in the face of trauma and loss but also the need for symbols of strength and endurance. On the other hand, there was the grief and mourning of many ordinary citizens, united in a new-found sense of weakness, wandering the streets looking for ways to support each other. For these there was an awakening of the desire to 'give': blood, food, time, comfort, encouragement. Two weeks later a friend, who had suffered no personal bereavement, e-mailed "why is this happening to me?". In the destruction of what was certain and familiar, New Yorkers, it seemed, were able to respond with thoughtfulness. *The Observer* (22 September 2001) reported that the popular mood was considerably less vengeful than elsewhere in the US.

In her discussions of the political implications of an ethic of care, Tronto (1994) identifies both a moral disposition and a practice and draws a crucial distinction between 'caring for' and 'caring about'. Both are necessary but it is the latter that lifts caring out of the mire of condescension and abuse of power with which it has sometimes been tainted. The former may be regarded as an activity that we pursue according to our circumstances. It is open to all of us equally to participate in the latter. However, a productive conjunction of the two dimensions of caring fails to develop in the context of the boundaries which separate morality from politics, particular from universal judgement and public life from the private and parochial.

Tronto sees care as a complex social construction, subject to the limitations of the culture that must sustain it, and warns against idealisation and sentimentalisation. She argues that it requires attentiveness, responsibility, competence and responsiveness. Sevenhuijsen (1998) similarly cautions against Held's (1993) attempt to ground an ethic of care in romanticised images of motherhood. She prefers to explore its potential within a socio-legal frame of citizenship. In posing the problem in terms of social and political construction, both writers insist on the affective aspect of care and register the potential for inequality, exploitation and abuse which has been so eloquently denounced by the disability movement. However, this perversion of relationship tends to be explained in terms of inequalities in power and denigration of attributes that are conventionally associated with the feminine. There is perhaps something of the catch-all in these explanations. Attention needs to be paid to the ways in which particular welfare arrangements sustain this denigration and how it comes to be articulated in the interpersonal dynamics of caring and the development of the capacity to care – a subject about which the Kleinian and object relations tradition has a great deal to say.

In seeking to explain why dependency has become so problematic in the late 20th and early 21st century, Hoggett (2000), drawing on the work of the Italian Marxist Sabastiano Timpanaro (1975), argues that it 'jars' with the active voice and evokes a repressed passivity, which is so antithetical to the spirit of late modernity and the ultimately inescapable helplessness that comes from being a part of nature and hence confined to a body that must die. He wonders whether major strands of political social science have not been caught up in a denial of this awkward truth and cites as examples the ongoing nature/nurture debate; a view of freedom as the overcoming of necessity; an infatuation with modernisation; and a narcissistic impatience with all forms of constraint. The denial of vulnerability and dependency distort our sense of ourselves as a part of nature no less than our relations to one another with often disastrous ecological and social consequences and yet:

> inside each one of us there is a drifter and nomad, a failure, a non-survivor and all the other personas that the passive internal voice can assume. A good society would be one which could provide a place for such selves to be, without always seeking to empower them or thrust cures upon them. Sometimes people just want to rest and be taken care of, sometimes people just want to drift along without having to think too much. It follows that there is something seriously wrong with a society in which the bestowal of full citizenship is contingent upon fitness to join a labour market which increasingly has the feel of a jungle. (Hoggett, 2000, p 169)

Related to this is an intolerance of problems that cannot be 'solved'. Up until the restructuring of social services under the 1990 NHS and Community Care Act, a very substantial part of many social workers' caseloads was made up of people who were effectively being maintained at a just about adequate level of functioning by the intermittent low or medium level support from a social or community worker, health visitor, or one of the many small-scale voluntary projects that had emerged to fill in the gaps left by official services. These people's problems were by no means trivial and always had the potential to spiral into crisis but by dint of careful watchfulness, support, cajoling, nagging, advice, practical help and a certain amount of carefully calibrated threat, it was possible to avoid the loss of children, home, sanity and self-respect. Working with such people yielded few spectacular rewards and outcomes were barely discernible if conceived in terms of measurable change. The work was long term, low profile, intensely frustrating and would perhaps continue on and off for most of their lives. It generated considerable anxiety – particularly where the quality of care for children was involved. There were some very dejected parents whose meagre internal and external resources were stretched to breaking point by the demands of their role. Supporting them imposed the strain of perpetual finely tuned judgement over small details – entirely different from the more dynamic, high profile child protection work. Other groups who called for this painstaking attention included the chronically mentally ill; people with personality disorders and permanently disarranged lives; and those who were old, weak, depressed and intractably resistant to care plans, however carefully devised. 'Progress', if it occurred, was faltering and ever subject to reversal. The resilience required for such work should not be underestimated. It depends very much on a capacity for containment analogous to the process that Bion (1970) describes when he refers to the way in which the mother receives the disorganised, undigested projections from the infant and by absorbing in a particular emotionally attuned way, makes it possible for them to be held in mind. She can then 'return' them in a form that the baby can use. Supporting long-term clients often meant standing by as a steadying and emotionally integrative presence – providing the boundaries within which sense could be made of chaotic and disturbing experience.

It is not clear to me what now happens to such people. This kind of work came to be frowned on as the 'what works' movement gained momentum and time-limited interventions became synonymous with effective practice. I suspect many of them have dropped out of sight to muddle along fairly miserably. Many will have joined the burgeoning ranks of the homeless or have chronic, unattended physical and mental health problems. Most will appear in general poverty statistics and swell the ranks of the long-term unemployed. Others survive through petty theft, delinquency, alcohol and drugs. The children raise the toll of school exclusions. I could go on but the point is that these groups who formerly received support have been a casualty of the idealisation of a narrowly conceived culture of 'efficiency' demanded of public institutions by government and the Exchequer. In asking whether inefficiency might not have its own virtues, Dartington (2001) points out that an over-valuation of efficiency may be allied to delusions of infinite perfectibility which operate as a defence against disappointment. This is the shadow side to a performative culture that defines itself in concepts of continuous development, lifelong learning, flexibility, change and growth. Since efficiency breeds a culture of comparison and inspection, it prefers to target problems that yield to bureaucratic responses – the infinitely perfectible organisation requires an infinitely perfectible client.

It should be clear by now that there are several layers to the argument that a welfare system based on consumer rights cannot sustain relationships of compassion and recognition. It perpetuates individualism at the expense of individuation, which requires both differentiation and solidarity. It addresses the problem of equality but not that of value and leads to an over-valuation of justice at the expense of care. It does not provide adequate containment for the anxieties of living in a risk society and instead offers a defensive retreat to prediction, regulation and control. This fosters a breakdown of the tension between self and other, paving the way to narcissistic omnipotence and omniscience and relations of domination. All of these tendencies are concretely embodied in the excessive rationalism of modern managerialist cultures, in the downgrading of face-to-face relationship-based practice, in the fetishisation of outcome and measurement, and in the subordination of meaning to goals.

Practices grounded in mutuality, recognition and response certainly exist (else they would be unimaginable). The politics that fosters them assumes the equal moral worth of individuals and demands a move towards a more substantive social, economic and legal equality. It asserts the necessity of social bonds that draw their vitality from the particular contributions of freely participating subjects. Something of the quality of such attachments finds expression in good friendships – a theme that has been developed by Friedman (1989). Within welfare agencies they depend on an attempt to repair the split between knowledge and values on which both modern managerialism and earlier bureaucratic forms of coordination are premised. While understanding the importance of attachment and affiliation to communities and associations of choice, they depend on face-to-face, communicative relationships.

Note

[1] At the time of writing the adjective compassionate has been coupled with conservatism to lend moral authority to the agenda of the Anglo-American Right.

SEVEN

Beyond welfare: recognition, practice and the organisation

We must plan the summer afternoon somehow
Of the swallow and the slow-worm and the sow
We must find some exercise
In the winter for the flies
We must organise the free time of the cow. ...

In the water too we should be interested
For the algae should be quarantined and tested
And every drop of rain
Should be packed in cellophane
And moonlight saved and carefully reinvested.
W.H. Auden, *Notebook* (1936-37)

The fantasy of regulation

This chapter falls into two parts. In the first, I highlight the increasing uncertainty of the environment and the response in terms of regulation and a quest for methodologies that offer certainty and predictive power. I contrast this approach with a rather neglected tradition that insists on the art-like dimensions of practice. In the second part, I give an extended example of a community project in which the arts have played and continue to play a seminal role. From this I attempt to draw out some of the ingredients of a reparative organisational culture.

For better or worse, the New Right assault on public sector professionals which gathered pace in the eighties, has borne fruit in a complex array of regulatory bodies whose activities are central to the modernisation agenda. Increasing regulation is justified on the grounds that it guarantees consumer rights and better quality services. Jordan (2000) reviews the modernisation agenda for social services and identifies a distinctively top-down Third Way model of governance which attempts to impose heightened levels of accountability on managers and local government officers, and tighter regulation of professionals. The General Social Care Council, for example, is to register practitioners, oversee training, set codes of conduct and standards of practice in both social work and social care. Occupational representatives on this body will be in a minority. The proposed regulatory and supervisory framework attempts to extend the reach of enforcement agencies into intimate areas of social care and family life where they have never successfully operated before. The government has faith in regulation and inspection as a means of promoting inclusiveness, listening, respect for diversity and general responsiveness. Yet 'improved commissioning' of services foresees a model of care management in which the distinctive contribution of the front-line practitioner has been all but removed. Jordan argues that this strategy is misconceived in that it fails to understand that face-to-face caring cannot be so mechanistically prescribed. It is a 'blood-and-guts' activity motivated by ties of

> affection, gratitude, guilt, greed, interdependence, obsession, power or powerlessness.... Into this maelstrom of mixed feelings and often conflicting interests, a care manager arrives to assess resources and risks, and purchase a package of care. The success or failure of this in sustaining the relationships between carer and cared for, in managing the transition towards greater dependence and eventual 'social death' (Miller and Gwynne, 1972) – the loss of a viable life in the community, often long before physical death – and the parting itself, relies on complex understandings and skills, well beyond the reach of Benthamite regulation. (Jordan, 2000, p 89)

For the individual practitioner it is not just understandings and skills that are at stake but the need to relinquish the delusion that all unhappiness or discomfort or ill-health can ultimately be dispelled. This widespread fiction sustains optimism for a while but at a high price: the loss of contact with the painful reality of suffering and the knowledge that many of the people who seek help from social and healthcare services have problems so severe that they will never be 'saved' or 'cured'. At best their difficulties may be moderately alleviated by small, practical measures, and by the patient, unspectacular process of emotional 'holding'. This is not a counsel of despair but a recognition that the goal-oriented activism fostered by the 'what works' culture is premised on the omnipotent assumption that a solution can always be found if personal ingenuity, material resources and the will to change can only be mobilised. The danger in this delusion is that the therapeutic potential of the helping relationship is disregarded, the time it takes is underestimated, and what *can* be done is not valued.

The theme of modernisation (DoH, 1998) occupied the millennial conference of the Association of Teachers in Social Work Education which, rather than opening with the customary address on teaching or practice, devoted its initial keynote session to a presentation on the planned work of the National Training Organisation for Personal Social Services. This is charged with workforce planning, setting of standards and overseeing a National Vocational Qualification framework, which will further extend and rationalise competency-based training at pre- and post-qualifying levels. The lack of debate from the floor seemed to indicate an audience that was distinctly underwhelmed. However, on the second day, Michael Leadbetter, Director of Essex Social Services, helped to restore the power of speech by asking a series of questions:

- Why were we producing newly qualified social workers devoid of psychological understanding?
- Why was their intellectual ability to analyse complex issues so low?
- Why did they appear to have such limited self-awareness?
- Why were they so inflexible, beaten down and ill-prepared to cope with a performative environment?
- Where were the vision, drive and creativity?
- Why was it nowadays assumed that practitioners only needed line management, rather than professional, supervision?

Regulation clearly *is* one way to hold professionals accountable although it may substitute for an internalised sense of authority and responsibility. However, it has now become a movement for standardisation, particularly of the training curricula, and is unlikely to do much to stimulate creativity and vision. As such it is entirely in line with a preference for outcome-led enquiry, quantitative measurement and instrumental orientations to task which have characterised reforms in the education of helping professionals over more than a decade. This is a topic which has been well aired elsewhere (for example, Clarke, 1995; Pietroni, 1995; Dominelli, 1996; Froggett, 1997).

Defences against uncertainty

There is cause for concern that regulation has itself become a socially structured defence against the anxieties of a world perceived as insecure and uncertain. It is provoked by the unpredictability of the socio-economic environment, and also by a desire to control the untidily diverse and fallible 'human resources' on which health and welfare services depend. Rather than regarding differences of approach as indicative of imaginative potential, there is an attempt to codify knowledge, skill and behaviour, and prescribe the framework within which they are transmitted. Yet divergences within and between health and welfare professions remain startling.

Huntington's (2000) vertical study of a social services department, undertaken in the late nineties, examined the interpretation of legislation relating to children and families at different levels in the organisation and found significant differences of perspective on the meaning and feasibility of the reforms. Froggett's (1999, 2000) study of an attempt to change the organisational culture of a department highlighted the ways in which such differences can complicate the best-intentioned efforts. Davies (2000a) points to the rifts that opened up between practitioners and managers with the restructuring of both health and social services in the eighties and early nineties. Since policy can be evaluated so differently by executives with career interests in aligning themselves with political power, and practitioners who implement it on the ground, she asks whether policy making was ever a rational process. She refers to Simon's (1958) notion of 'good-enough' rationality, which informs the art of the possible rather than idealised pictures of rational choice. Although formal techniques of statistical modelling and expert option appraisal are nowadays very much in vogue, sceptical studies of the policy-making process (Lindblom, 1959) have described it as 'the science of muddling through'.

There is little reason to suppose that this has changed. Policy-led predictions are seldom borne out because implementation encounters complex variables and conflicting agendas. Some are well elaborated – others barely acknowledged, even by contenders themselves. One has only to consider the complex constellation of opinion that informed the community care legislation. Competing priorities related to costs, quality of care, de-institutionalisation and public safety. It is doubtful whether anyone accurately anticipated the results. Concerns have focused on the homelessness, dangerousness and fecklessness of people released from long-stay institutions and the indifference of the public, or the niggardly resources available to help people achieve a reasonable quality of life.

It may be better to acknowledge that the illusion of predictive power reinforces a desire for certainty and the security of procedures, standards, benchmarks, guidelines, and externally validated mechanisms of quality assurance. However, this may ultimately undermine the capacity of practitioners to deal with the uniqueness and complexity of each case and of what Clarke and Stewart (2000) call the 'wicked issues' – those which yield neither to measurement nor to standardisation and yet probably account for the bulk of their work. Handling these issues requires acknowledgement of the partial nature of our understanding even as we endeavour to grasp the whole and the ability to tolerate not knowing even though we must act. This is the basis for an openness to new situations and other people which allows learning from experience. The difficulties of maintaining this openness are compounded by the shifting professional boundaries in lateral relations between practitioners while the vertical relations of established organisational hierarchies remain rigid, precisely because of their concern to implement the top-down approaches to professional governance which are in vogue. Finlay (2000) argues that these hierarchies will need to change, giving way to flexibility between health and welfare occupations, holistic approaches to patient and client care and eventually reductions in professional territorialism. However, my own interprofessional students complain that things on the ground get no easier. Arguments over financial responsibility at managerial level are complemented by competing approaches to practice, and pervasive irritability and mistrust. Pressures towards equalisation of relationships with service users in a cost-cutting environment lead to the use of unqualified and low paid care workers, overseen by trained colleagues who have ever fewer opportunities for hands-on work. Assertions that professionals are over-invested in their own disciplines continue, and allegations of blinkered, demeaning and stigmatising practice have become repetitive. Under what conditions might differences come to be regarded as a resource rather than an obstacle to fruitful collaboration?

Reflective practice

Reflective practice is sometimes advanced as a response to these difficulties. It represents an alternative to proceduralism and excessive reliance on regulation, and may well be a more realistic response to risk and uncertainty. Ixer (1999) provides an overview of recent work starting with Schon's (1983) seminal contribution. Schon, who considered a number of professions, distinguished the technical rationality of the academy from the experientially grounded knowledge of the practitioner. In asking how practitioners use experience in practical decision making, he posed the problem of how knowledge already acquired from past practice is brought to bear on each novel situation without a lengthy recapitulation of prior learning. As Ixer points out, Schon's formulation of 'reflection-in-action' evokes something of the sensation of thinking on one's feet, and the absence of explicit theorising – but does not really clarify the nature of reflection itself. Boud et al (1985) introduce the question of affect and suggest that reflection involves a return to experience and attention to the feelings that it arouses. Brockbank and McGill (1998) implicitly recognise the problem of resistance, arguing that once challenged – for example in relation to racism – one is faced with a choice: to retreat, or to accept learning at a deeper level. In other words, learning involves moral thinking in the context of personal biographical experience, conducted in an inner conversation and in dialogue with others.

Strangely enough, there is no reference in this debate to Mattinson's (1975) work, which considers the reflective process by taking the reflection metaphor seriously. Although rational, critical thinking may be an aim, she shows that its experiential basis lies in the unconscious communications whereby the practitioner picks up and mirrors, without knowing it, the feeling states of the client. The supervisor may in turn mirror the social worker and if this is not recognised it will lead to collusion – for example in scapegoating, or the denial of negative feelings. However, in good psychodynamic supervision, the supervisor considers her own feelings together with the information presented. She brings a particular kind of attention to bear on the matter, which can be reflected back and made available for interpretation. In this way the reflective chain involves an iterative movement between inner and outer experience, between emotion and cognition. The words to express it are found through dialogue.

R was summoned to visit the mother of a young man, who had suffered a number of schizophrenic episodes and who was managing, with her help, in a small flat. It seemed a good arrangement, and the few skirmishes with neighbours and landlord over loud music and late rent, were common enough among young people. R was exasperated at having to meet and talk about these trivialities – the mother seemed over-protective and there were more pressing things to do. She arrived to find a small precise woman with a neat front room who revealed no personal information but quietly repeated that she wanted social services to take charge of a list of minor practical problems. Despite the open window, R felt suffocated by a deadness in the air and wanted to get away from her. She left feeling oppressed by the small problems and ungenerously concluded that the mother was enough to make anyone ill. Later, in supervision, R felt remorse for being so unfair, and determined to take her requests seriously (by which she meant literally). She reported them without comment, said she would think about how to accommodate them, and tried to change the subject. Her supervisor, however, picked up her sense of deathliness and invited her to consider what it might mean. She went back in a more questioning frame of mind. This time the mother told her story. She had cancer and was dying. She expected it to be soon. She had not been able to bring herself to tell her son, and she was concerned about much more than his ability to cope with the mundane details of day-to-day living. She was asking for help with a significant, practical and emotional task.

The emphasis on reflective practice may offset tendencies to mechanistic and formulaic proceduralism. It may even validate critical thinking. However, its potential will be dissipated if it is piously nominated as a self-evident virtue with little understanding of the effort it requires in respect of emotional and analytical engagement, or the organisational resources necessary to sustain it. In the example above, R was not just acting on 'intuition' or 'following a hunch'. She was being invited to identify and overcome her own resistance, and consider it in the light of other information. Specific projections and counter-projections were in play. She was a harassed practitioner warding off a sense of powerlessness in relation to chronic and incurable conditions through a self-important activism, while this self-contained and reticent woman was conveying, in terms which she could neither comprehend nor ignore, a deathly anxiety. Although R could not immediately articulate this and her initial response was avoidant, she had access to an interpretive process to help her – or rather impel her – to think about it. The dialogue was not primarily an intellectual exchange but arose out of a disjunction between the shape of the mother's narrative, or lack of it, the feelings it induced and her palpable reluctance to consider these – her attempt to foreclose on thought by deferred action. Although the purpose of the conversation was to bring this to conscious awareness and express it in words, the process was by no means confined to language.

A renewed emphasis on language and meaning is to be wholly welcomed and is one of the strengths of social constructionism. Parton and O'Byrne (2000) ask what social constructionism might mean for practice, and acknowledge that this line of thinking has lent itself more readily to critique than to positive contributions. Following Rosenau (1992) they have embraced an 'affirmative' post-modernism. This differs from the despair of the sceptics whose obsession with the destructive elements of modernity has echoed in the nihilist tenor of their manifesto: death of the subject, death of history, death of metaphysics. Rather, it is a postmodernism that seeks out the creative opportunities in an environment of risk and uncertainty. From this perspective, Parton and O'Byrne reaffirm the importance of process and the possibility not just of deconstruction, but of reconstruction. The understanding that human beings are creatures of context leads to an insistence not only on their differences from one another, but on their irrevocable interdependence. Above all, the discrediting of claims to a simple, and unitary truth demands of them responsibility and moral choice.

One of the emancipatory implications of social constructionism is that it subverts taken-for-granted assumptions about the world. Recognition of the socially constructed nature of boundaries, customs and the moral order gives rise to demands for the right to be different and a refusal to privilege a quest for certainty and rectitude. The approved state of mind for the postmodern subject is ambivalence – thus equipped she is able to forego the reassurance of foundational truths and accommodate the inescapable ambiguity, doubt and complexity that characterise the human condition. All knowledge is fluid, all is contestable and permanently open to revision. With the demise of external sources of authority, whether in science or historical tradition, there is a turning away from the foundational impulses of welfarism: community and solidarity. The reference points from which the post-modern subject takes her bearings are 'choice, self-realisation and self-agency'. Following through the logic of their interpretation of postmodernism, Parton and O'Byrne orient themselves towards this fully differentiated self whose interdependence with others is constructed pre-eminently in the realm of conversation and shared meaning. They appreciate the role of the practitioner in engaging with the 'storied' nature of lives, and the possibilities of personal reinvention through the narrative reconstruction of selves.

Although their point of departure is different to mine and I have reservations about their lack of depth psychology, their quest for an emancipatory practice, their grounding in interpretive social science and their accent on interdependence leads them in directions which in some ways, though not others, are similar. I regard this as another indication of an emergent paradigm based on (differentiated) attachments and (reflective) solidarity. Most importantly, their preoccupation with language and meaning leads them to emphasise the communicative nature of social work and to advocate dialogical approaches to practice based on active listening, reflection and conversation. In particular, they recover two major themes that I regard as central to a psychosocial understanding: an ethic of care and an insistence on the artistry of practice, and especially its affinity for narrative. However, despite my sympathy for these indications, I share with Clarke (1998) an unease about the unreal 'weightlessness' of social constructionism.

A fascination with language may leave pre-linguistic dimensions of experience obscured from view so that emotions are merely language games, the problem may be unrelated to the solution, and while the past is acknowledged, one skips lightly on to new possibilities. In Parton and O'Byrne's version, constructionism comes very close to the wish for 'constructiveness', which is reflected in the allure of brief solution-focused therapy, as if clients are all suffering temporary setbacks, inconvenient habits or bounded problems in living, and can easily rethink their situation. The performance of the self can always be restaged and identities reinvented. The two case studies provided as exemplars of constructive social work are equally light and bounded. The first deals with the troubles of an essentially stable family with their two adopted teenagers; the second with the painful decision of a young woman agreeing to the adoption of her baby. While these are extremely delicate situations, they are considerably less complex than the work that takes place with disturbed people who have multiple problems, histories of abuse or neglect, and highly chaotic lives. They are also relatively free from coercion and hostility. There is little sense of the intensity of emotions, of the fact that moving on requires mourning for lost attachments and versions of the self in which we may be deeply invested. Equally there is little indication of how to work with the negative. We do not simply overcome our limitations and let go of our hatred and destructiveness because we alight on a better story of who we are. Nor do we easily transcend material and social lack. Social constructionism tends to lose sight of the fact that there are parts of the self that are hidden from view and hard to reach, and deprivations that leave permanent scars. Clarke draws attention to the fact that discourse and social constructions may be mutable but they also solidify, or contain traces of the past which leave imprints, a substratum of experience that is resistant to reconstruction. Poverty, he reminds us, "is a truth produced by particular discursive strategies, it is a social construction – and people die from it" (1998, p 183).

Interdependence, dialogue, creativity, engagement and tolerance of uncertainty are in danger of becoming new clichés which will be emptied of meaning if they are disconnected from their anchors in experience. They are deceptively easy to invoke, but extraordinarily difficult to achieve. Attempts to equip the novice practitioner reveal the depth of the problem, because they are not competencies but capacities that can only be developed within a relational context which is not well supported by current institutional structures or training protocols. Posing the problem at the level of cognition and language assumes that acknowledging that we are all interdependent makes it really feel so, or exhorting someone to tolerate uncertainty means they can simply adopt this as a useful attitude when contemplating the unknown. The nurses, social workers and voluntary sector staff attempting to deliver aspects of healthcare within a particular area know very well that their work should interconnect and that it would be better to trust one another. They may even work in structures that lay the framework for interprofessionalism, but this is not enough to make it happen. As for dialogue, who in a democracy would be opposed? Who would seriously argue nowadays against the engagement that is required to make partnership a reality? Is there anyone left who does not extol the virtues of creativity? It seems to me that there is nothing to be gained in understating the sheer psychological difficulty of developing and maintaining these capacities. Changing systems and structures can go part of the way towards facilitating a new mindset but can also divert attention from inner sources of resistance. The ability to think holistically, entertain new perspectives and bring in outsiders, all require a willingness to cross intellectual, social and emotional boundaries to make new links.

Some of the obstacles to the thinking required come from what Bion (1967,1970) called 'attacks on linking'. In his attempt to understand the internal constraints on thought, Bion observed that linking is not only obstructed by intellectual limitations, but by internal censorship induced by anxiety. In this instance, the anxiety of crossing boundaries and encountering other professional cultures is potent. It occurs when organisations or professional disciplines fail to provide an environment that offers containment for the fragmented projections of its members. In such situations it is unlikely that they can achieve the integration of thought and feeling essential to reflective practice. As described in Chapter Two, Bion's model for the container was the nursing mother who responds to the disorganised projections of her baby with a particular kind of attentiveness which he calls reverie. It is as if she transforms or 'metabolises' the child's primitive and undigestible proto-thoughts through emotionally attuned reception. They can then be made available to the infant in a less threatening form and re-introjected as a basis for thinking. Because these fragments have now been contained, they can be brought into relation with one another – thereby losing their character as random, threatening 'bizarre objects'. As the infant's anxiety reduces s/he is eventually able to link experiences to thoughts and thoughts to words. A dynamic and useful relation is established between container and contained which eventually allows the playful process of symbolisation and its expression in language to begin. Central to this is the capacity both to distinguish and make links between inner and outer worlds and between representation and reality.

In adult life we constantly make use of containers, creating them for ourselves when we feel stressed, disoriented and unable to see the connections between things that do not add up. Examples might be music, hot baths, walks in the countryside, people who listen to us. I once worked in a child protection team that had been in a state of high anxiety about the introduction of yet more child protection procedures, escalating workloads, and the development of a blame culture. People were struggling with the frictions of joint working with police and health professionals. There was a widespread feeling that management neither understood nor cared about the nature of the pressures, and careers were on the line if mistakes were made or forensically significant evidence was missed. Particular fearfulness surrounded the interviewing of children who had disclosed sexual abuse. In this climate one might have thought that any clue would be seized upon, and indeed social workers were being accused in the press of imagining child abusers in every closet. Nevertheless, an experienced and usually meticulous colleague came into the office one day in a state of agitation. She had been at home, musing in the bath on a conversation with a small boy, and realised that he had been communicating to her that he was being abused by a family member. It was only by recreating a containing environment and a state of mind which allowed the emotionally engaged attentiveness that recalls reverie, that she was able to make the links. This capacity for linking inner and outer experience and for representing it in language or some other symbolic form is something that the practitioner shares with the artist.

The uncertain arts of practice

Talk of practice as a form of artistry has receded with the resurgence of empiricism, behaviourism and the increasing momentum of an evidence-based research agenda. However, postmodernism has led to a renewed awareness of the aesthetic dimensions of experience and their contribution to emotionally grounded reflection and reflexivity. In particular, the use of stories to arrive at shared meaning has been explored in social work and welfare (Bach, 1993; Saleeby, 1994; Sheppard, 1995; Booth and Booth, 1996; Parton and O'Byrne, 2000), in nursing (Benner, 1984), in medicine (Tannenbaum, 1994), and in psychotherapy (Held, 1995). Casework is an intrinsically biographical method, where the intersection of the narratively structured experience of practitioners and clients informs the process of therapeutic reflection, and indeed the momentum and modality of the work. Although there are variations in narrative approaches, there are important commonalities of concern – notably the insistence on the dialogical, communicative nature of practice and the importance of the relationship between participants. The narrative turn is supported by developing research interests in biographical methods: for example, Chamberlayne and King's (2000) micro-sociological study of the impact of social change on the lives of individual carers and the work of the Centre for Biography in Social Policy at the University of East London. Hollway and Jefferson (2000) have bravely pushed the boat out further by proposing the 'free association narrative interview', in which unconscious dynamics can be foregrounded. Chamberlayne and Froggett (forthcoming) are currently using biographical methods in organisational evaluation.

Debates as to whether practice is an art or science have a venerable history. Martinez-Brawley and Mendez-Bonito Zorita (1998) trace them from the earliest years of welfare work. They show that while the art-like dimensions of practice have sometimes been regarded as a strength, they have been undervalued since the rise of the scientific paradigm in the thirties, and then with renewed emphasis from the sixties onwards. Sheldon's (1978) scientific approach, aiming at precise knowledge and predictive power, was countered by Jordan's (1978) insistence that practitioners must be open to confusion and doubt, and might more usefully be informed by literature and poetry. This debate has rumbled on and acquired renewed salience in the context of the 'what works' mindset that informs much current evaluation. In engaging with the limitations of scientific perspectives and behaviourist models of practice, post-positivists have searched for methods that are congruent with the uncertain and imperfect data that practitioners work with. Munro (1998), for example, has proposed the use of Bayesian probability theory in an attempt to develop statistical methods able to deal with such data. However, a stream of authors (for example, Timms, 1968; Imre, 1984; Weick, 1990; Kilty and Meenaghan, 1995) have argued that scientific methods are not well suited to uncertain and unstructured domains such as the human emotions and relationships that are at the centre of practitioners' concerns, and have done little to make social workers into better helpers. Insofar as these are removed from the particularity of experience, the effect has been to distance practitioners from the interaction of the helping relationship. Critical non-positivist social science – which is potentially closer to social work in that it is occupied with meaning, culture and interpretation – may continue to influence the academy but is progressively marginalised in a field where it yields to managerialist preoccupations with outcome measurement.

Views of practice as a form of artistry drew on Polanyi's (1967) insight into the importance of tacit knowledge. With this understanding, practice knowledge could be construed as bringing together intuition, craft and logical discipline-based reasoning. The subjectivity of the practitioner or researcher came into the frame and hence an appreciation of reflexivity. Writers on the artistic dimensions of good practice have been alert to the fact that while talented practitioners must work within clearly defined parameters, they are often reflectively idiosyncratic in their approach to individuals, drawing as much on their own biographical resources as those of the people they try to help. A number of authors (Rapoport, 1968; Timms and Timms, 1977; Heineman, 1981; Goldstein, 1990) have lamented the loss of confidence in the art-like qualities of professional practice, since it is these that accommodate indeterminacy and complexity. However, the most detailed and authoritative argument, within social work at least, has come from England (1986).

England bemoaned the 'inflated respect' for the social sciences and saw confinement within them as a form of penance for the supposed intellectual 'softness' of social work as a discipline. He considered that this had led to the neglect of other more relevant areas of knowledge. Although references to the artistic dimension of practice have recurrently peppered the literature, they have too often been to its unfathomable aspects, so that the use of the term 'art' becomes a dustbin for the subjective, synonymous with 'flair'. Note that England is not recommending an instrumental use of art as yet another item in the toolkit, he is suggesting that it has an *immanent* relationship to practice. While this is a complex matter, his argument relates to the use of the whole self in perception, interpretation and the communication of meaning. For England, the artist and the good social worker share an ability to mobilise all of their faculties in order to understand and express experience with intense and imaginative force. The aim in both perception and interpretation is always to behold the object in as nuanced a way as possible, to make sense of it and to express this with a vitality that draws in the other. This is a recognisable description of the purpose of literature, visual art and the essentially dramaturgical arts of practice.

Although England does not himself venture into psychoanalytic theories of aesthetic experience, his work leads the reader in that direction. Such approaches have the virtue of allowing us to specify with more precision the ways in which the faculties are brought into play when 'the whole self' is given over to sense-making. They also shed some light on the ways in which aesthetic sensibility enables us to grasp the complex 'layered' nature of experience. Robinson (1997) considers Freud's (1907) conception of the 'tolerance of artistic intelligence' is useful in thinking about the different kinds of mental process that are involved. He sees it as an ability to access and shape inner states through "a controlled simultaneity of conscious and unconscious processes" (p 516), which the artist then makes available in symbolic form. This involves bringing together the non-discursive primary process that is so often glossed over as 'merely' intuitive or emotional, and discursive, rational, secondary process. It is this linking – a forcing together of different levels or domains of experience – that can be so disturbing in art. As so many have done, Robinson turns to the complexity of Shakespeare's sonnets and Hamlet's character and motivation for an example, but for sheer economy and wit I cannot resist quoting from Geertz's *Notes on the Balinese cock-fight* (the punning apparently works to the same effect in English and Balinese):

> The disquietfulness arises, 'somehow' out of a conjunction of three attributes of the fight: its immediate dramatic shape; its metaphoric content; and its social context. A cultural figure against a social ground, the fight is at once a convulsive surge of animal hatred, a mock war of symbolical selves, and a formal simulation of status tensions, and its aesthetic power to force together these diverse realities. The reason it is disquietful is not that it has material effects (it has some, but they are minor); the reason that it is disquietful is that in joining pride to selfhood, selfhood to cocks, and cocks to destruction, it brings to imaginative realisation a dimension of Balinese experience normally well obscured from view. (1973, p 444)

Although I cannot compare with anything so immediately colourful, it seems to me that practice situations often produce similar conjunctions– surges of primitive feeling and the effort to bring them to an adequate symbolic expression – usually in language, but sometimes in tacit 'rituals' and the use of these to enact and explore differentials of power and status.

One teenage girl who struggled with terrifying levels of rage was in complete denial about the abuse that she had suffered in her family. She was easily tipped into what the staff in her children's home called 'tantrums', although the term was – if such a thing is possible – an aggressive euphemism, which infantilised her while masking the fear, among those who were in its path, of her violence. For a long time the staff who worked with her felt frustrated and disheartened. When the shift occurred it was indicated not by a cessation of attacks– which were usually on the fabric of the home – but by a change in their 'random' quality. She began to throw plant pots, to the extent that there was a move among the staff to remove them all. They decided instead to explore their latent meaning: a metaphor of growth, or self-containment, or dependence and care, or middle-class taste. They also recognised value in the ritualisation of aggression. This 'binding' of emotion to a particular object and sequence of behaviour had begun to acquire a dramaturgical shape, a symbolic structure, which could be explored and thought about.

Kaminsky (1985) relishes the opposing stereotypes of the 'wild man' of art: the irritable, rebellious, impassioned misfit, and the social worker: intelligent, humane but basically conformist. He looks for the common ground on which their 'marriage' might be based and finds it in their respective roles as 'secretaries of the interior'. Whereas social workers stand on the boundary as society's 'delegates' to the hinterland of the ghettoised, marginalised and excluded, the artist brings back material from the "inner wilderness that's been pushed beyond the borders of our sanitised urban lives" (p 21). The sympathies of the artist have often been aroused by a concern for poverty. Kaminsky cites Blake, Wordsworth, Whitman, and William Carlos Williams who was both obstetrician and poet. The list is potentially much longer. However, a bohemian fascination with low life should also be taken into account, even though this need not have any altruistic motive. Many artists seem to have been compelled both to move among the excluded and to mine the excluded parts of the self. In Segal's (1986, 1991) view the artist is drawn to mental suffering, confronts it and represents it in work, which is therefore an attempt to repair or give form to loss or to a damaged inner world. Williams Carlos Williams described his mission as a poet "to salvage, to complete, to repair" (cited in Kaminsky, 1985, p 23).

So far in this chapter and the previous one I have drawn attention to the emergence or re-emergence of a number of themes in current thinking about the future of welfare, all of which attempt to move beyond the limited equity and individualising effects of the modernisation agenda. This consists of top-down governance of the welfare professions, pervasive regulation, centralised command management, technical–rational models of service delivery, standardised competence-led training curricula, consumer rights and interest-based models of partnership and participation. The alternative ideas discussed do not as yet cohere into a programme. They bear on the ethical basis for welfare, the pitfalls and possibilities of partnership and participation, the importance of language, meaning and narrative, and the art-like dimensions of practice. They are inspired by the notion of differentiated equality and the hope that alternative forms of welfare might promote greater social solidarity based on recognition and interdependence. A central argument of this book is that however persuasive the principles, they will only inform the development of a reparative culture if the commitment to collective welfare arises from, and fosters, a particular state of mind characterised by genuine acceptance of difference, compassion, generosity and an ability to value the vulnerable and dependent aspects of self and others. In Kleinian terms, this state of mind arises from depressive capacities for relatedness which arise in the course of ordinary human development, but which are difficult to maintain in groups and organisations and even more difficult in political life.

Community and the third sector

Practices of recognition have been found within the voluntary sector whose partial insulation from the political pressures which drive statutory organisations has sometimes allowed a little room for manoeuvre. Such agencies have made use of this leeway in order to treat users as subjects around whose needs and aspirations individualised support could be invented. The negotiation of clearly defined service contracts has curtailed this area of relative freedom and imported personnel with business and accountancy skills, rather than a sense of active citizenship (Davies, 2000b). Nevertheless, voluntary projects lose their rationale if they cease to define themselves in terms of dialogue and responsiveness to the people they exist to help. Older organisations within the sector have struggled to hold onto established roles. Family service units, for example, attempt to combine a preventive role with social facilities, counselling and training in parenting skills, while working in conjunction with statutory services who are preoccupied with their coercive and correctional responsibilities. However, even within services wholly funded and managed by local authorities, there have been differentiated forms of provision such as outreach work, family centres, day centres and community-based leisure projects, which have allowed the preventive to co-exist with the protective. These have often been used to imaginative effect but are vulnerable to excessive regulation. Ensuring the preservation of supportive and therapeutic principles together with individualised and flexible forms of care demands considerable creativity. The juxtaposition of different kinds of services in allowing a division of labour between informality and nurturing on the one hand, and the exercise of formal statutory responsibilities on the other, allows for varied models of partnership and participation.

Much has been written of participation – a critical ingredient in the development of any welfare democracy that aims to ensure individualised responsiveness while sustaining social bonds. For example, Barnes and Prior (2000) have identified an emergent new paradigm of participatory services based on the notion of active citizenship. Peterson and Lupton (1996) have written of the centrality of citizen participation in the new public health. Both have drawn attention to the tension between the inclusive rhetoric of some recent initiatives and the potentially coercive overtones of the duty to participate. The problem may lie in the juxtaposition of a discourse of participation with one of contractual rights and entitlements. An abstract and individualised framework of rights cannot sustain either the idea of genuine individuation (which may include one's desire not to participate, partner or be empowered) or the social commitment which gives meaning to these activities. What this discourse lacks is a means of identifying the psychosocial linkages that allow people to move from a privatised sense of their predicament to a free assumption of partnership with a public agency. A precondition for a personally meaningful participation is a sense of recognition, which in turn depends on the knowledge that one moves in a compassionate rather than coercive environment, and that this demands neither pity nor charity but the space to be a subject – the 'source' rather than the 'object' of understanding (Smith, 2000).

In a useful discussion of recognition in social policy, Williams (1999) underlines the importance of democratic welfare politics and civil campaigns in raising the questions and demands which have effectively placed this issue on the agenda. She identifies a number of principles for welfare which arise from the everyday claims-making activities and values of groups and communities. These often challenge or supplement expert knowledges and in doing so become a force for democratisation in provider–user relations. The principles identified include an acknowledgement of interdependence as an alternative to enforced or denigrated dependency; the reassertion of care as a relationship rather than merely an (undervalued) activity; an understanding that the connection between intimacy and care should invoke commitment, negotiation, consent, and trust; respect for bodily integrity; acceptance of the transnational nature of welfare and voice for the many diverse groups who use or need services.

In order to make an otherwise abstract and speculative discussion more concrete, I shall refer in some detail to a particular community-based project which has attracted considerable interest and funding, and claims to have a distinctive way of working. I do not suggest that a whole welfare system should be built on this particular model, but I do identify some of its more promising principles and features.

Hughes and Mooney (1998) juxtapose different discourses of community: on the one hand, the conservative moral communitarianism that achieved some popularity in the late 20th century and influenced Blair governments; on the other, the radical Left pluralism that emphasises the constantly shifting nature of communities as a source of activism and alternative vision. The former emphasises the organic solidarity of family and surrounding networks held together by tradition, place and a strong sense of moral obligation. The latter recognises the fluid ground of grass-roots organisations, movements, and campaigns that make demands of the state and find expression in self-help, advocacy, voluntary and campaigning organisations. It is clear that in either case, community is a normative concept lending itself at times to sentimentalisation. In one or other of its forms, it appears to be indispensable for the imagination of new social relations of welfare. The pervasive emotional investment in the idea of community must derive from its connotations of social attachment and solidarity, even where the reference is to virtual communities of choice, in which face-to-face relations are minimal or non-existent. Although the current understandings of community must be in part a political and social construction, dependent on a long line of government-led social policy initiatives, they are widely associated with projects of public participation. Their legitimating power depends on an assumption that communities are, or ought to be, built on relationships of trust where the operation of the market is attenuated or at least subordinated to higher ethical goals.

The Bromley by Bow Centre in the London Borough of Tower Hamlets is not easy to locate in terms of the moral communitarian/radical pluralism dichotomy, crossing boundaries in this, as in other, respects. It draws on early welfare traditions of mutualism and self-help, takes an increasingly proactive role in modelling alternative forms of services, yet it incorporates a GP practice, community nursing and midwifery teams, alongside health networking, arts-based community care projects, craft workshops, a café, surrounding park, luncheon clubs, complementary health facilities, youth projects, and more. It has expanded, partly because it has built workable partnerships, forging alliances with other service providers as well as local businesses; partly because it succeeded in making participation a reality. At the time of writing, it is involved in over a hundred initiatives, with a thousand people from different ethnic communities using its facilities each week. It has also developed a remarkable ability to draw on the biographical resources of its surrounding population, creating local networks which co-opt users and volunteers into projects that they design and carry forward to meet locally identified need. The account that follows depends partly on data that was collected in the course of a biographical study of flagship agencies (Chamberlayne and Rupp, 1999), and partly during the planning of a depth evaluation of the Centre's work.

Art, stories and care

The Centre began in 1984 and initially developed its activities from a rundown church building. From those modest beginnings it has become an integral part of a wider regeneration project involving a range of partnerships with private enterprise and public bodies. It describes its five 'pillars' as health, education, arts, enterprise and the environment and with these broad foundations it works on the principle that everyone has something to contribute. By the standards of most community projects, it has achieved enviable continuity and growth of funding and high levels of involvement from one of the most deprived and ethnically diverse communities in the UK. A tour of the Centre is an experience of high quality architectural design and a place brimming with energy and imagination, yet like all initiatives in the third sector it is obliged to expend immense amounts of time and effort on maintaining and justifying its funding stream, and at times it has been locked in combat with statutory services.

The evaluation in progress (Chamberlayne and Froggett, forthcoming) will try to identify the generalisable features of the model but the Centre has its own view: that the key to their method is the attention paid to interpersonal relations within the project that facilitate the involvement of local people and staff, often dissolving the distinctions by absorbing volunteers into paid work. They have evolved a model of partnership and membership which involves the painstaking, time-consuming acquisition of local experience, and a willingness to take risks and break moulds. On the face of it, some of Williams' (1999) 'good enough principles for welfare' seem to find expression in their work. Most obviously, a determination to give voice to members of the community underlies democratic work processes and is considered as the key to ensuring involvement and ownership. An understanding that the connection between intimacy and care should invoke commitment, consent and trust is reflected in a negotiated rather than procedural approach to information sharing, where ethical dilemmas are likely to be debated through 'cluster' meetings. Respect for bodily integrity acquires a broader meaning by bringing the health-based activities of the Centre into close relation with the creative and social dimensions of life. An acknowledgement of interdependence is perhaps implicit in most third sector projects whose knowledge of the fragility of existence is drawn from their own struggle for survival and their need to form a symbiotic relationship with their constituency. Certainly, the assertion of care as a relationship rather than merely an activity is central, and care is understood in the widest possible sense of caring about the detail and developmental potential of individual lives. As a result, the medical records system has been redefined to include crucial quality of life information such as leisure activities and social networks.

This concern is also immediately visible in an aesthetic self-presentation: in the most degraded of urban environments the Centre is a visual adventure, from the award-winning design of the buildings themselves, to the sculptures which adorn the park, the community garden, the hand-made furniture, the Mediterranean-style courtyard, the minimalist café and even the small ceramic tiles set into the walkways which were designed and fired on the premises. Furthermore, the arts are put to explicitly therapeutic use: the problem of attracting older residents of the area to leg ulcer clinics is addressed via the seductions of a 'young@art group', and the community care project is heavily craft based.

Storytelling, another means of defining an organisational aesthetic, has been of utmost importance to the life of the project. Development of a narrative sensibility conditions its emotional climate. This has operated in a number of ways, enabling the Centre to define its own identity through its signature stories and learn from its own critical incidents, which then contribute to a constructive organisational mythology. It has been more likely to work from its own experiences, relayed as narratively structured exemplars, than from policy. For instance, among the foundational events was the collective caring for a terminally ill woman for whom local authority services had simply not been forthcoming. Members drew a network of people around her and negotiated the care of her children with her extended family. In doing so they worked with a very disturbed woman, validating her wish to offer care, while dealing with her delusion that she was 'called' to be the children's guardian. This experience is reiterated as a seminal part of the collective learning process.

Formative events such as these have become woven into the Centre's memory. In stark contrast to the here-and-now self-presentation of statutory services, its account of itself is predominantly biographical, referring both to its own 'life story' and to those of the individuals who have been a part of it. A sense of movement through time and space has influenced the collective imagination and therefore the practical implementation of its projects. A dance motif was so strongly present in its early period, and with such spectacular success, that the classes coalesced into a school which then hived off to become a separate self-sustaining business. Movement is reflected in the organisation's spontaneous metaphors: flexibility is a form of 'dancing either side of the line' – the crossing and recrossing of boundaries. The Centre conceives of itself as creating 'eddies and flurries of energy'. The moveable canopy that covers the area of the hall normally reserved for worship represents fluidity and light. The nursery lives on the periphery of this space with the children's play providing an energetic counterpoint to the stillness of the central arena. The architectural spaces, many of which are multifunctional, appear to flow into one another. Art work is conceived as 'getting the creative juices going'. One of the founding projects was building a boat, and the Centre's course is seen as a journey. An important phase of rest and reflection was thought of as 'drawing breath'.

It is the visual and narrative aesthetic that seems to bring Honneth's (1995) three dimensions of recognition: love, rights and solidarity, into a coherent relation with one another. Love is revealed as an acknowledgement of the sensual as well as the spiritual nature of human need. Working at the Centre is for many of the staff a vocation, calling for a compassionate attentiveness to both individuals and surroundings and an inclusiveness which has succeeded in drawing in some of the most disturbed people in the community. For some it is also the outward expression of religious faith. The aesthetic informs a respect for the rights of the poorest of people to receive services that are in every way comparable with the best that can be offered, compatible both with dignity and delight. Solidarity is built through creative project work, incorporating users and volunteers in the planning and decision-making processes. It is strikingly evident in the bringing together of communities that do not comfortably share the same cultural space outside of the Centre.

Depictions of inspirational elements of organisational life sometimes sound overly pious and remote from many people's experiences of working with meagre resources in the grim day-to-day reality of deprived communities. Bromley by Bow initially learnt to manoeuvre within the harshly competitive environment of new conservatism. The Thatcher government's determination to roll back public services propelled it towards the business sector while the climate encouraged a local survivalism: the street-level hustling where each muddles through at the expense of the other. This was hostile to the spirit of mutualism and community ownership that the Centre aspired to foster. Since then it has worked out a distinctive interpretation of the New Labour discourse of 'social entrepreneurship', 'social investment' and 'social capital building', but has had to reckon with the relentless extension of regulation, which runs counter to its ethos of innovation. At the same time, it works hard to maintain support from a culturally and ethnically diverse community and from individuals whose involvement in its activities is less to do with politics or 'vision' than 'getting by'. The approach has remained resolutely bottom-up and locally based while taking account of the parameters determined by increasingly prescriptive professional bodies. In addition, it has become a centre for employment and training, drawing in volunteers, validating their skills, providing them with paid work and encouraging them to move on to other opportunities elsewhere. Some of the volunteers have used their work as a route for a Higher National Certificate (HNC) in Public Arts Management. Plans are afoot to develop the training of the health networking team for validation as a HNC by a local university.

Although Bromley by Bow is a particularly ambitious example of an organisation that began as a modest arts-based initiative and has now achieved a national profile, there is no shortage of interest in this kind of work. The community arts-for-health movement, which has grown exponentially in the last decade, has moved beyond its experimental pioneer phase and projects are increasingly undergoing systematic evaluation in order to respond to funding criteria and generalise from their experience. While there are tensions between established evaluation methodologies and the participatory and process-oriented nature of the organisations themselves (Angus, 1999), the increasing interest of government, local authorities and charitable trusts is promising. Such organisations tend to be impatient of the rigid professional boundaries and demarcation disputes that seem to bedevil statutory public bodies. Their small-scale, voluntary nature places them in a position that is privileged, precisely because it is loosely defined. Bromley by Bow's second Director, Alison Trimble, recalls that her job description was a blank sheet of paper and she was advised to put all her plans to one side while for the first three months she watched and listened. Active listening is highly prized because it contains the tensions that arise from the fault lines within communities, and between communities and statutory sources of monitoring and assistance. Although Bromley by Bow is by no means immune to these difficulties, it claims to have created a genuinely dialogical environment, evolving a working style which is well able to accommodate difference (over 50 languages are spoken in the borough). While it incorporates some projects that are group specific or ethnically based, it has allowed a high degree of openness, tolerance and carefully gauged confrontation – even with views to which it is averse. For example, it has dealt with overt racism among users of the Centre in a softer manner than would be admissible in local authority organisations, and claims to have negotiated this most difficult of territories by focusing on the preservation of face-to-face relationships of care. Granted, it operates in a space which is immune to many of the pressures bedevilling statutory services, but small-scale projects are often undermined by factionalism and fission – exacerbated by anxieties about survival.

Beyond the ideal leader

Non-sectarian religious inspiration appears to sit comfortably with social entrepreneurship and motivates a number of the staff. The project could be situated within a long tradition of radical non-conformist work among the poor. Early in its life, Santiago Bell, an exiled Chilean craftsman, imported the influence of liberation theology and the methods of Paolo Friere (1996) but this has not impeded the full participation of people from other faiths and those with no faith. The local Bengali population are particularly well represented among users. Andrew Mawson, the charismatic first Director, and former vicar of the church, was highly critical of the obstructive 'Sargasso Sea' in which public service bureaucracies and churches were equally prone to flounder. Convinced that these institutions created as much poverty as they alleviated, he gathered around him a group of powerful personalities with unusual biographies to take the work of the Centre forward. These were the 'social entrepreneurs', characterised by Leadbeater and Goss (1998) as "restless, creative, lateral thinking rule breakers" (p 15), social dreamers with the capacity to mobilise and create out of thin air.

The romantic heroism in this characterisation begs a number of questions – notably whether the organisation can gain the confidence and momentum to survive a change of leadership and develop a self-sustaining culture that can change and grow. Charismatic leaders have an unusual ability to appeal to the unconscious phantasies of group members, combined with the will to bring them to consciousness and translate them into reality (Gabriel, 1999). They can also be highly narcissistic individuals prone to omnipotence and grandiosity and able to mobilise people precisely through their own identification with such traits. Such people have little ability to cope with failure, often lapsing into contempt for others who appear not to have fulfilled their hopes. Arts-based voluntary projects are often dependent on particular personalities, with serious implications for their continuity (Angus, 1999). However, it may be that in an increasingly regulated and bureaucratised environment, individuals with the capacity to flout convention are essential if the system is not to atrophy. Jordan (2000) counterposes the dreary, rule-bound technocrat sponsored by the regulators to the charisma of the street-credible front-line practitioner. He suggests that it is only through the energies of the latter that 'tough love' policies can be realised. The important issue is whether such people are able to eschew the excitement of 'outlaw' status and work at the boundaries of the possible, without being entirely co-opted and losing their originality and capacity to excite. For this they must ideally be surrounded by a mature work group in which omnipotence and vulnerability check each other so that members can dabble in illusion while continually testing the waters of reality.

Alford (2002) suggests that mature leadership is interpretive and its goal is to make it possible for members of a group to differentiate without defensively opting for a schizoid compromise. In this state the valued individuated part of the self is preserved by withdrawing from the group while the participating self is emptied of vitality. The interpretive leader aims to create and make use of a holding environment, in which these split parts of the self can be reunited, allowing members a more spontaneous personal engagement and creative reality-testing in which they are less inclined to attribute all shortcomings either to one another, to outside rivals, or to the insufficiency of the leadership itself. At issue, is the ability to make use of leadership while maintaining a provisional relationship to it. This seems unlikely in the case of the charismatic in that the seduction of charisma lies in its power to induce followers to transfer onto the leader desires that are related to a primary identification with the pre-oedipal mother (Gabriel, 1999). This identification, which must eventually be ruptured by the realisation that mother is separate and other, remains as an unconscious memory and wish: to be absolutely accepted and perfectly understood by one who is loved and admired as a mirror of one's own perfection. The experience of such leadership is an extraordinarily potent affirmation of the narcissistic longings of followers to be held in unconditional positive regard. Productive use of such a phantasy is only possible to the extent that the transiently creative fiction that one is at the centre of the world, gives way to a realistic ambivalence that recognises limits without being imprisoned by them.

As Hirschorn (1988) points out, the danger of charismatic leadership is that it may lead to excessive dependence, where the idealised leader must be protected at all costs from hostility to authority. This is achieved by splitting and projecting aggression elsewhere. In the case of voluntary organisations, the public sector is an obvious target because of its constrained remit, hierarchical structure, and sharply defined boundaries. There is a temptation to caricature all differences of approach and role as owing to the sclerotic nature of bureaucracy and self-serving interest. The problem is how to create a work culture in which the introjected goodness represented by the charismatic leader can be projected onto the work itself which then becomes the source of fulfilment, reinforced by the fact that it is cherished by others. The leader can then safely depart. The most potent indicator comes through the direct face-to-face approval of those who have valued what one has created. Neither polite praise nor the achievement of disembodied objectives can in themselves confer this recognition of the worth of the product. Welfare organisations that succeed in forming working alliances with those whom they exist to help, may benefit from the credible affirmation that comes from relationships of recognition. This can be trusted because it encompasses knowledge of the struggles and failures on the way. The Centre is now able to periodise its relations to the public sector as falling into three phases in which initial engagement and conflict was followed by a 'stand-off' which in turn has given way to a new search for workable partnerships. It may be that this will allow projections to be retrieved and conflicts over dependency and authority owned by the members. It is notable that the current leadership does not rely particularly on charismatic identification, and the functions of lateral thinking, risk-taking and responsibility seem to be more widely diffused.

Despite some difficulties, the Centre appears to have weathered major changes in leadership style, negotiating the divisions that inevitably open up when unifying personalities leave. It has continued to demonstrate a capacity to identify and nourish potential – not only among the conventionally and recognisably talented, but in the large reservoir of the community, and particularly in its volunteers. The sense that everyone has something to contribute – it is only a matter of finding it – elicits an attentiveness to the qualities and capacities of individuals, an eye for detail and a sense of the obstacles that people routinely face. A fuller understanding of why they are able to continue to do this while so many public and voluntary organisations fail must await further investigation.

The transformative environment

Although the Centre has not theorised its preoccupation with space and boundaries, its commitment to maintaining such beautiful surroundings reveals an intuitive grasp of the importance of a benign environment in unleashing its creative work. In Winnicott's terms, belief in the environment, initially the containing environment mother, is the precondition of all development. This was described in Chapter Two as the continuity and reliability of the facilitating mother as she presides over a potential space in which she takes care not to intrude. Her child is thus allowed to experiment with the relation between internal and external reality, to symbolise, and to discover an imaginative faculty. The potential space is a sphere of illusion in which the infant 'creates' what it finds out of its own desire. It is therefore fundamental to a sense of agency and, according to Winnicott, the psychosocial source of religion, the arts and cultural life. The mother's task is to preserve this arena where "fantasy is more primary than reality, and the enrichment of fantasy with the world's riches depends on the experience of illusion" (Winnicott, 1955, p 153). Picking up on this theme, Hoggett (2000) stresses the importance of illusion within work groups because it allows an 'as if' relation to reality, without which there can be no true innovation. Groups that cannot allow themselves to dream of who they are and what they might do are condemned to routinism and only too often bedevilled by cynicism. In the case of the Bromley by Bow Centre, an insistence on high quality and aesthetically pleasing buildings and materials makes a powerful statement that, alongside its very serious business, it is a space where imaginative potential can be released, effectively a space in which to play.

It seems likely that the Centre functions for many of its participants as a transformational object (Bollas, 1987). In considering the nature of aesthetic experience and its power to induce change, Bollas implicitly develops a justification of profound importance to the arts-for-health movement. He considers the psychodynamics of aesthetic recognition and asks where it comes from. Why is it that a beautiful building, garden, story or poem induces such a moving sensation? Might it be that it acts not so much as an object of desire but as a container of the wish for personal change, stimulating unconscious memories of the first transformational object – the facilitating mother? The primary aesthetic is thus irrevocably linked to an experience of care. The baby internalises the mother's particular attentiveness communicated through the holding, stroking, cooing and feeding and creates out of this a personalised 'aesthetic of being' which patterns all future ways of handling the self and being with others.

When something 'hooks' us as a work of art it evokes an uncanny sense of fusion that holds out a promise of future change. In doing so it stands as an existential reminder of a past anticipation of being transformed by an object, which, although it may never be repeated with such intensity, is unconsciously re-enacted in the giving and receiving of care in later life. This provides a powerful rationale for giving art a central place in caring organisations aiming to be vehicles for personal and social change. Be that as it may, Bromley by Bow's insistence on the aesthetic quality of the space and its equipment has not met with the wholehearted approval of the local public services, constrained by niggardly capital spending budgets and struggling to maintain minimum standards. In this climate it is tempting to lapse into appeals to utility. I was shown the lovely little handmade wooden chairs in the nursery with the slightly apologetic justification that "after all, they have lasted 12 years".

Boundary management and risk

Bromley by Bow is very conscious of its boundaries and the finely tuned judgement constantly required to maintain and breach them as necessary. The commitment to crossing boundaries is the key to their networking and partnership arrangements but constantly imposes risks and strains of its own. In psychodynamic terms, the boundary of an organisation represents the point where the inner and outer worlds meet – effectively the encounter with the reality principle. The task of working at the boundary is then the task of protecting the creative fantasy life of the organisation within, while working through the anxieties that arise as a consequence of the unpredictable world without. In hierarchical, paternalistic organisations this task of boundary maintenance falls to management, leaving the workforce relatively protected from the need to respond to the risks and uncertainties of an uncontrollable environment. While this may reduce the need for defences to manage risk among the workforce, it can also lead them to a certain disengagement from the harshness of reality, paving the way for resentment on the part of the management at their indifference or irresponsibility.

Bromley by Bow operates with the flattish management and diffused decision-making structures, characteristic of post-industrial network-based agencies. Their model of participation stresses the systematic absorption of volunteers and users of the Centre into internal organisational processes. For example, when it became necessary to set up a steering group to oversee the strategic development of a participatory research project, the organisation's instinctive approach was to co-opt the health networkers – themselves the subject of the research – so that it became part of their HNC training experience. Although the theory of participatory research can certainly justify this kind of reflexive approach, I confess I experienced a momentary sense of vertigo at the prospect of loss of control so early in the project, an urgent need to re-establish the locus of responsibility, and fear that working methods in which I had confidence might be derailed by the unknown agendas of others.

All these anxieties had a realistic dimension – after all I was accountable as the budget holder to the funders, as an employee to my university, and as a researcher to my partners and to a wider academic community. At a more primitive level, the fear was to do with lack of trust, a desire to avoid complexity and a reluctance to expose myself to so many imagined sources of aggression. Furthermore I was suddenly burdened by a sense of what it might be like for the next three years to negotiate the culture clash between my own large bureaucratic institution and this open networking organisation which had little regard for orthodox qualifications and authority structures. There was already a worry about how far the university's recruitment policy would conflict with the Centre's hope that local people, possibly without higher education, might be employed within the research project. It dawned on me that something important was being communicated about the nature of obstacles that members of the Centre routinely confront when interfacing with public service bureaucracies – something which had, in fact, been a formative experience for them. I was taking on the feelings that were being made available to me in an unconscious initiation ritual: loss of control, the aggression of others and weariness at the prospect of swimming against the tide. I recognised that also in play were my own counter-projections onto this fantasised group in relation to which I, the outsider, risked rejection and persecution. I relate this not because I am more fearful of this kind of situation than the next person, but to illustrate just some of the difficulties which arise when boundaries are called into question.

An organisation that can juggle adeptly with such issues and turn them to advantage must have a sophisticated ability to negotiate inner and outer dimensions of mental and organisational space. Hirschorn (1988) makes it clear that the boundary is the most anxiety-provoking point of the organisation and there is always a temptation to retreat from it into the interior where one can relinquish responsibility to a benevolent caretaker. However, he also suggests that the post-industrial milieu continually tests the social defences in that the complexity and uncertainty of the work environment imposes on people the need to confront others without the relative safety of stable roles or procedures. Insofar as it succeeds in helping its staff and volunteers to work creatively under these conditions, the Centre appears to facilitate what Miller (1993) calls a 'post-dependency culture' which relies on the development and exercise of personal authority by its staff and a commitment to task over and above the agency. Miller considers that such a culture is facilitated by the post-industrial environment itself. He suggests that declining expectations of long-term, full-time jobs encourage the workforce to adopt increasingly instrumental attitudes to employing organisations. Such a stance suggests the absence of a need for organisational containers and is problematic in the field of social care. It is certainly not in evidence at the Centre, which works hard to maintain them, relies on vocational commitment and often draws staff, their families and social networks into its orbit.

The difficult question, then, is how to create a culture that is both reparative and developmental, and able to contain the anxieties that inevitably follow from a continual engagement with risk and uncertainty. Organisations able to manage this have a crucial role to play in a risk society, not only in picking up the casualties but also in developing and modelling a new work culture and politics. In effect, Bromley by Bow must keep its focus on an ever-changing task that constantly requires new resources and initiatives. This is not achieved through the denial of dependency needs but rather through a mature acceptance of interdependence both within and across boundaries. The sophisticated boundary management offers containment for members and safeguards internal functioning while remaining outwardly responsive to the whole of the social field in which they operate. It also allows the organisation to remain grounded in its own accumulated experience and use this as the basis of an imaginative and compassionate relation to an unpredictable wider world.

> As we have seen, a reparative culture rests on the twin pillars of risk and love. Development through work is impossible unless we expose our competence and judgement to the test of those who buy our goods and services. But today too many people face the risks of social degradation and homelessness and never face the more subtle tests of their competence and value. We need to design a system of social supports that helps shape a forgiving economy, that helps people recover from failure and gives them second chances. (Hirschorn, 1988, p 239)

Elements of the reparative culture

This extended example illustrates some of the key features that may allow organisations to establish and sustain relationships of recognition with people who participate, use, and organise their services. Much work remains to be done both in understanding the reparative nature of the Bromley by Bow model itself and the even more complex question of its transferability. However, there are strong indications. All of the following features identified in the preceding sections require and sustain a predominantly depressive relation to reality which avoids splitting, polarisation and scapegoating. The problem is to find and maintain a third position in situations of negotiation and conflict, which continually arise:

- An approach which encourages participants to understand their own welfare in terms of a wider vision of individual and social well-being.
- The capacity to build on the creative possibilities of lateral rather than hierarchical relations, specifically the ability to avoid idealisation and sustain productive partnerships.
- An understanding of how to maintain appropriately porous boundaries, and cross them as necessary.

- A capacity to make use of, and then move beyond, the inspirational potential of good leadership.
- The achievement of a potential space in which the inner organisation can develop its imaginative life while constantly realigning itself with external realities.
- The development of a distinctive organisational aesthetic and ability to become a transformational object for the people who use it and work for it.
- A narrative sensibility that encourages storytelling, reworks the organisation's history, and gauges movement through time.
- An ability to interpret the rights of vulnerable people within a pervasive ethic of care.
- A commitment to individual and community development understood in biographical terms, rather than as the acquisition of skills and competencies.
- Inclusion based on highly individuated recognition of needs and capacities.
- An ability to function in an environment of extreme uncertainty.

Together, these features suggest a reparative organisation that promotes a developmental culture. 'The learning organisation' has unfortunately become something of a management cliché, but the idea has value if it is understood as an attempt to come to an ever-closer understanding of the task. Learning is facilitated not so much by technique or staff development programmes as by an orientation which accepts that complete understanding of the object will always elude the inquirer but that an attitude of ambivalence allows one to see the good, the bad and the indifferent. The process of learning cannot be foreshortened by splitting and projection, with all the attendant over-simplifications. Above all, it requires the ability to suspend omniscience, adopt a basically dependent position of not knowing, and be open to guidance. The emotional climate that allows members to maintain a depressive relation to reality provides a context in which the attendant anxieties can be worked through, splitting maintained at a minimum and the narcissism of leaders and individuals held in check. In organisations oriented to the welfare of others, reparative dynamics are also the interpersonal ground on which an ethic of care can be sustained.

EIGHT

Beyond welfare: the political environment

A Master Swimmer was walking along the side of a swimming pool. He was very handsome and very strong and – it goes without saying – very, very competent in his profession. He had already saved countless people from the waters of the pool and even from the wild sea. Because of his ability to save human lives, everyone loved him.

He was also a political man who never stopped thinking about the people: the people of his little village, the people of his country, the disinherited people of the entire world, especially from Ethiopia and Bangladesh. Because of his political convictions, everyone loved him. He consecrated his life to the people and the people loved him.

This particular day, he was walking along the side of the swimming pool reading the complete works of Marx, Engels, and Mao Tse Tung when, all of a sudden, he heard the cries of a man about to drown because he had fallen into the pool and did not know how to swim. He cried in anguish for help. Instinctively, the Master Swimmer got ready to save him, but on second thought, remembering that he was a political Master Swimmer – and not just any Master Swimmer – he stopped and said to the drowning man:

'Excuse me, dear Sir, but I am a political Master Swimmer and you are nothing but a single individual, when there are at least twenty of you drowning together, then I will be at your service, ready to help you and save your life.'

Augusto Boal, *Playing Boal: Theatre, therapy, activism* (1998a, p 134)

What are the wider political conditions that might facilitate the growth of a reparative culture within welfare organisations? The issues of equality, citizenship and solidarity remain of central importance and demand a framework within which reconciliation of universal welfare provision with a particularistic understanding of individuals and their needs can be achieved (Thompson and Hoggett, 1996). This implies a thick psychosocial understanding of 'differentiated needs' (Williams, 1993) in which material and psychological deprivation are understood to intersect and condition one another. As helping professionals and educationalists constantly rediscover – even apparently generous and enlightened provision often misses its mark and remains unused, at least in the manner intended. Some headway has been made in identifying cultural barriers to accessible services (Froggett, 2001), but this obstacle clearance approach also misses half the point. A theory of recognition directs our attention to the relational nature of human well-being in which the three dimensions of love, rights and solidarity identified by Honneth (1995) are indispensable. A substantive, rather than formal, equality of access to services and resources can only be meaningfully realised in a context that establishes and preserves interpersonal attachments and a culturally mediated sense of belonging to a wider collectivity. The cases of the most poor and marginalised of people can illustrate this most strikingly.

Hussain (2000) investigated the use, or rather non-use, of mental health services among older Pakistanis in a northern English town. Many of them were illiterate, unskilled and living on very meagre incomes. The local health and social service providers had made strenuous efforts to produce culturally appropriate information and recruit professionals from the Pakistani community. Yet these older people preferred to visit healers who advised them in the context of a spiritually significant relationship, together with a variety of charms, potions, exorcisms, incantations and poetic rituals. Although none of Hussain's sample had ever been offered any form of talking therapy, he considered that they were effectively making use of informal culturally attuned 'counselling'.

This was an immigrant population whose life experience had been marked by a profound sense of rupture from kin and country of origin. Life within a Western secular society, along with the daily humiliations of poverty and racism, had imposed considerable strains on their families who were their chief source of support. The sense of fragmentation was particularly toxic within a culture where the experience of daily life would normally be suffused with an awareness of spiritual unity and of the underlying connections between individual and collective, mind and matter, psyche and soma. A rift between any of these could itself be experienced as a form of madness. Exposure to the conventions of Western bio-medicine which assumes just such polarisations only compounds the distress. The healers understood this predicament and aimed to restore a psychosomatic unity through the use of rituals and artefacts which re-established continuity with a viable, yet changing, culture. Equitable service provision is by no means irrelevant to such a marginalised people but it can only be realised through the re-forging of attachments to communities and social networks, and through them, to a valued way of life. In taking their problems to local healers, the older people were seeking recognition of their distress in the context of a relationship that could restore a sense of belonging to a moral and spiritual order.

The fourth section of the grid (Figure 1) suggests the possibility of moving towards social relations of welfare premised not only on equality but, as I have been arguing, on attachment between individuals and communities as the basis of wider networks of social solidarity. In the last decade or so there has been widespread international debate over the role of civil society, and specifically of civic associations, in sustaining the horizontal relationships of cooperation and trust that are thought to be at the root of a healthy democracy. The discussion has been particularly vibrant in America, stimulated by Putnam's (1993) thesis that that there is a close correlation between effective governance and high levels of civic participation. His original research referred to Italian regional government institutions, which looked superficially similar, yet performed very differently:

> You tell me how many choral societies there are in an Italian region, and I will tell you plus or minus three days how long it will take you to get your health bills reimbursed by its regional government. (Putnam, interview, 1995a)

Putnam's argument was that civic associational life, as measured by membership of voluntary civic organisations, was a critical factor not only in promoting individual well-being and localised goodwill, but in building reservoirs of social capital which in turn contribute to social cohesion and political and economic development. The list of possibilities is long and varied: citizens' forums, swimming clubs, women's organisations, boy scouts, charities, amateur dramatics, single-issue campaigns, user groups, tenants associations and many more. In *Bowling alone* (1995b) Putnam turned his attention to the US itself, arguing that modern work patterns, consumerism, privatism and dominance of television as a leisure activity were all resulting in a withdrawal from the civic life that de Tocqueville (1947) had identified with the strength of American democracy in the first half of the 19th century.

This thesis attracted attention from liberals and conservatives alike and influenced the moral communitarianism of the Clinton and Blair administrations. It reflected anxieties about the malignant side of modernisation: its intrinsic indifference to social integration. The hope invested in civil society was that it would result in an era of civic renewal as the basis for social identity and communities of value in a globalised economic order. The 'democratic deficit' would be countered by drawing individuals into active citizenship and thence into political engagement. Informal networks, voluntary organisations and social movements would nourish a dynamic public sphere where processes of collective will-formation could feed into public policy. There is some empirical support for the proposition that membership of civil associations leads to competent pluralist political behaviour, which can be further enhanced by active participation (Almond and Verba, 1989; Dekker and van den Broek, 1998). The assumption is that social networks may be motivated by self-interest but the cumulative effects of repeated engagement, and experience of the reliability of others, establishes trust and a norm of 'generalised reciprocity'. It creates the conditions in which a latent altruism can flourish.

Although public support for explicitly socialist programmes appears to have faltered in the last two decades, new social movements have argued for an expanded civil society in which grass-roots politics can once again flourish. It is hoped that expectations of solidarity and equality might be rekindled in institutional life, and that their horizontal diffusion might re-ignite activism. For Conservatives, preoccupied with the decline of the family and traditional communities of place as a source of moral socialisation, civil associations promise alternative arenas for the transmission of norms and values. For market liberals, the freedom of association facilitates the development of a social entrepreneurship which complements cherished economic freedoms. From all of these viewpoints – though with varying degrees of radicalism – there is the expectation that an extended civil sphere would lead to a retraction of the state and large public service bureaucracies.

In the search for sites of solidarity within pluralist Western democracies there is perhaps a tendency to idealise civil society and to understate the difficulties of overcoming divisions due to very real differences of interest and power. In the political arena, such differences are traditionally expressed through representation and in terms of ideological conflict over alternative programmes. Civil association can in no sense substitute for this contest, where particular interests can be publicly scrutinised with reference to a general good. Political argument moves beyond immediately perceived needs and stimulates the formation of new relations and alliances. The attempt by the New Centre to transcend Left/Right opposition has been associated with reduced levels of electoral engagement and acquiescence of the political classes in the de facto hegemony of global neo-liberalism. However, the drawbacks of party politics are well known: the overshadowing of the process by powerful interests; the incentive for manipulation, bordering on deceit; the limited accountability afforded by elections; and on a global level, the desperation of the permanently excluded. In contrast, civil society promises a more subtle and differentiated expression of opinion from below. Of course, there are no guarantees that this is benign, nor that particularism is free of intense and often violent conflict: the National Rifle Association in the US, the hunting lobby in the UK, the pro-life movement, the animal rights movement, and for that matter football clubs, can all mobilise intensely primitive emotions in their members and opponents. Such associations can create insider mentalities, allowing us to recoil from recognition of the other. It is not just power and the structuring of disadvantage at stake here but the nature of unconscious phantasy:

> We cannot understand the Otherness of the gay male for the heterosexual in this way, or the otherness of the Downs Syndrome child for the child with no learning difficulties. For the other is also a container for my own fear, her difference to me perturbs me at a deeper level, for her Otherness is a reminder to me of what I have repressed in my own identity – my sense of inferiority, my bisexuality, my fear of physical imperfection, my fear of aging and death. In this sense the Other exists as a container for that which I cannot bear, for that which the individual or collective body lacks the capacity to understand as a part of itself. (Hoggett, 2000, p 61)

The problem in civil society, then, is how to establish norms of engagement that preserve the possibility of recognising the self in the other who represents a threat both to identity and passionately held belief. This threat urges dissolution into competing factions, and defensively drawn social boundaries. It poses the dilemma that marks our entry into social life – how to cope with the difference of the other. It returns us to the divisions within the self.

Civil society and the ideal of deliberative dialogue

There is insufficient space here for an extended discussion of democracy and its relation to civil society and welfare institutions. This would be beyond the scope of this book and divert attention from its chief focus: the psychosocial dimensions of welfare practice and organisations. However, it is worth asking what kind of political processes and institutions might facilitate the development of a reparative welfare culture. Clearly, bottom-up influences must play a central role. Interest in the third sector has been stimulated by the perceived failure of large state bureaucracies in the West and the opening up of East European political cultures since 1989. Apart from a widespread disenchantment with big government and recognition of the limitations of representative institutions, its cultural basis has been exploration among community and social movements of direct forms of democracy (Brickell, 2000) and determination to carve out deliberative and associational space.

Theorists of deliberative democracy (for example, Benhabib, 1996; Cohen, 1996) maintain that its purpose in a highly pluralistic society is to transcend the partiality of many viewpoints and maintain a forum dedicated to the pursuit of universal values. In contrast to interest-based democracy, the deliberative ideal relies on a rationalist mode of argumentation which assumes that citizens can directly address the conflict between particular interests from the perspective of a common good. Commitment to open dialogue and adherence to procedures for examining claims and disentangling good from bad reasons allows the emergence of deliberative spaces where public interest is the basis for just decision making. Procedural fairness, providing it is universally upheld, creates the conditions where the 'force of the better argument' can supersede other points of view. Underlying the deliberative process is an assumption that our essential interdependence implies a shared interest in cooperation as a basis for judgement. Although a measure of cooperation is essential for social life, it cannot deny conflicting interests. The deliberative ideal implies an acceptance that one's own viewpoint is partial and will be transcended in the course of collective decision making.

The model retains the fundamental principle of moral respect for individuals and equal rights to participation but differs from liberal democracy in its emphasis on the *process* of collective will formation. It is this that shelters the voices of weaker parties from the undue weight of powerful interests. Commitment to plural values is sustained not by seeking to resolve differences but by universal agreement on the means whereby the confrontation takes place, and the binding nature of decisions so reached. For example, Habermas's (1983) theory of discourse ethics makes a heuristic appeal to the 'ideal speech situation' in which participants strive to remove all non-rational constraints to communication exerted by undue operation of power. Discrimination on grounds of race, gender or other disqualifying ascriptions cannot survive such a test. Blaug (1995) suggests that this can usefully inform anti-discriminatory practice, if systematically applied to decision making in health and social services.

All participants to discussion must ask themselves if the communication is free from the distortions of power, whether this derives from knowledge, status or prejudice. The notion of ideal speech challenges the pervasive instrumentalism of welfare bureaucracies and policy processes which assume the overriding importance of cost containment. It accents the communicative process, which may be more circuitous and take longer than is consistent with efficiency. It supports reflective rather than managerial models of supervision, insists on defensible judgement rather than prescriptive guidelines, and questions an over-reliance on the scientific paradigm. The ideal speech situation is implicitly evoked in the principle of informed consent, which requires optimal understanding of the implications of a course of treatment or action.

Buckinghamshire Health Authority – citizen's jury on back pain

Fifteen jury members were recruited by an independent market research company to reflect the characteristics of the county's population. Their task was to make recommendations on whether the health authority should fund osteopathy and chiropractic for back pain by moving some resources from physiotherapy services. They sat for four and a half days and heard evidence from a range of witnesses. The jury needed to weigh up a complex array of evidence on clinical effectiveness, patient experiences, professional opinions, financial information and epidemiology. Witnesses included two local back-pain sufferers, a GP, an orthopaedic surgeon, a director of public health, a researcher, two finance directors (one purchaser, one provider), a physiotherapist, an osteopath, a chiropractor and a representative from the Back Pain Association. The jury was invited to call extra witnesses of its own choosing. Jurors worked in pairs or small groups to assess what they had heard and prepare questions – this helped to enable everyone to participate. Two independent facilitators helped the jurors to work as a group and supported them through the whole process. The jurors' recommendation was for an integrated evidence-based service for back-pain sufferers incorporating osteopaths and chiropractors as part of a multidisciplinary team. Jury members were subsequently invited by the health authority to join a project group to take this plan forward. (Davies, 2000a, p 313)

Although features of deliberative democracy may be weakly present in larger representative institutions, there is a greater affinity between self-governing associations and the deliberative procedural ideal. Scale is important as there may well be a limit to the size of assemblies that do not distort the reasoning process (Benhabib, 1996). A plurality of modes of association thus widens opportunities for self-expression, particularly within smaller voluntary associations such as citizens' forums, or social movements where the urge towards unity arises from a common mission. Deliberative procedures appear to underlie some local government activity such as the use of public consultation exercises:

> It is through the interlocking net of these multiple forms of associations, networks, and organisations that an anonymous 'public conversation' results. It is central to the model of deliberative democracy that it privileges such a public sphere of mutually overlapping networks and associations of deliberation, contestation, and argumentation. The fiction of a general deliberative assembly in which the united people express their will belongs to the early history of democratic theory; today our guiding model has to be that of a medium of loosely associated, multiple foci of opinion formation and dissemination which affect one another in free and spontaneous processes of communication. (Benhabib, 1996, pp 73-4)

The vision draws its force from an overarching metaphor of the 'network society'. It builds on organisational forms that are sometimes successful in mobilising civic engagement. However, when conflicts in the public domain are depoliticised, such engagement proves difficult to sustain. Public consultation exercises are notorious for attracting desultory levels of participation, mainly from articulate members of the community who benefit through the promotion of private interests such as planning applications. Misuse is evident in 'nimby' ('not in my back yard') phenomena such as opposition to the location of homes for people with learning disabilities or mental health problems.

The acknowledgement that a democratic project must be able to accommodate disagreement regarding visions of the good leads to an 'agonistic' model of deliberative democracy (Benhabib, 1996). The democratic project can be seen as a 'mode of being' which allows us to let go of the conviction that conflicts arising from group identities are capable of ultimate resolution. Benhabib foresees a pluralistic society where rights are actively asserted and contested and subject to perpetual reinterpretation. For Honig (1996) this means giving up the "dream of home" – the yearning to return to "a womblike universe, unriven by difference, conflicts or dilemmas, a well-ordered and welcoming place" (p 270). The loss of this dream is one of the principal losses that characterise risk societies – of rootedness in a stable social and territorial environment. The pay-off is that the choice of how and where to live, and with whom to associate, allows an expression of diversity through which subjects come to know themselves better. The solidarities that are constructed are based on fluid conceptions of self and other, subject to constant processes of realignment. Reflective solidarity allows one to sacrifice the comforting delusion that we can exclude the unfamiliar and ignore what we cannot understand.

The question, however, is whether the rationalist vision of deliberative democracy outlined above can help us to admit imperfection and tolerate uncertainty. First, the presumption of unity as either a condition or an outcome of the deliberative process suggests that it is driven by an ideal of perfection – an acceptable end point where division is transcended. Second, contestants in the rational agonistic debate implicitly strive towards the unanswerable argument and the closure that it brings. Third, the adversarial nature of the process, however well contained, pitches parties into a win–lose situation that is unlikely to foster a reflective (or depressive) relation to the issue in hand. Ambivalence is unlikely to attract listeners or to be accorded much respect. In practical terms, this form of communication is most easily adopted by the well-educated middle class and turns many people off. Bromley by Bow has observed that 'people just don't want to talk like that' and many voices are effectively stifled. Brickell (2000) takes New Labour to task for its assumption that grass-roots regeneration initiatives such as Sure Start and New Deal for Communities can effectively increase participation through a model that amounts to 'neighbourhoods in committee'. The failure of such measures to involve relatively powerless people has been proven time and again. Instead, Brickell defends working alongside people in direct practical action for change. This allows deeper levels of engagement in which needs are understood and articulated in a relational context. He cites the restoration of 'Bob's Park' – a derelict patch of ground adjacent to the Centre. The formal consultation on its renewal attracted just two members of the public. However, the eventual design and execution of a community garden, playground and recreational space involved dozens, and the eventual outcome reflected the influence of some of the community's most vulnerable members: those with mental health problems and learning disabilities.

In seeking to illustrate further the limitations of the deliberative model, I reflected on my own political experience in the radicalised milieu that formed in the industrial and student unrest of 1968. As a young activist attempting to engage with tenants' organisations, I was dismayed by the way in which initial mobilisation was followed by a rapid decline in participation which left the arena to a restricted (mainly male) band of articulate and experienced militants. Although a few of these hectored, I do not recall that this was the norm. Considerable care was taken to encourage people to express themselves. Tenants' struggles drew in a wide cross-section of people – including women and pensioners – and no one wanted to spoil them. Early meetings were colourful social occasions in which anger was counterbalanced by anecdotes, jokes, and a lot of friendly banter. This expressive spontaneity could survive formal process that promoted fairness and kept participants to task. People were driven away not so much by procedure as by adversarial argument. The involvement of political groups such as my own was premised on winning support for a 'correct' position and however democratically pursued, this led to a goal-oriented debating style. It altered the communicative climate in a way which was uncongenial for those whose understanding of their struggle was more personalised, and whose involvement was motivated by giving voice to their experience, especially the new forms of purposeful sociability and fellow-feeling.

Some years later when I was living in Italy I watched from the sidelines as a wave of feminist trade unionism challenged both the political content and style of the traditional movement, in an effort to find forms of engagement that corresponded more closely to their experiences of life and work (Froggett, 1981). In abandoning the deliberative model, these women experimented with different modes of communication, from consciousness-raising, unstructured discussion and storytelling, to new forms of pedagogy that explored the relationship between work, health and family. Their aim was to dissolve boundaries and to give voice within an institutional framework to the fluidity and interconnectedness of women's lives. Above all, it was to inject a politics of experience into trade unionism. The book that recorded this experiment was called *L'acqua in gabbia* (water in a cage) (Bocchio and Torchi, 1979) and explored the absurdities of a culture where women speak of "their fears, mothers, cycles, love and fevers, and then write cold little pamphlets on employment and rationalisation" (p 37, author's translation). For most of the people who participated in this wave of activism there was never an either/or situation in that the deliberative model of trade unionism was recognised as necessary and effective in progressing disputes and finding solutions. The women identified the union as the site of their 'emancipation'. Liberation, however, required something more: a way of thinking and speaking that reached beyond deliberative democracy to a more fluid communicative environment in which dimensions of experience normally relegated to private life could inform a political outlook (Froggett, 1981).

Interpersonal narrative voice

Iris Marion Young (1996) attempts to establish a case for a 'communicative democracy' in which forms of interaction that are constitutive of the lifeworld can be accorded a place. She points out that a growing body of literature demonstrates that the deliberative style is well rooted in the culture of the white Western middle classes, but that even among them many people – especially women – find it intimidatory. Although she does not pursue the psychological implications of this in depth, she argues that the dynamics of victory or defeat are likely to usurp or colonise the reflective or questioning faculty. She observes that conventions such as greeting, rhetoric and storytelling give access to differences in culture and social perspective and can stimulate people to try and understand each other in new ways. Such devices are not to be thought of as alternatives to rational argument, rather the problem is how to accord them a place in institutional life and to recognise their democratic, communicative value.

The first of these, greeting and leave-taking, frames the interaction in terms of warmth, anticipated sympathy, formality, social proximity and respect. It brings the body into the encounter through the use of gesture, smiles, handshakes, kisses or the offering of refreshment. By so doing it opens the channel through which recognition of the embodied other can be established and their value affirmed. Rhetoric such as humour, wordplay and figures of speech, claims the attention of the other, situates the communication, and invests it with libidinal energy – giving it colour and "making the discussion pull on thought through desire" (p 131). Perhaps most significant of all, storytelling is a widely preferred mode for communication of subjective experience across personal and social distance. It allows speakers to express values in a uniquely intelligible way to others who have little in the way of common culture or experience but can share meanings through the narrative form. Since narrative is of such importance for a psychosocial approach to welfare organisations and practice, I shall consider its use in more depth in the final section of this book and for the moment will content myself with highlighting its importance within civil institutions.

If communicative democracy is conceived as politics rooted in particular experience, there is a great need for experiment to find reflective forums in which this experience can be articulated and translated into political agendas. The 'legislative theatre' developed in Brazil by Augusto Boal (1998b) is one such example. Boal's trajectory can be described as a project of democratisation: from theatre, to therapy, to politics. His early work among the poor in the *Theatre of the oppressed* (1979) was extended during the years he spent in Europe to accommodate forms of subjective oppression such as 'fear of emptiness', which called for a psycho-political interpretation. *The rainbow of desire* (1995), which emerged from this period, began to bridge the divide between the therapeutic and political consciousness. His aim throughout has been to develop a theatre of dialogue in which the subject, desire, and more recently the law, can find expression. In these forums, the life experiences of individuals and groups and their aspirations to participative citizenship are enacted, problematised and made available for collective discussion. The technique of dramatisation depends on the formation of nuclei which may be constituted around geographical communities or communities of interest, and aims to promote the citizen-as-artist. This means overcoming inhibitions such as reticence to perform, or to speak publicly of problems which, more often than not, are both personal and political. The position of the animator as 'joker' is pivotal because s/he is licensed to question and reframe, mix fact and fiction, and jump in and out of role. This makes it possible to see how the predicaments of individuals can be pluralised. The task of the theatre is to recognise the uniqueness of the subjective experience yet discover and enact those aspects of it that can be shared. The aim is always to preserve the experiential link. If a person is cheated by a colleague, for example, it is the experience of betrayal or abuse that resonates throughout the group and needs to find symbolic expression in a larger political context.

The aesthetic space is used to create the distance through which citizen actors can observe themselves playing a range of possible solutions to an agreed problem. The preferred course of action can then, with the help of legal draughtsmen, inform concrete proposals which can be brought before the legislative assembly. (This process was elaborated while Boal himself was serving as an elected representative.) Other techniques may be used to stimulate this 'transitive democracy': interactive mailing lists and 'Chamber in the Square' consultations whereby, with careful preparation, the functions of the assembly are re-enacted in a public space so that the text of the law can be scrutinised and voted on. The first law to be approved using these means stemmed from a 'third age' theatre group, incensed at the ignorance of local doctors in relation to the health problems of older people. Law 2384/95, required all municipal hospitals to have doctors specialising in geriatric medicine. Other examples have included prohibition on treatments for mental illness which have irreversible effects; raised platforms for telephone kiosks so that blind people can detect them with their canes, and avoid banging their heads; standardisation of motel charges for all couples, regardless of sexual orientation; and crèche facilities for teachers' children in state schools. Needless to say, local problems such as refuse collection can be addressed by similar means.

Civility and association

Concern over the health of a public sphere able to mediate between the state and civil society has been widespread in the last two decades. Falling levels of political participation – registered both in voting behaviour and the dwindling membership of political parties – is accounted for in terms of a widespread loss of trust in politicians and government, and in parliamentary process. The steepness of the decline suggests that this has little to do with the healthy scepticism extolled by Alexander (1996) when he argued that distrust and political conflict are rightly pervasive in a civil society since it rests on trust in universal values rather than particular historical actors. Contemporary anxieties seem to be related to the survival of welfare democracy itself, assailed by a rising tide of incivility that elicits a range of concerns: the personal integrity, greed and ambition of people who hold public office, the privatism and egotism of a consumer society, the seeming inability of large public institutions like the National Health Service to reform themselves, the centralisation of political power and its abuse in the manipulation of public opinion. It may well be that civil society is colonised or undermined by these processes but, for the purposes of my argument, the reverse hypothesis is more interesting since "we must recognise that civil society is always nested in the practical worlds of the uncivil spheres, and we must study the compromises and fragmentations, the 'real' rather than merely idealised civil society that results" (Alexander, 2000, p 98).

Certain types of welfare initiative can be conceived as just such 'nestings', precarious when buffeted, but under the right conditions able to transform the networks of social relationships that surround them. This is possible because of their potential to reassert universal solidary values in very particularistic contexts. A centre such as Bromley by Bow sees itself as operating at a number of distinctly uncivil front lines: hidebound public service bureaucracies, the amoral indifference of market forces, racialised hatred, and the rip-off culture of the streets. Nevertheless, its continued ability to nourish lifeworld activities suggests that it is possible – though sometimes fraught with difficulty – to maintain a communicative relation to sites of both systemic and random disrespect.

As Alexander (2000) argues, such civil institutions immediately face a contradiction: they operate not only from a 'space' but from a place, which then becomes uncivil because it is the territorialised location of an exclusionary group identity. On a larger scale, nationalism would be the most obvious historical example. But this is a process that constantly reasserts itself in agencies that try to work across cultural divides. The experience of Bromley by Bow suggests that the fixity of territory must be imaginatively overcome through the maintenance of a metaphorical sense of 'space' rather than a literal relation to 'place', even though this remains as a physical entity to be protected and cared for. Art has a key role in this because it develops the capacity for both visual and verbal metaphor. Recall that the collective imagination of the Centre is informed by fluidity and movement, expressed in its architecture, artwork and in the way it speaks about itself. At the same time the storytelling culture enables it to avoid another form of incivility – a fixed history which is unable to accommodate new influences, ideas and people, and the moral perspective of the other.

All this seems to call for a richer model of civil activity than that required of the citizen–elector or the citizen–consumer. The exercise of political rights or rational choice in relation to goods and services, in itself involves only restricted forms of participation. The processes whereby an organisation like Bromley by Bow promotes creative engagement are both more demanding and less formalistic, while remaining largely based on voluntary association. They are also of interest in that the Centre has managed to establish a viable amalgam of an NHS primary healthcare facility and a flourishing range of voluntary activities and services. It has often been impatient of conventional organisational forms, which are not perceived as particularly user-friendly by many people in deprived communities.

Debates over associational democracy in recent years (Hirst, 1994; Cohen and Rogers, 1995; Held, 1996; Hoggett and Thompson, 1998) have begun to explore the virtue of a wide range of self-governing democratic forms which may be rather more narrowly defined than the Bromley by Bow model in relation to members' interests or group identities. The most elaborated of these accounts (Hirst, 1994) envisages a drastically reduced role for state governance of services within a body of associational law. This would set broad parameters within which organisations would have to operate (for example, guaranteeing that members' ability to exert influence is preserved through robust defence of their rights of exit and voice [Hirschman, 1970]). It would also need to provide some regulatory mechanism to ensure that more powerful groups do not achieve undue political influence or the ability to commandeer a disproportionate level of resources. Forms of representation could be quite diverse. Some might continue to depend on formal electoral mechanisms, while in other cases more dialogical and participatory channels would be designed to allow members expression of opinion and preference. The crucial point is that groups have very diverse requirements in this respect depending, among other things, on their communicative conventions and credible means of constraining undue exercise of power.

There are considerable variations on this theme. For example, Amin and Thrift (1995) foresee the possibility of a complex of democratised networks, some of which would remain as national and local institutions of the state while others would be located within civil society. The purpose of these networks, which are conceived as intermediate between the market and the state, is to interact with both while increasing opportunities for citizen involvement in the overall direction of the local and national economy. Effectively they help to disperse decision making through a range of participatory institutions. The virtue of such arrangements lies precisely in the degree of differentiation that would be introduced into local political processes. Cochrane (1998) considers there are exciting possibilities in an enlarged conception of community government, where local councils play only a part, alongside a range of democratically accountable and collectively controlled provider organisations. Hirst (1994) underlines the important modelling effects of associations which might be regarded as examples of good practice and foresees both a bottom-up diffusion of new organisational forms and a gradual reform of legal and political institutions, together with a retraction of the state to accommodate them. Rather than the basis of an alternative society, he regards self-governing associations as an 'axial principle' of social organisation that can be generalised to a variety of different contexts.

Common to all of these views is an assumption regarding the need to remain closely linked to the requirements and sensitivities of members. Salomon (1995) warns of a number of dysfunctional myths that can afflict the sector and tilt it towards populism or paternalism. In particular 'the myth of pure virtue' which involves a romantic denial that self-governing organisations can fall victim to all the same problems that manifest themselves in large-scale bureaucracies. As initial levels of enthusiasm and activism fall off, the inexorable tendencies of routinisation and professionalisation need to be countered by processes of renewal based on active citizenship. Insofar as this involves continual reality testing, it is also a safeguard against the 'myth of voluntarism' which tends to position associations in eternal and idealised opposition to the state sector. It is for this reason above all that the discussion should focus not only on the forms taken by associations and their networks but on the emotional and motivational climate which, from the point of view of the individual, is often the defining factor in their desire to remain involved. The reparative culture requires not only the accommodation of difference but a deliberative space within which the tension between particularity and universality can be held. In the end it is the quality of human relationships and the conversations they make possible that keep us engaged: the sense that our voice will be heard, the knowledge that others will be patient with our efforts to see things from their point of view, and the sense of mutual regard across distances of perspective. All this allows us to suspend the urge towards a premature or manipulated consensus that sometimes makes organisational life so oppressive.

Because the achievement of more complex and substantive forms of equality requires a constant negotiation of tensions and sources of fracture within and between communities, it requires a communicative space within welfare organisations, the forums where needs are articulated and interpreted and where resources are mobilised by, with and for welfare subjects. Examples of organisations that aspire to create such a communicative space are not impossible to find, and although they arise with fewer constraints within the voluntary sector, statutory organisations may also attempt to create within themselves structures that promote reflection and dialogue. However, the internal communicative climate of an organisation cannot in the end be insulated from the surrounding political environment. Attempts to do this over the last 20 years or so have resulted in paranoid cultures of corporate secrecy and image management where obsession with loyalists and leakers substitutes for a spirit of critical internal debate. Such cultures fail to develop the porous boundaries required of a genuinely participatory, post-industrial milieu, but openness carries its own risks in the absence of vigorous, democratic public sphere, which sustains active citizenship. Its revitalisation is both a condition and consequence of ethically acceptable responsive welfare provision.

NINE

Beyond welfare:
vision, voice and story

Not long ago, I interviewed staff in a department that was trying to enact a process of cultural change by devoting resources to supervision (Froggett, 1999). Over time I was struck by differences in the narrative quality of the transcripts. It seemed that where people considered they had established a helpful, containing supervisory relationship they were inclined to describe it in a reflective story which captured a sense of development through time, often with humour and imagination. The contrast with accounts of 'poor' or 'hostile' supervision was palpable. It was as if a crucial connection between representation and relationship had been disrupted.

This connected with my experience of marking student assignments based on practice placements. It had increasingly worried me that in many of these pieces of written work there were no recognisable people – a list of observations, behaviours, risks, costs and projections, certainly, maybe even an off-the-peg value or two, but no identifiable helper or person to be helped. They seemed somehow to have fallen through the gaps in the assess/plan/intervene/evaluate framework. As an assessor I was left with snapshots of bits of activity and very little sense of the thinking, let alone the feeling, which had connected them. In rendering their actions visible, students had left out felt relations between people.

Vision, accountability and reflective thinking

Among the least challenged aspects in the cult of 'evidence' is the unquestioned priority of visibility. Indeed visibility and accountability go hand in hand, as if we are so little able to bear ambivalence that we must nurture a fantasy of an activity so lucid that it yields to the purest form of symbolic expression – the mathematical equation – incorporating formal logic, symmetry, standardisation of form, the peerless perfection of numbers. Older models of relationship-based work that do not yield to quantitative measurement are derided as opaque, mysterious – prone to deceive clients through the mystifications of jargon, the public through arcane professional exclusivity and managers through sheer obtuseness. This may well be an over-generalised stereotype, which misrepresents much of former practice. Nevertheless, any defence of obfuscation, would clearly be absurd. Calls for public accountability have emerged after exposure of corruption, sleaze and poor practice standards, which in several agencies have allowed the organised exploitation of people in institutional care. The principle of recording, monitoring and evaluation of practice is hardly something

I would question. However, in the absence of a credible culture of research and evaluation, sympathetic to its own priorities, social work and to some extent nursing have been subjected to models drawn from other disciplines that fulfil the criteria of those concerned with the governance of the profession, but not necessarily of practice values. Methods of evaluation should foster – or at the very least *do no damage* – to the capacity for ethical, reflective practice.

Hannah Arendt (1978) has been one of the relatively few Western philosophers concerned to examine the process of thinking rather than of knowing. She drew attention to the preoccupation with visibility within Western culture – a culture that regards sight as the preeminent sense in the apprehension of the object and has therefore tended to elide objectivity and visibility. The seduction of the visible may in itself run counter to the activity of thought. The intellectual vacancy and square-eyed oafishness of Harry Enfield's Kevin locks onto parental despair at the evaporating signs of intelligent life in their TV-addicted offspring.

Arendt suggests that the essential characteristic of thinking is the process whereby the thinker distances him- or herself from the world of appearance, and the common sense that depends on it. Our language for talking about mental operations is rich in visual metaphor: insight, representation, viewpoint, but the metaphor reconnects us with appearances only *after* a withdrawal which allows us to form and hold images in the mind – to release the mental activity we call imagination:

> The mind learns how to deal with things that are absent and prepares itself to 'go further', toward the understanding of things that are always absent, that cannot be remembered because they were never present to sense experience. (Arendt, 1978, p 77)

Thus *all* thinking involves a retraction of the mind from commonsense awareness of the immediacy of the given world and is in some sense reflective in that the mind becomes the 'screen' or 'container' where images and imageless thoughts are formed and refashioned. Similarly, all non-psychotic thinking returns from these mental containers to the world of external objects in a process of continual confrontation with reality which links inner and outer experience. Perhaps what we are really referring to when we speak of reflective thinking and practice is the ability to delay the return of thought to the outer world long enough to turn things around, experiment with perspective, infuse with emotion, manipulate, modify or enjoy them. This involves a tolerance of ambiguity.

Reflective thinking does seem to partake of the poet's privilege of thinking with no immediate practical effect. The capacity to tolerate uncertainties and doubt that Keats called 'negative capability' is not one readily accorded in modern, instrumental, task-driven organisations . And yet this is important in maintaining the critical and creative faculties. According to Arendt the mind must engage in a form of "intra-mural warfare between thought and common sense", moving continually to separate and reconnect the two. Organisational cultures that over-invest in appearances can disrupt this to-and-fro movement of thought, failing to provide the opportunity for the withdrawal that initiates reflection and effectively undermining scope for the activity of both memory and judgement – the ability to make links, to engage in process, to take time. The outcome imparts to thoughts a pre-sent quality that they are called to re-present through presentation and presenteeism.

The impact of technical information systems and the influence of binary models of computation encourage forms of thinking in which something either 'is' or 'is not'. President Clinton may have had the audacity to question the meaning of 'is' before the Grand Jury but he was roundly denounced for sophistry, and not only because of suspicion of his motives. Visually oriented cultures are impatient of any suggestion that the self-evident may be a deception. What is at risk then is the power of metaphor which, Arendt tells us, deals not in resemblances between things but in resemblances between relations. The poet's language is 'vitally metaphorical' – it allows us to perceive relations between things that cannot be otherwise apprehended. However, this is by no means the exclusive preserve of the poet but a function that allows us to find images from the world of the senses that bind or clothe our thoughts. Far from being a matter of style, a poetic flourish, its use bridges thought and reality and is essential in the articulation meaning. Its unique effectiveness both as a means to understanding and communication arises from its intrinsically pleasurable aesthetic quality – perceptions take form and are recognised. Meanings can be shared.

If over-reliance on visibility and the impoverishment of language go hand in hand (and the decline of the paragraph in favour of the bullet point in corporate documents could be regarded as symptomatic), this is more than a question of style. The ways in which we look and speak are likely to be affected, and for those who are looked at and spoken to this may be a matter of psychic survival. Marks (2000) has written of disabled people's experiences in this regard. She suggests that the clinical gaze, which distances professional observers from bodies deemed to be abnormal, might be more abusive than the 'freak show'. There is at least within the latter the possibility of actively moulding perceptions through the art of performance. The dwarf dance/striptease troupe who called themselves The Half Monty brought into play an ironic commentary on the predicament of non-disabled men, obliged by lack of work to reclaim self-esteem by making a spectacle of themselves – traditionally one of the few routes available to people whose appearance deviates from aesthetic norms. At the same time their pride in their own physique and the assertive nature of the show directed the audience to look with new eyes at bodies which were functionally unimpaired but socially disabled. By manipulating response to their own commercial and artistic advantage they imposed themselves as subjects. This is not to deny the prurient inquisitiveness that may have motivated the audience, merely to point out that there are opportunities for engagement which are absent in the clinical gaze. It is this that can overwhelm the ability of disabled people to experience self and body as a psychosocial unity.

In terms of the main argument of this book – that ethically viable relationships in the welfare domain depend on mutual recognition of the parties to the helping relationship – the question is how far do the conditions under which we deliver welfare sustain the clinical gaze and how far do they allow us to move beyond it and recognise others as subjects? At present, metaphors of looking, and the distance this places between the observer and observed, are strongly present in the culture of effectiveness which emphasises clarity, focus and visible outcomes. Minsky (1995, 1998) pointed out that the ways in which contemporary culture privileges 'sight' over 'insight' can be likened to a form of 'womb envy', a mistrust of that which is within, hidden from view, and inaccessible even to the penetrating power of the visible organ. She revealed the culturally gendered inflection of 'seeing' and of the particular status of this sense in our attempts to explore the world around us. I have previously pointed out that this may go some way to explain the dominance of metaphors of vision in masculinised management cultures (Froggett, 1996).

The privileged position of vision has the effect of positioning people in the dimension of vision – that is in terms of their spatial relationships to other people, institutions and the environment. To the extent that this fixes and objectifies them – and this is a long-standing complaint of oppressed peoples – it corrodes their sense of past and future and the fluidity and movement that comes with insertion into a personal and collective history. Bauman (1998) has drawn attention to the way in which this has become one of the main forms of global exclusion. He suggests that we are witnessing an effective division of populations into 'tourists' and 'vagabonds'. The tourists, or mobile elites, enjoy forms of power, travel and cultural media such as cyberspace, which means that they are no longer confined to territorial locations. They are the successful consumers who move through the world in time (of which they are always short). Space no longer confines them. The vagabonds on the other hand, the failed consumers or welfare candidates, tainted with the suggestion of dangerousness and resented for the costs they impose on the public, live primarily in their localities as the world moves by them and conspires to hinder their movements through a myriad of restrictions: immigration controls, residence laws, welfare regulations and zero tolerance. Confinement to space becomes a form of humiliation. Fear and mistrust of these largely urban poor seep into the organisation of urban environments. The anti-crime ecology demands not only 'defensible space' designed to pre-empt the possibility of ambush, but also elimination of 'civic' space where people might loiter, encounter one another and converse. The vagabonds are displaced to those arenas of seduction and surveillance, the shopping centres, where they act as a warning to the middle classes that unless they keep moving, changing and consuming, they too might become vagabonds.

The use of generalised visual surveillance was an organising theme of Orwell's *1984*, where it was portrayed as the most potent instrument of his totalitarian dystopia – the two-way screen in every home that watches the watcher. However, a variety of authors have analysed the less overt extension of surveillance in modern liberal democracies. Foucault's (1975) metaphorical development of the idea of the panopticon extends to the operations of power in Jeremy Bentham's architectural ideal of the perfect prison, where all inmates are forever within sight of the guards without knowing whether they are being actively watched. The point, however, is that within contemporary societies a physical apparatus of external surveillance is a marker of social exclusion, necessary only for those who fail to internalise the injunction to self-scrutiny, thereby turning the panoptical vision inwards. While the excluded have a battery of health and welfare professionals to supplement the disciplinary gaze of the forces of law and order, the included, the successful consumers, watch themselves.

Lasch (1979) finds this obsession with self-image to be the root of a culture of narcissism. In his view the value now ascribed to images fosters a particular kind of personality which searches for a reflection of itself in the commodities with which it is surrounded. Constant acquisition of new artefacts provides a mirror through which the self can be observed and evaluated according to the visible indicators of successful consumption. The projection of desire onto objects, which are then used to bolster and measure the self, encloses the consumer in a narcissistic loop where the outside world exists principally to support that self. The value of others is as fuel for fantasy, and it is this, rather than acquisitiveness, that is the searing point of Lasch's critique. The consequences are superficial relationships, the impossibility of intimacy that presupposes an ability to connect with an outside other, ultimately a sense of meaninglessness that seems to evoke a postmodern pessimism that we must sustain our fascination with appearances because there is nothing beyond.

Voice and personal recognition

It is perhaps no accident therefore that marginalised groups do not ask to be 'seen' so much as to be 'heard'. By claiming 'voice' they demand to represent themselves. The voice comes from within and is a medium of self-representation that allows the speaker a more direct influence over the ways in which they are heard. Ree (1999) explores these issues through his philosophical study of deafness and hearing. He points out that voice has always been seen as the privileged medium of self-expression, of interiority, involving breath, which in the spiritual imagination is linked to the soul. But this is not merely a movement from inner to outer. Unlike light, the movement of sound is not linear and unidirectional:

> Beams of light pass chastely through each other without being affected at all whereas sound-waves are constantly colliding and combining and mutually interfering. (Ree, 1999, p 31)

Whereas 'seeing' often stands for the singularity of clear, distinct reasoning and deliberative argumentation, 'voice' offers us a better metaphor for understanding in interpersonal contexts, and a corrective to the prevailing emphasis on ways of seeing across the spatial distances which isolate individual subjects.

Furthermore, an over-reliance on the visible can lead to a focus on the immediately available surface of things, whereas:

> The objects of hearing are essentially multiple, and the world of hearing has a kind of perceptible depth which has no equivalent in vision. (Ree, 1999, pp 32-3)

Modern management cultures have led to a resurgence of positivist methodologies in which the detachment of professional observers and the spatial separation of those who manage, command and coordinate the relationships of practice have become institutionalised. Within this world there is a consistent logic to the argument that social workers should withdraw from face-to-face work in favour of the supervision of social care workers (Higham, 1998). It is worth considering what happens to communication when those who predominantly observe are separated from those who mainly listen, especially where there are significant power and status differentials between them and one mode of perception is culturally preferred. The likelihood is that the 'art' of listening with its 'perceptible depth' is abandoned in favour of the 'science' of observation, leading in practice to a crude and reductionist behaviourism and shallow one-sided evaluations based exclusively on visible indicators.

Lived time and storytelling

There are very few forms of mental activity which lend themselves to the establishment of communicative and analytical links between different ways of life, between individuals and moral communities and across social divides. Narrative is one such form and it is peculiarly democratic, being implicated in the development of moral sensibility from an early age and across a range of cultures, whether formally as in the bedtime ritual, or informally, in the everyday tales of right and wrong through which we reproduce the norms of social life. Children seem to have a particular attraction for stories that act as a social lubricant, easing them into cultural life, while for older people reminiscence is vital in the construction of a meaningful personal biography. It must also be added that stories are inclusive, accessible, enjoyable, creative, dense with meaning, and ubiquitous.

It may therefore be no accident that historically social work's defining methodology was social casework that allows people to describe lives lived in time via the telling and reconstruction of personal histories. This is now being progressively abandoned precisely because it is held to be wasteful of time and careless of immediate discernible outputs. Over the last decade or so, interest in narrative form, function and methodology has been gathering pace across a wide range of disciplines. But with a strange kind of perversity, social work, which has shown a historical affinity for narrative knowledge, and has little to gain from insularity, underrates it. Worse still, social work organisations and training models have adopted codes of communication which disrupt the processes of storytelling. The psychosocial case history may be a near forgotten art. Most students can complete an assessment pro-forma but fewer can give a reflexive account of an interview.

Saleeby (1994) observes that the subjugation of other peoples (the colonised both within and outside a society) typically begins with two basic violations. In the first instance, the degradation of the body and its passions. Consider the construction of the 'negro' as bestially sensual and grotesque; of the Jew as filthy louse in Nazi ideology, of homosexuals as depraved and now probably diseased, of disabled people as asexual and deformed. In the second instance, it involves the suppression of voice and story. For this reason, liberation movements almost always involve the recovery of tradition through folklore, myth and history. Plummer (1995) points out that for some groups of people there are stories waiting to be told – that is, awaiting the moment when there will be an interpretive community willing and able to receive them. In this way the emergence of the story at a particular moment in time, for example of domestic violence or of childhood sexual abuse, inserts a group's existence into public consciousness and allows it to elaborate an account of its own existence. The realisation of the narrative is the precondition of an emancipatory impulse. For stigmatised groups who have been in receipt of much negative projection it allows for retrieval of past humiliations and response under conditions which make them amenable to reworking. Specifically it is the denigrated otherness of lesbian and gay people, of 'victims', of disabled or black people, which is called into question as they reposition themselves through the story as subjects.

Saleeby (1994) points out, very pertinently for social work, that the colonisers too have their stories along with privileged powers to impose them as official history. The caseworker myths have included tales of heroism and rescue, often through a mixture of science and supernatural insight. Modern methods may be disruptive of storytelling, but managerialism has nevertheless drawn legitimacy from its own tales of modernising entrepreneurial vitality.

At the level of the individual, a tolerably coherent personal biography seems to be at the root of a sense of identity. But perhaps most importantly, in the context of the spatialisation of culture, it is the process by which events are ordered and construed in time.

> The major dimension of human existence is time, and the discourse on human action is pervaded by an awareness of the centrality of time and change. Narrative is always controlled by the concept of time and by the recognition that temporality is the primary dimension of human existence. (Polkinghorne, 1988, p 20)

Similarly Bruner (1987) observes that we seem to have no other way of describing 'lived time' than as narrative.

Narrative captures sequence and is implicated in the production of memory. This is never clearer than in the recall of traumatic events when such powerful responses of despair, terror, and hatred are evoked that the narrative function, which links events in time and finds expressions for these linkages in language, is overwhelmed. Thoughts become fixated at the moment of trauma leading to nightmarish flashbacks in which the event represents itself concretely and repetitively. Or else, it is so little amenable to the distancing and reworking activity of thought that it becomes not only unspeakable but also unimaginable. Recovery involves learning to tell the story in which the pain is located, recognised, and acknowledged in the context of a much larger narrative of a particular life – so that it is no longer a catastrophic breach but part of an intelligible flux. Much of social work involves reconfiguration of bits of plot alongside and through the practical day-to-day activity of putting together a workable set of living arrangements as a backcloth against which a life-story can unfold. This location of events in real time is part of the process through which the private world of the unconscious finds expression in the realm of communicable experience, which takes place in shared historical time. The particular texture, tenor, tension and pace of the narrative, and most especially its integrative power, depends on what the narrator brings to it – lives can be made intelligible in many ways and it is the individuality of the telling that reveals a personal creative intelligence.

People who have experienced very traumatic childhoods are often very little able to present a coherent historical account of their lives. Memories are fragmented and disjointed.

> Eva, who had had three babies in close succession in her teens, would tell people with a curiously bland little smile how she had 'lost' them to social services, just as she had 'lost' touch with their fathers and with dozens of fleeting liaisons before and since. She had also managed to 'lose' a succession of flats, jobs, friends, and most strikingly of all, her own childhood. There was a gap of about ten years, from which she could occasionally pull out a seemingly inconsequential event, remembered as one might remember a scene from a movie whose plot-line was long forgotten. She was unfailingly pleasant, never even showing a hint of irritation with her mother who accompanied her to appointments insulting her to all who would listen, or towards the social worker who had taken her children into care, or to her brother who had sexually abused her four-year-old, or to friends who had cheated her and lovers who had beaten and abandoned her. She lived in space but not in time, in a seamless present in which things were either here or gone, but in which she could identify no meaningful succession. She had never knowingly made a significant choice in her life. She was also young, pretty, fertile and once again pregnant.

With people like Eva, the contemporary emphasis on choice and empowerment does not get past first base without painstaking psychodynamic work. The flattening out of all emotional response and the absence of any ability to take up a position in historical time are intimately bound up with one another. Learning to tell the outlines of her own story did not in the end involve much in the way of recovered memory. Rather it allowed her to reconnect a few fragmented events in such a way as to give form to a 'lost' emotional range from rage to hope. She made her first ever decision – not to 'lose' but to leave her family of origin for a spell. She was able to keep and raise her fourth child and she chose not to have any more.

Saleeby (1994) is clear that in social work the role of narrative goes beyond the face-to-face encounter or group consciousness in that it can enable us to make links between culture, theory and individual life-stories. He characterises practice as an intersection of meanings, many of which are delivered in narrative form: the personal accounts of clients, the myths and rituals of culture and the symbolic constructions of the practitioner. He is not the only one to have drawn attention in different ways to the importance of linking in social work. This arises from its very position 'at the margins' (Henkel, 1995) and as I have argued elsewhere (Froggett, 1997) is intrinsic to the nature of social work knowledge. This linking is jeopardised in conditions that produce very defensive reactions among professionals and, at the same time, structures those defences in organisationally approved ways through proceduralisation. It also promotes an over-reliance on methods favouring goal-directed, instrumental ways of thinking and communication. This undermines the capacity to move between public institutions and private experience with the result that responsiveness to individuals, which is the basis for recognition, is eroded. Narrative provides a form in which interpretive links can be made in dialogue. Although it too can be presented in the esoteric languages of expertise, its structure is intrinsically communicative and better adapted to the lived experience of families and communities.

In the current debate over the status of social work knowledge and admissible forms of evidence, the narrative tradition points to an alternative frame to the discourse of effectiveness and outcome. Listening to someone's story involves paying attention to their version of events and comparing it with other perspectives on reality. It also allows them to star in their own drama and, crucially, it is the quality of the attention that helps draw forth the performance. In narrative, content and form become intertwined in a personalised aesthetic which reveals its own process of production, a process which has to reckon with external conditions. Narrative conveys much more than information – it reveals a certain quality of effort mobilised in its production – or the lack of it. It comes to us with urgency, excitement, boredom, apathy, bewilderment, pensiveness, rage, disappointment, providing us with windows on successive states of mind of the narrator. Because of this it is a sensitive analytic tool, an interpretive filter influencing what is attended to and defining the boundaries of meaning.

The narrative form does not insert us into the flow of time only to leave us afloat in space. Ricoeur (1981) suggests that it involves both sequence and configuration. It therefore allows us to exist in both dimensions. Polkinghorne (1988) notes that narrative meaning always emerges from the recognition that something is part of a whole and that causal relations can only be accounted for in terms of the relations between its elements. To ask what something means is to ask how it is connected to something else and how it contributes to the movement towards an end. The resolution implied is a process of making sense as the plot unravels – pleasure in dénouement is the pleasure gained from a more harmonious re-ordering of reality – a moment when understanding and events appear to be aligned, making possible a rapport between storyteller and the audience. The pleasure then is in the congruence between the faculties and the world in which they are exercised. But the satisfaction goes deeper, in Kleinian terms representing a movement into a depressive relation to reality whereby the contradictory tensions in the plot are relaxed, the holes filled in and the schisms repaired. The resolution of a narrative appears to dispel illusion through a momentary reconciliation with reality, which impels emotional growth. Often this learning leaves us sadder and wiser and comes at a price of recognition that the primal illusion of the narcissist – that of perfect unity, control and comprehension – is irrecoverable.

Narrative movement is quite distinct from prediction. The quest for predictability in the social world can be understood in terms of a desire to stabilise an uncertain environment. In critiques of scientific methodology the point has often been made that prediction is motivated by control. Narrative forms, however, raise the possibility of movement towards resolution without domination. Ricoeur (1981) refers to directedness but points out that this is not the same as prediction – a thousand contingencies can intervene. He suggests that uncertainty, even suspense, about the conclusion is intrinsic to the narrative function. Predictability empties the story, divesting it of interest. To say that a person is predictable is to suggest that they invite contempt. An inability to surprise is also an inability to delight. The acceptability of a conclusion must come with hindsight. This is a far cry from the predictability that aims to control the future and render it safe. Narrative forms allow for intentionality, clarification and movement towards a conclusion, while accommodating ambiguity in the process. Uncertainty is valued, for real life plots may never achieve closure. As Saleeby says, narratives bind experience without fixing it and the best stories surprise and unsettle us.

Ending

> The Good Conversation is never the one that we wanted to have. It allows
> something to emerge that henceforth exists.
>
> H. Gadamer, *Truth and method* (1975)

This book is not the one that I started out wanting to write. It has emerged out of many good conversations – with colleagues, friends, family and students. I continue to worry about it. I worry about what I have put in and what I have left out, about lapses in style and judgement and about whether it speaks with too many voices or too few. I worry that it looks like a work of systematisation that leads to a small argument – that it starts as grand theory and ends with little narratives. Naturally I worry that in posing the problems in this way I am setting up binary oppositions and failing to sustain the tension between them.

Narrative methods in the context of more equal social relations of welfare can help to sustain relationships of recognition. Such methods, often untheorised, have always been at the heart of responsive practice. The casework tradition implicitly grasped this but seldom articulated it and has been unable therefore to mount an effective argument for its own value. Critical attention has been directed at shortcomings which have more to do with the relations under which casework has been practised than with narrative methods themselves. The loss of focus on personal interactions within the helping relationship has hastened the decline. Hall's *Social work as narrative* (1997), for example, considers mainly professional texts. It is now easier to appreciate the importance of stories because of work that has been done outside of the social welfare field. For example, the collection edited by Christopher Nash (1990) includes essays on the importance of storytelling in economics, law, literature and the natural sciences. Tannenbaum's (1994) study of narrative in physician's reasoning is of particular interest because it revealed the inability of the probabilistic models favoured by the outcomes movement to capture the processes of thinking and communication used in medical practice. Indeed, she concludes that "the best doctors are the most skilful storytellers" (p 33) in that they incorporate the conventions of scientific enquiry and validation but subordinate them to individualised accounts which accommodate the irregularities and inherent uncertainties of particular cases.

The SOSTRIS project (Social Strategies in Risk Societies) (Chamberlayne and Rustin, 1999) has used socio-biographical methods in a comparative European study of social exclusion. The researchers were informed by the work of Beck and Giddens on risk and reflexivity and the emergent emphasis on 'active welfare'. They were concerned to examine the salience of these concepts for analysis and policy formation and focused both on the individual accounts of life displacements and transitions among excluded groups and on the biographical resources of 'flagship' agencies attempting to work with them. They contend that in attempting to 'read' lives from formal systems, traditional social policy analysis has produced over-standardised and over-generalised accounts of social transformation. Their case studies suggest that "social change is overwhelmingly experienced individually rather than perceived as a collective process, and that the shift towards the private sphere involves a worrying erosion of collective identities, an individualising of imaginative world and horizons" (p 13). They point out that designing social policy around probabilistic notions of actuarial risk neglects the nature of individual experience where problems are filtered through inner worlds and where "hidden blockages may lie in repetitive patterns within the family, in experiences of family rupture, or in paralysing cultural rifts" (p 14). They emphasise the importance of listening and finding methods which build biographical strategies out of people's own resources. In short, their conclusion, which underlines the importance of relational and processual skills in practice and service delivery, is in line with the argument presented here for a welfare politics of recognition based on a concern to address inequalities and sustain social attachments.

There was once a social worker – no better or worse than many others – who had plenty of worries. Like many of her colleagues she often felt over-stretched, undervalued and wracked by uncertainty. But mostly she was concerned about two teenage boys. One was her son, Jo, the other was a client, Dan. Jo took up plenty of her home time, and in the normal sort of family-knockabout way this had its ups and downs, but was a huge source of pleasure. Dan took up large tracts of work time – too much it seemed. He moved in a world of bleak chaos where he and his sadistically abusive family contrived to throw up continual unscheduled crises. These played havoc with her diary and confounded her best-laid plans. Her relationship with these two was, quite properly, very different. Jo had first been put into her arms as a squawking blood-streaked new-born who had promptly clamped his little mouth on her nipple and settled down. She met Dan as a well-developed 14-year-old in a children's home. He was curled up in a foetal position, alternately sucking his thumb and chewing his arm until it bled.

Jo had quickly taught her about maternal passion and about the intense personalised attentiveness that flows from it. Dan at the start had filled her with anxieties that bordered on dread. She had enough experience to know all about professional boundaries and authority, and how to use good supervision. But she felt that nothing had prepared her for Dan, for the ferocity of his psychological assaults, or for the growing tenderness she felt for him as the work progressed.

She was daily struck by the contrast between their life-chances. The welfare state had clearly benefited her son, but its contribution to Dan's well-being was much less certain. Jo had been born into a financially secure, well-educated, stable family. She and her partner were public sector professionals who looked out for his interests and were determined that he would get the best out of the health and education services. Dan was very much a child of the so-called 'underclass'. His homes had changed constantly – after fires, evictions or burglaries. Schools and doctors had seen little of him, but social services had a drawer full of files. Anyone could have predicted where both boys would be by the age of 21. Jo would be at a good university somewhere, preparing to take his finals. Dan would be living on benefits, or in prison, or possibly dead.

All this took place in the changing times of the mid-to-late eighties. Long-term casework remained the norm for people like Dan but the writing was clearly on the wall with increasing pressure to 'deliver' and move on. Like many of her colleagues, our social worker was wilting under the growing weight of a critical public, hostile press, and ever-diminishing resources. She asked herself how much truth there was in the contradictory stereotypes of her profession: over-identified with their clients, hopelessly lax, rigid and interfering, controlling and nannying. In any case, she wondered, who was going to regulate or nanny the furious, unruly Dan, other than by locking him up? What contract would ever restrain him? And just who would be foolhardy enough to ignore the manifest dangerousness of his world? The accumulation of child protection guidelines was designed to protect the department and guard against sloppiness, but in no sense did this lessen the responsibility, or the anxieties he aroused in her.

At first all she could manage was to survive his attacks and endure. He danced on the roof of her car and lobbed bricks through her office window. Often he was ambivalent – he would lunge at her, but only when he was certain that someone else would restrain him. At times she was beguiled by his charm and humour and at his little gestures of protectiveness towards her – like the day he stopped his friend from stealing her purse, or the time when he refused to celebrate his birthday without her. He would rarely cooperate with any arrangements she made, but slowly she detected a change – from intense and primitive expressions of love and hate to the beginnings of thoughtfulness. He was teaching her how to care for him in the only way he could accept, using their time together to help him extract some meaning from his crazy life. In her regard for him, he began to recognise the outlines of a self worthy of respect and bit by bit a sordid tale of abuse emerged. Eventually, the perpetrators were prosecuted and imprisoned and Dan got some compensation, which was soon gone.

Jo and Dan never met, and it is unlikely they ever will. They could be living on different planets. Dan lives on benefits, writes to her from time to time at work and makes it clear that from his present vantage point, the tangible legal outcomes of his case seem to be neither here nor there. What matters most are being his own person, friendships and getting by. Jo is reading philosophy at a good university. When asked what matters most he gives roughly the same answer.

References

Abel-Smith, B. and Townsend, P. (1965) *The poor and the poorest*, London: G. Bell & Son.

Ainsworth, M. (1982) 'Attachment: retrospect and prospect', in C.M. Parkes and J. Stevenson-Hynde (eds) *The place of attachment in human behaviour*, London: Routledge.

Ainsworth, M. (1989) 'Attachments beyond infancy', *American Psychologist*, vol 44, pp 709-16.

Alexander, J. (1996) 'Some notes on the misunderstanding of civil society as capitalism', presented at The Direction of Contemporary Capitalism, University of Sussex, April, cited by Hess, A. (2000) 'After success: the politics of civil society', *Soundings*, vol 16, pp 90-5.

Alexander, J. (2000) 'Contradictions: the uncivilising pressures of space, time and function', *Soundings*, vol 16, pp 96-112.

Alford, C.F. (1989) *Melanie Klein and critical social theory*, New Haven, CT: Yale University Press.

Alford, C.F. (1994) *Group psychology and political theory*, New Haven, CT: Yale University Press.

Alford, C.F. (2002) 'Leadership by interpretation and holding', *Organisational and Social Dynamics*, vol 1, no 2, pp 153-73.

Almond, G.A. and Verba, S. (1989) *The civic culture*, Newbury Park, CA: Sage Publications.

Amin, A. and Thrift, N. (1995) 'Institutional issues for the European regions: from markets and plans to socioeconomics and powers of association', *Economy and Society*, vol 24, pp 41-66.

Angus, J. (1999) *An enquiry concerning possible methods for evaluating arts for health projects*, Bath: Community Health UK.

Arendt, H. (1978) *The life of the mind*, London: Secker and Warburg.

Armstrong, D. (1991) *The 'institution in the mind': Reflections on the relation of psychoanalysis to work with institutions*, London: The Grubb Institute.

Armstrong, D. (1995) 'The analytic object in organisational work', Paper presented to ISPSO Conference, London.

Armstrong, D. (1996) 'The recovery of meaning', Paper prepared for the International Society for the Psychoanalytic Study of Organisations' 'Organisation 2000: Psychoanalytic Perspectives', New York, June.

Association of Directors of Social Services Research Group (1996) 'Guidelines for researchers', ADSS Research Group.

Auden, W.H. (1936-7) 'Education' (from *Notebook*, Berg Collection), cited in K. Bucknell and N. Jenkins (1994) *The language of learning and the language of love*, Oxford: Oxford University Press, pp 86-7.

Bach, M. (1993) *Welfare work: Discursive conflicts and narrative possibilities*, Aldershot: Edward Elgar.

Barnes, M. and Prior, D. (2000) *Private lives as public policy*, Birmingham: Venture Press.

Bauman, Z. (1988) *Modernity and ambivalence*, Cambridge: Polity Press.

Bauman, Z. (1998) *Globalisation*, Cambridge: Polity Press.

Beck, U. (1992) *Risk society: Towards a new modernity*, London: Sage Publications.

Beck, U. (1994) 'The re-invention of politics: towards a theory of reflexive modernisation', in U. Beck, A. Giddens and S. Lasch, *Reflexive modernisation*, Cambridge: Polity Press.

Bell, D. (1997) 'Primitive mind of state', *Psychoanalytic Psychotherapy*, vol 10, no 1, pp 45-57.

Bellah, R. (1988) *Habits of the heart: Middle America observed*, London: Hutchinson Education.

Benhabib, S. (1996) 'Towards a deliberative model of democratic legitimacy', in S. Benhabib (ed) *Democracy and difference*, Princeton, NJ: Princeton University Press.

Benjamin, J. (1990) *The bonds of love: Psychoanalysis, feminism, and the problem of domination*, London: Virago.

Benjamin, J. (1995) *Like subjects, love objects*, New Haven, CT: Yale University Press.

Benner, P. (1984) *From novice to expert: Excellence and power in clinical nursing practice*, Menlo Park, CA: Addison-Wesley.

Berger, B., Berger, P. and Kellner, H. (1974) *The homeless mind*, Harmondsworth: Penguin.

Beveridge, W. (1942) *Social insurance and allied services: A report by Sir William Beveridge*, Cmd 4604, London: HMSO.

Bion, W. (1961) *Experiences in groups*, London: Tavistock.

Bion, W. (1967) *Second thoughts: Selected papers on psychoanalysis*, London: Karnac Books.

Bion, W. (1970) *Attention and interpretation*, London: Tavistock.

Blaug, R. (1995) 'Distortion of the face to face: communicative reason and social work practice', *British Journal of Social Work*, vol 25, no 4, pp 423-39.

Boal, A. (1979 edn) *Theatre of the oppressed* (trans C.A. and M.L. Mcbride), New York, NY: Unizen, first published in 1974.

Boal, A. (1995) *The rainbow of desire*, London: Routledge.

Boal, A. (1998a) 'The political master swimmer', in M. Schutzman and J. Cohen-Cruz (eds) *Playing Boal: Theatre, therapy, activism*, translated from French by J. Cohen-Cruz, London: Routledge p 34.

Boal, A. (1998b) *Legislative theatre*, London: Routledge.

Bocchio, F. and Torchi, A. (1979) *L'acqua in gabbia: Voci di donne dentro il sindicato*, Milano: La Salamandra.

Bollas, C. (1987) *The shadow of the object*, London: Free Association Books.

Bollas, C. (1992) *Being a character*, Canada: Harper Collins.

Booth, T. and Booth, W. (1996) 'Sounds of silence: narrative research with inarticulate subjects', *Disability and Society*, vol 11, no 1, pp 55-69.

Boud, D., Keogh, R. and Walker, D. (1985) 'What is reflection in learning?', in D. Boud, R. Keogh and D. Walker (eds) *Reflection: Turning experience into learning*, London: Kogan Page pp 7-40.

Bowlby, J. (1969, 1973, 1980) *Attachment & loss*, vols 1, 2 and 3, London: Hogarth Press.

Brewer, C. and Lait, J. (1980) *Can social work survive?*, London: Temple Smith.

Brickell, P. (2000) *People before structures: Engaging communities effectively in regeneration*, London: Demos.

Britton, R. (1989) 'The missing link: parental sexuality in the Oedipus complex', in R. Britton, M. Feldman and E. O'Shaughnessy (eds) *The Oedipus complex today*, London: Karnac, pp 83-101.

Brockbank, A. and McGill, I. (1998) *Facilitating reflective learning in higher education*, Buckingham: The Society for Research into Higher Education, and Open University.

Bruner, J. (1987) 'Life as narrative', *Social Research*, vol 54, no 1, pp 11-32.

Bruner, J. (1990) *Acts of meaning*, Cambridge, MA: Harvard University Press.

Buckler, S. and Dolowitz, D. (2000) 'New Labour's ideology: a reply to Michael Freeden', *Political Quarterly*, vol 71, no 1, pp 109-62.

Burack, C. (1994) *The problem of the passions: Feminism, psychoanalysis and social theory*, New York, NY: New York University Press.

Butterworth, E. and Holman, R. (eds) (1975) *Social welfare in modern Britain*, Glasgow: Fontana/Collins.

Chamberlayne, P. and Froggett, L. (forthcoming) *Evaluation of the Bromley by Bow Centre's work with older people*.

Chamberlayne, P. and King, A. (2000) *Cultures of care: Biographies of carers in Britain and the two Germanies*, Bristol: The Policy Press.

Chamberlayne, P. and Rupp, S. (1999) *'Only connect': Report on the Bromley by Bow project*, London: Centre for Biography in Social Policy, University of East London.

Chamberlayne, P. and Rustin, M. (1999) *From biography to social policy: Final report of the SOSTRIS project*, London: Centre for Biography in Social Policy, University of East London.

Chodorow, N. (1978) *The reproduction of mothering*, Berkeley, CA: University of California Press.

Clarke, J. (1993) 'The comfort of strangers: social work in context', in J.A. Clarke (ed) *Crisis in care*, London: Sage Publications, pp 5-21.

Clarke J.(1995) 'Competence and discipline in professional formation', *British Journal of Social Work*, vol 25, pp 563-80.

Clarke, J. (1996) *Capturing the customer: Consumerism and social welfare*, Working Papers on Managerialism and Social Policy, Milton Keynes: Open University Press.

Clarke, J. (1998) 'Thriving on chaos: managerialisation and social welfare', in J. Carter (ed) *Postmodernity and the fragmentation of welfare*, London: Routledge, pp 171-86.

Clarke, J., Hughes, G., Lewis, G. and Mooney, G. (1998) 'The meaning of the welfare state', in G. Hughes (ed) *Imagining welfare futures*, London: Routledge, pp 1-12.

Clarke, M. and Stewart, J. (2000) 'Handling the wicked issues', in C. Davies, L. Finlay and A. Bullman (eds) *Changing practice in health and social care*, London: Sage Publications, pp 337-86 .

Cochrane, A. (1998) 'Globalisation, fragmentation and local welfare citizenship', in J. Carter (ed) *Postmodernity and the fragmentation of welfare*, London: Routledge, pp 252-66.

Cohen, J. (1996) 'Procedure and substance in deliberative democracy, in S. Benhabib (ed) *Democracy and difference*, Princeton, NJ: Princeton University Press, pp 95-119.

Cohen, J. and Rogers, J. (eds) (1995) *Associations and democracy: The real utopias project*, vol 1, London: Verso.

Cooper, A. and Lousada, J. (2003, forthcoming) *The meaning of welfare*, London: Karnac.

Cooper, D. (1967) *Psychiatry and anti-psychiatry*, London: Tavistock Publications.

Cormack, U. and McDougall, K. (1950) 'Case-work in social service', in C. Morris (ed) *Social case-work in Great Britain*, London: Faber & Faber.

Cowling, M. (ed) (1978) *Conservative essays*, Cassell: London.

Craib, I. (1994) *The importance of disappointment*, London: Routledge.

Dalley, G. (1996) *Ideologies of caring: Rethinking community and collectivism*, second edn, Basingstoke: Macmillan, first published 1988.

Dalrymple, J. and Burke, B. (1995) *Anti-oppressive practice: Social care and the law*, Buckingham: Open University Press.

Dartington, T. (2001) 'In defense of inefficiency', Paper presented at Organisational and Social Dynamics conference, OPUS.

Davies, C. (2000a) 'Understanding the policy process', in A. Brechin, H. Brown and M.A. Eby (eds) *Critical practice in health and social care*, London: Sage Publications, pp 211-30.

Davies, C. (2000b) 'Frameworks for regulation and accountability', in A. Brechin, H. Brown and M.A. Eby (eds) *Critical practice in health and social care*, London: Sage Publications, pp 296-317.

Deakin, N. and Walsh, K. (1996) 'The enabling state: the role of markets and contracts', *Public Administration*, vol 74, pp 34-48.

Dekker, P. and van den Broek, A. (1998) 'Civil society in comparative perspective: involvement in voluntary associations in North America and Western Europe', *Voluntas*, vol 9, no 1, pp 11-38.

DoH (Department of Health) (1998) *Modernising social services: Promoting independence, improving protection, raising standards*, Cm 4169, London: The Stationery Office.

de Tocqueville, A. (1947 edn) *Democracy in America* (translated by H. Reeve), Oxford: Oxford University Press, first published 1836, Paris: Libraire de Charles Gosselin.

Dinnerstein, D (1976) *The mermaid and the minotaur: Sexual arrangements and human malaise*, New York, NY: Harper Colophon.

Dominelli, L. (1988) *Anti-racist social work*, London: Macmillan.

Dominelli, L. (1996) 'Deprofessionalising social work: anti-oppressive practice, competencies and postmodernism', *British Journal of Social Work*, vol 26, no 2, pp 153-75.

Dominelli, L. (1998) 'Anti-oppressive practice in context', in R. Adams, L. Dominelli and M. Payne (eds) *Social work: Themes, issues and critical debates*, Basingstoke: Macmillan, pp 3-22.

Douglas, M. (1992) *Risk and blame: Essays in cultural theory*, London: Routledge.

Driver, S. and Martell, L. (1997) 'New Labour's communitarianisms', *Critical Social Policy*, vol 17, pp 27-46.

Edgar, D. (1986) 'The free or the good', in R. Levitas (ed) *The ideology of the New Right*, Cambridge: Polity Press, pp 55-79.

England, H. (1986) *Social work as art*, London: Allen & Unwin.

Esping-Andersen, G. (1990) *Three worlds of welfare capitalism*, Cambridge: Polity Press.

Etzioni, A. (1994) *The spirit of community*, New York, NY: Touchstone.

Etzioni, A. (1997) *The new golden rule: Community and morality in a democratic society*, London: Profile Books.

Everitt, A. and Hardiker, P. (1996) *Evaluating for good practice*, Basingstoke: Macmillan.

Figlio, K. (1989) 'Unconscious aspects of health and the public sphere', in B. Richards (ed) *Crises of the self*, London: Free Association Books, pp 85-99.

Finlay, L. (2000) 'The challenge of professionalism', in A. Brechin, H. Brown and M.A. Eby (eds) *Critical practice in health and social care*, London: Sage Publications, pp 73-95.

Finlayson, A. (2000) 'The feeling state and the emotionally literate self', in W. Wheeler (ed) *The political subject: Essays on the self from art, politics and science*, London: Lawrence and Wishart, pp 137-59.

Fischer, J. (1976) *The effectiveness of social casework*, Springfield, IL: Charles C. Thomas.

Flax, J. (1990) *Thinking fragments: Psychoanalysis, feminism and postmodernism in the contemporary West*, Berkeley, CA: University of California Press.

Flax, J. (1993) 'The play of justice', in *Disputed subjects: Essays on psychoanalysis, politics and philosophy*, London: Routledge.

Fonagy, P., Steele, M., Steele, H., Higgitt, A. and Mayer, L.S. (1994) 'The Emmanuel Miller memorial lecture 1992: the theory and practice of resilience', *Journal of Child Psychology and Psychiatry*, vol 35, no 2, pp 231-58.

Foster, A. (1998) 'Psychotic processes and community care', in A. Foster and V. Zagier Roberts (eds) *Managing mental health in the community*, London: Routledge, pp 61-70.

Foucault, M. (1975) *Discipline & punish*, Harmondsworth: Penguin.

Fox, N. (1995) 'Postmodern perspectives on care: the vigil and the gift', *Critical Social Policy*, vol 15, pp 107-25.

Fraser, N. (1995) 'From redistribution to recognition? Dilemmas of justice in a post-socialist age', *New Left Review*, vol 212, pp 68-92.

Fraser, N. (2000) 'Recognition of identity or recognition status?', Paper presented at Recognition: Psychoanalysis and the politics of identity conference, Institute of Psychoanalysis.

Freeden, M. (1999) 'The ideology of New Labour', *Political Quarterly*, vol 70, no 2, pp 128-38.

Freud, S. (1907) *Creative writers and day-dreaming*, in *The standard edition of the complete psychological works of Sigmund Freud*, 24 volumes, 1953-74, London: Hogarth Press.

Freud, S. (1930) *Civilisation and its discontents*, in *The standard edition of the complete psychological works of Sigmund Freud*, 24 volumes, 1953-74, London: Hogarth Press.

Friedman, M. (1962) *Capitalism and freedom*, Chicago, IL: University of Chicago Press.

Friedman, M. (1989) 'Feminism and modern friendship: dislocating the community', *Ethics*, vol 99, pp 275-90.

Friere, P. (1996) *Pedagogy of the oppressed*, (revised edn translated by R. Shaull), Harmondsworth: Penguin, first published 1921, translated by M. Bergman Ramos.

Froggett, L. (1981) 'L'acqua in gabbia: a summary and discussion', *Feminist Review*, vol 8, pp 35-42.

Froggett, L. (1996) 'Instrumentalism, knowledge and gender in social work', *Journal of Social Work Practice*, vol 10, no 2, pp 119-27.

Froggett, L. (1997) 'Containment, connection, creativity and competence', *Issues in Social Work Education*, vol 17, no 1, pp 65-81.

Froggett, L. (1998) 'The future of social work lies in face-to-face work', *Professional Social Work*, November, p 5.

Froggett, L. (1999) 'Sustaining tensions in practice supervision', *Social Services Research 1*, pp 33-42.

Froggett, L. (2000) 'Staff supervision and dependency culture: a case study', *Journal of Social Work Practice*, vol 14, no 1, pp 27-35.

Froggett, L. (2001) 'From rights to recognition: mental health and spiritual healing among older Pakistanis', *Psychoanalytic Studies*, vol 3, no 2, pp 177-86.

Froggett, L. and Sapey, B. (1997) 'Communication, culture and competence in social work education', *Social Work Education*, vol 16, no 1, pp 41-53.

Gabriel, Y. (1993) 'Organizational nostalgia', in S. Fineman (ed) *Emotion in organizations*, London: Sage Publications, pp 118-41.

Gabriel, Y. (1999) *Organisations in depth*, London: Sage Publications.

Gadamer, H. (1975) *Truth and method*, translated and edited by G. Barden and J. Cumming, London: Sheed and Wand.

Garland, C. (ed) (1998) *Understanding trauma*, London: Duckworth.

Geertz, C. (1973) 'Deep play: notes on the Balinese cockfight', C. Geertz, *The interpretation of cultures: Selected essays*, London: Hutchinson & Co, pp 412-53.

Giddens, A. (1992) *The transformation of intimacy: Sexuality, love and eroticism in modern societies*, Cambridge: Polity Press.

Giddens, A. (1994) *Beyond Left and Right: The future of radical politics*, Cambridge: Polity Press.

Giddens, A. (1998) *The third way*, Cambridge: Polity Press

Gilligan, C. (1982) *In a a different voice*, Cambridge, MA: Harvard University Press.

Gilligan, C. (1988) 'Remapping the moral domain: new images of self in relationship', in C. Gilligan, J.V. Ward and J. McLean Taylor, *Mapping the moral domain*, Cambridge, MA: Cambridge University Press, pp 3-19.

Goldstein, H. (1990) 'The knowledge base of social work practice theory: theory, wisdom, analogue or art?', *Families in Society: the Journal of Contemporary Human Services*, vol 73, pp 48-55.

Gould, L. (2001) 'Love and hate in the partnering pair: the capacity for sophisticated BaP', Paper presented at OPUS conference Organisational and Social Dynamics, London.

Habermas, J. (1980) 'Psychic thermidor and the rebirth of rebellious subjectivity', *Berkeley Journal of Sociology*, no 24-25, pp 1-12.

Habermas, J. (1983) *The theory of communicative action*, Oxford: Polity Press.

Hall, C. (1997) *Social work as narrative: Storytelling and persuasion in professional texts*, Aldershot: Ashgate.

Hall, S. (1983) 'The great moving Right show', in S. Hall and M. Jacques (eds) *The politics of Thatcherism*, London: Lawrence and Wishart.

Hall, S. (1998) 'The great moving nowhere show', *Marxism Today*, November/December, pp 9-14.

Halton, W. (1995) 'Institutional stress on providers in health and education', *Psychodynamic Counselling*, vol 1, no 2, pp 187-98.

Hayek, F.A. (1944) *The road to serfdom*, London: Routledge & Kegan Paul.

Hebdige, D. (1979) *Subculture: The meaning of style*, London: Methuen.

Hegel, G.W.F. (1969) *The phenomenology of mind*, New York, NY: Harper & Row, first published 1807.

Heineman, M.B. (1981) 'The absolute scientific imperative in social work research', *Social Service Review*, vol 55, pp 371-97.

Held, B. (1995) *Back to reality: A critique of postmodern theory in psychotherapy*, New York, NY and London: Norton.

Held, D (1996) *Democracy and the global order: From the modern state to cosmopolitan governance*, Cambridge: Polity Press.

Held, V. (1993) *Feminist morality: Transforming culture, society and politics*, Chicago, IL: Chicago University Press.

Henkel, M. (1995) 'Conceptions of knowledge in social work education', in M. Yelloly and M. Henkel (eds) *Learning and teaching in social work*, London: Jessica Kingsley, pp 67-82.

Higham, P. (1998) 'The future of social work lies in social care', *Professional Social Work*, November, p 4.

Hinschelwood, R.D. (1989) 'Social possession of identity', in B. Richards (ed) *The crises of the self*, London: Free Association Books, pp 75-83.

Hinschelwood, R.D. (1998) 'Creatures of each other', in A. Foster and V. Zagier Roberts (eds) *Managing mental health in the community*, London: Routledge, pp 15-26.

Hirschorn, L. (1988) *The workplace within*, Cambridge, MA: MIT Press.

Hirschman, A. (1970) *Exit, voice and loyalty*, Cambridge, MA: Harvard University Press.

Hirst, P. (1994) *Associative democracy: New forms of economic and social governance*, Cambridge: Polity Press.

Hoggett, P. (1998) 'Hatred of dependency. Where are the people? Expertise and experience', Psychoanalysis and the Public Sphere 11th annual conference, University of East London.

Hoggett, P. (2000) *Emotional life and the politics of welfare*, Basingstoke: Macmillan.

Hoggett, P. and Thompson, S. (1998) 'The delivery of welfare: the associationist vision', in J. Carter (ed) *Postmodernity and the fragmentation of welfare*, London: Routledge, pp 237-51.

Hollway, W. and Jefferson, T. (1997) 'The risk society in an age of anxiety: situating the fear of crime', *British Journal of Sociology*, vol 48, no 2, pp 255-66.

Hollway, W. and Jefferson, T. (2000) *Doing qualitative research differently: Free association, narrative and the interview method*, London: Sage Publications.

Holmes, J. (1996) Attachment theory: a secure base for policy?', in S. Kraemer and J. Roberts (eds) *The politics of attachment*, London: Free Association Books, pp 27-42.

Home Office (1998) *Compact on relations between government and the voluntary and community sector in England*, Cm 4100, London: The Stationery Office.

Honig, B. (1996) 'Difference, dilemmas and the politics of home', in S. Benhabib (ed) *Democracy and difference*, Princeton, NJ: Princeton University Press.

Honneth, A. (1995) *The struggle for recognition: The moral grammar of social conflicts*, Cambridge: Polity Press.

Howe, D. (1992) 'Child abuse and the bureaucratisation of social work', *Sociological Review*, vol 40, no 3, pp 491-508.

Howe, D. (1993) *On being a client: Understanding the process of counselling and psychotherapy*, London: Sage Publications.

Howe D. (1995) *Attachment theory for social work practice*, Basingstoke: Macmillan.

Howe, D. (1996) 'Surface and depth in social work practice', in N. Parton (ed) *Social theory and social change in social work*, London: Routledge, pp 77-97.

Howe, D. (1998) 'Relationship-based thinking and practice in social work', *Journal of Social Work Practice*, vol 12, no 1, pp 43-55.

Hughes, G. (ed) (1998) *Imagining welfare futures*, London: Routledge.

Hughes, G. and Mooney, G. (1998) 'Community', in G. Hughes (ed) *Imagining welfare futures*, London: Routledge, pp 55-102.

Hughes, L. and Pengelly, P. (1997) *Staff supervision in a turbulent environment: Managing process and task in front-line services*, London: Jessica Kingsley.

Huntington, A. (2000) 'Differing perceptions of legislative and policy change in children's and families' services: a vertical analysis', PhD thesis, University of Central Lancashire.

Hussain, N. (2000) 'Experience and perceptions of mental health among older Asians in a northern English city', Unpublished research paper, University of Central Lancashire.

Ignatieff, M. (1994) *The needs of strangers*, London: Vintage.

Illich, I. (1977) *Limits to medicine*, Harmondsworth: Penguin.

Imre, R.W. (1984) 'The nature of knowledge in social work', *Social Work*, vol 29, no 1, pp 41-5.

Ixer, G. (1999) 'There's no such thing as reflection', *British Journal of Social Work*, vol 29, pp 513-27.

Jacoby, R. (1975) *Social amnesia*, Hassocks: Harvester Press.

Jones, C. (1983) *State social work and the working class*, London: Macmillan.

Jordan, B. (1978) 'A comment on "theory and practice in social work"', *British Journal of Social Work*, vol 8, no 11, pp 23-5.

Jordan, B. (2000) *Social work and the third way: Tough love as social policy*, London: Sage Publications.

Kaminsky, M. (1985) 'Daily bread: or, the marriage of art and social work', *Social Work with Groups*, vol 8, no 1, pp 17-23.

Kearney, P. (1996) *The management of practice expertise project report*, London: National Institute of Social Work.

Kilty, M. and Meenaghan, T.M. (1995) 'Social work and the convergence of politics and science', *Social Work*, vol 40, no 4, pp 445-53.

Klein, M. (1975) *Collected works of Melanie Klein*, vols 1-4, London: Hogarth Press and Institute of Psychoanalysis.

Kohlberg, L. (1981) *The philosophy of moral development: Moral stages and the idea of justice: Essays on moral development*, San Francisco, CA: Harper & Row.

Kohlberg, L. (1984) *The psychology of moral development: Essays on moral development 2*, San Francisco, CA: Harper & Row.

Kristol, I. (1978) *Two cheers for capitalism*, New York, NY: Basic Books.

Kundera, M. (1984) *The unbearable lightness of being*, London: Faber & Faber.

Langan, M. and Day, L. (1992) (eds) *Women, oppression and social work: Issues in anti-discriminatory practice*, London: Routledge.

Lasch, C. (1979) *The culture of narcissism: American life in an age of diminishing expectations*, New York, NY: W.W. Norton.

Leadbeater, C. and Goss, S. (1998) *The rise of the social entrepreneur*, London: Demos.

Levitas, R. (1986) 'Competition and compliance', in R. Levitas (ed) *The ideology of the New Right*, Cambridge: Polity Press.

Lewis, G. (1998) 'Citizenship', in G. Hughes (ed) *Imagining welfare futures*, London: Routledge, pp 103-50.

Lindblom, C. (1959) 'The science of "muddling through"', *Public Administration Review*, vol 19, pp 78-88.

Maclean, M. and Groves, D. (1991) *Women's issues in social policy*, London: Routledge.

Mahlouf, A. (1999) *Ports of call*, London: Harvill.

Marcuse, H. (1969) *Eros and civilisation*, London: Sphere Books.

Marks, D. (2000) *Disability*, London: Routledge.

Marshall, T.H. (1963) 'Citizenship and social class', in *Sociology at the crossroads and other essays*, London: Heineman, pp 67-127.

Marshall, T.H. (1971) *Social policy in the twentieth century*, London: Hutchinson.

Marshall, T.H. (1981) 'The right to welfare', in T.H Marshall (ed) *The right to welfare and other essays*, London: Heinemann.

Marsland, D. (1996) *Welfare or welfare state*, Basingstoke: Macmillan.

Martinez-Brawley, E. and Mendez-Bonito Zorita, P. (1998) 'At the edge of the frame: beyond art and science in social work', *British Journal of Social Work*, vol 28, pp 197-212.

Marx, K. (1965) *Capital*, vol 1, London: Lawrence and Wishart, first published 1887.

Mattinson, J. (1975) *The reflection process in casework supervision*, London: Tavistock Institute of Marital Studies.

Mayo, M. (1997) 'Partnerships for regeneration and community development: some opportunities, challenges and constraints', *Critical Social Policy*, vol 17, no 3, pp 3-36.

Mead, G.H. (1934) *Mind, self and society from the standpoint of a social behaviourist*, Chicago, IL: University of Chicago Press.

Menzies-Lyth, I. (1988) 'The functioning of social systems as a defence against anxiety', in *Containing anxiety in institutions, vol 1, selected essays*, London: Free Association Books.

Miller, E. (1993) *From dependency to autonomy: Studies in organisation and change*, London: Free Association Books.

Miller, E. and Gwynne, G. (1972) *A life apart*, London: Tavistock.

Minsky, R. (1995) 'Reaching beyond denial: sight and insight – a way forward?', *Free Associations*, vol 5, no 3, pp 326-51.

Minsky, R. (1998) *Psychoanalysis and culture: Contemporary states of mind*, Cambridge: Polity Press.

Mitchell, J. (ed) (1986) *The selected Melanie Klein*, Harmondsworth: Penguin.

Mitchell, J. (2000) *Mad men and Medusas*, London: Allen Lane.

Morris, J. (1993) *Independent lives: Community care and disabled people*, London: Macmillan.

Morris, J. (2001) 'Social exclusion and young disabled people with high level support needs', *Critical Social Policy*, vol 21, no 2 , pp 161-83.

Munro, E. (1998) *Understanding social work: An empirical approach*, London: Athlone.

Murray, C. (1984) *Losing ground*, New York, NY: Basic Books.

Nadas, P. (1998) *A book of memories*, translated by I. Sanders and I. Goldstein, London: Vintage.

Nash, C. (ed) (1990) *Narrative in culture: The uses of storytelling in the sciences, philosophy, and literature*, London: Routledge.

Obholzer, A. and Zagier Roberts, V. (1994) (eds) *The unconscious at work*, London: Tavistock.

Ogden, T.H. (1992) *The matrix of the mind*, London: Karnac.

Oliver, M. and Sapey, B. (1999) *Social work disabled people*, 2nd edition, Basingstoke: Palgrave.

Orbach, S. (1998) 'A crying shame', *Marxism Today*, November/December, pp 61-2.

Pahl, R. (1996) 'Friendly society', in S. Kraemer and J. Roberts (eds) *The politics of attachment*, London: Free Association Books.

Park, J. (2000) 'The feeling state and the emotionally literate self', in W. Wheeler (ed) *The political subject: Essays on the self from art, politics and science*, London: Lawrence and Wishart.

Parton, N. (1998) 'Risk, advanced liberalism and child welfare: the need to rediscover uncertainty and ambiguity', *British Journal of Social Work*, vol 28, pp 5-27.

Parton, N. and O'Byrne, P. (2000) *Constructive social work*, Basingstoke: Macmillan.

Payne, M. (1991) *Modern social work theory*, Basingstoke: Macmillan.

Payne, M. (1996) *What is professional social work?*, Birmingham: Venture Press.

Pearson, G., Treseder, J. and Yelloly, M. (1988) *Social work and the legacy of Freud*, Basingstoke: Macmillan.

Peterson, A. and Lupton, D. (1996) *The new public health: Health and self in the age of risk*, London: Sage Publications.

Phillips, S. and Benner, P. (1994) *The crisis of care*, Washington, DC: Georgetown University Press.

Philp, M. (1979) 'Notes on the form of knowledge in social work', *Sociological Review*, vol 27, pp 83-111.

Pietroni, M. (1995) 'The nature and aims of professional education for social workers: a postmodern perspective', in M. Yelloly and M. Henkel (eds) *Learning and teaching in social work*, London: Jessica Kingsley.

Plummer, K. (1995) *Telling sexual stories*, London: Routledge.

Polanyi, M. (1967) *The tacit dimension*, London: Routledge.

Polkinghorne, D.E. (1988) *Narrative knowing and the human sciences*: Albany, NY: State University of New York Press.

Pope, A. (1733) *Essay on Man, Epistle 2, Argument of the nature and state of man with respect to himself as an individual*, in B. Dobrée (ed) *Collected poems of Alexander Pope*, 1956 edition, London: Dent.

Putnam, R. (1993) *Making democracy work: Civic traditions in modern Italy*, Princeton, NJ: Princeton University Press.

Putnam, R. (1995a) 'Bowling alone: interview with Robert Putnam about America's collapsing civil life', *Bulletin of the American Association for Higher Education*, September.

Putnam, R. (1995b) 'Bowling alone: America's declining social capital', *Journal of Democracy*, vol 6, no 1, pp 65-78.

Rapoport, L. (1968) 'Creativity in social work', *Smith College Studies in Social Work*, vol 38, pp 139-61.

Ree, J. (1999) *I see a voice*, London: Harper Collins.

Rhodes, M.L. (1985) 'Gilligan's theory of moral development as applied to social work', *Social Work*, March-April, pp 101-5.

Ricoeur, P. (1981) 'Hermeneutics in the human sciences: essays on language action and interpretation', translated by J. B. Thompson, Cambridge, MA: Cambridge University Press.

Robinson, K. (1997) 'The tolerance of artistic intelligence: shaping the unconscious', *Free Associations*, vol 6, no 4, pp 513-29.

Rogers, C. (1951) *Client-centred therapy: Its current implications and theory*, Boston, MA: Houghton Mifflin.

Rogers, C. (1970) *On encounter groups*, New York, NY: Harper & Row.

Rojek, C., Peacock, G. and Collins, S. (1988) *Social work and received ideas*, London: Routledge.

Rose, H. (1994) *Love, power and knowledge*, Cambridge: Polity Press.

Rosenau, P.M. (1992) *Postmodernism and the social sciences: Insights, inroads and intrusions*, Princeton, NJ: Princeton University Press.

Ruddick, S. (1989) *Maternal thinking: Towards a politics of peace*, Boston, MA: Beacon Press.

Rusher, W.A. (1975) *The making of the new majority party*, Ottawa, IL: Green Hill.

Rustin, M. (1996) 'Attachment in context', in S. Kraemer and I. Roberts (eds) *The politics of attachment*, London: Free Association Books.

Sackville-West, V. and Nicolson, H. (1945) *Another world than this...* (anthology), London: Michael Joseph.

Saleeby, D. (1994) 'Culture, theory and narrative: the intersection of meanings in practice', *Social Work*, vol 39, no 4, pp 351-59.

Salomon, L. (1995) *The global associational revolution*, London: Demos.

Schon, D.A. (1983) *The reflective practitioner: How professionals think in action*, New York, NY: Basic Books.

Scruton, R. (1980) *The meaning of Conservatism*, London: Penguin.

Segal, H. (1986) 'A psychoanalytical approach to aeshetics', in H. Segal, *The work of Hannah Segal*, London: Free Association Books.

Segal, H. (1991) *Dream, phantasy and art*, London: Tavistock.

Sennett, R. (1998) *The corrosion of character: The personal consequences of work in the new capitalism*, New York, NY: W.W. Norton.

Sevenhuijsen, S. (1998) *Citizenship and the ethics of care: Feminist considerations on justice, morality and politics*, London: Routledge.

Shakespeare, T. (2000) *Help*, Birmingham: Venture Press.

Shapiro, E. and Carr, W. (1991) *Lost in familiar places*, New Haven, CT: Yale University Press.

Sheldon, B. (1978) 'Theory and practice in social work: a re-examination of a tenuous relationship', *British Journal of Social Work*, vol 8, no 1, pp 1-22.

Sheppard, M. (1995) *Care management*, London: Whiting and Birch.

Simon, H. (1958) *Administrative behaviour*, New York, NY: Macmillan.

Smith, C. (2000) 'Social work as rights talk', in J. Harris, L. Froggett and I. Paylor (eds) *Reclaiming social work: The Southport papers vol 1*, Birmingham: Venture Press.

Stroufe, L.A. (1988) 'The role of infant–caregiver attachment in development', in J. Belsky and T. Nezworski (eds) *Clinical implications of attachment*, NJ: Lawrence Erlbaum.

Tannenbaum, S. (1994) 'Knowing and acting in medical practice: the epistemological politics of outcomes research', *Journal of Health Policy, Politics and Law*, vol 19, no 1, pp 27–44.

Taylor, C. (1992) 'The politics of recognition', in A. Gutman (ed) *Multiculturalism and the politics of recognition*, Princeton, NJ: Princeton University Press.

Taylor-Gooby, P. (2000) 'Blair's scars', *Critical Social Policy*, vol 20, no 3, pp 331–48.

Thompson, S. and Hoggett, P. (1996) 'Universalism, selectivism and particularism: towards a post-modern social policy', *Critical Social Policy*, vol 16, no 1, pp 21–43.

Timms, N. (1968) *The language of social casework*, London: Routledge & Kegan Paul.

Timms, N. and Timms, R. (1977) *Perspectives in social work*, London: Routledge & Kegan Paul.

Timpanaro, S. (1975) *On materialism*, London: New Left Books.

Titmuss, R. (1968) *Commitment to welfare*, London: Allen & Unwin.

Titmuss, R. (1970) *The gift relationship*, London: Allen & Unwin.

Tronto, J. (1994) *Moral boundaries: A political argument for an ethic of care*, London: Routledge.

Turney, D. (1997) 'Hearing voices, talking difference: a dialogic approach to anti-oppressive practice', *Journal of Social Work Practice*, vol 11, no 2, pp 115–25.

Ungerson, C. (1987) *Policy is personal: Gender and informal care*, London: Tavistock.

Volkan, V.D. (1980) 'Narcissistic personality organisation and "reparative leadership"', *International Journal of Group Psychology*, vol 30, pp 131–52.

Ward, D. (1998) 'Groupwork', in R. Adams, L. Dominelli and M. Payne (eds) *Social work: Themes, issues and critical debate*, Basingstoke: Macmillan.

Watson, C.W. (1997) 'Born a lady, became a princess, died a saint', *Anthropology Today*, vol 13, no 6, pp 3–7.

Webb, A. and Wistow, G. (1987) *Social work, social care and social planning: The personal social services since Seebohm*, London: Longman.

Weick, A. (1990) 'Knowledge as experience: exploring new dimensions of social work inquiry', *Social Thought*, vol 16, no 3, pp 36-46.

White, S. (1997) 'Beyond retroduction? – hermeneutics, reflexivity and social work practice', *British Journal of Social Work*, vol 27, pp 739-53.

Wilkinson, R. (1996) *Unhealthy societies*, London: Routledge.

Williams, F. (1989) *Social policy: A critical introduction: Issues of race, gender & class*, Cambridge: Polity Press.

Williams, F. (1993) 'Gender, "race" and class in British welfare policy', in A. Cochrane and J. Clarke (eds) *Comparing welfare states: Britain in international context*, London: Sage Publications.

Williams, F. (1999) 'Good-enough principles for welfare', *Journal of Social Policy*, vol 28, no 4, pp 667-87.

Williamson, J. (1995) *Consuming passions*, London: Marion Boyars.

Wilson, E. (1977) *Women and the welfare state*, London: Tavistock.

Winnicott, D.W. (1955) 'Group influences and the maladjusted child', in D.W. Winnicott (1964) *The family and individual development*, London: Tavistock.

Winnicott, D.W. (1958) *Through paediatrics to psychoanalysis*, London: Hogarth Press.

Winnicott, D.W. (1965) *The maturational process and the facilitating environment: Studies in the theory of emotional development*, London: Hogarth Press and the Institute of Psychoanalysis.

Winnicott D.W. (1971) *Playing and reality*, London: Tavistock.

Wootton, B. (1959) *Social science and social pathology*, London: Allen & Unwin.

Wordsworth, W. (1798) *Lines composed above Tintern Abbey on revisiting the banks of the Wye during a tour*, in M. Arnold (1879, reprinted 1969) *Poems of Wordsworth*, London: Macmillan, St Martins Press, pp 250-1.

Young, I.M. (1996) 'Communication and the other: beyond deliberative democracy', in S. Benhabib (ed) *Democracy and difference*, Princeton, NJ: Princeton University Press, pp 120-35.

Index